ANNE HOOPER'S

ULTIMATE

SEX
GUIDE

ANNE HOOPER'S

ULTIMATE

SEX
GUIDE

*A therapist's guide to the
programmes and techniques that will
enhance your relationship and
transform your life*

A DORLING KINDERSLEY BOOK

Dorling  Kindersley

LONDON, NEW YORK, SYDNEY, DELHI,
PARIS, MUNICH and JOHANNESBURG

Original edition
Created and produced by
CARROLL & BROWN LIMITED

Revised edition
Senior Managing Art Editor Lynne Brown
Senior Managing Editor Corinne Roberts
Senior Art Editor Karen Ward
Senior Editor Julia North
Production Bethan Blase

First published in Great Britain in 1992

This revised edition published in 2001 by Dorling Kindersley Limited,
9 Henrietta Street, London WC2E 8PS

A CIP catalogue record for this book is
available from the British Library.

ISBN 0 75133 355 7

Reproduced by Colourscan, Singapore

Printed in Italy by L.E.G.O.

See our complete catalogue at
www.dk.com

FOREWORD

Over my years as a sex therapist and as the director of a clinic for sexual problems, I have met with a great variety of people needing to improve and expand their sex lives. The most sensible, intelligent and successful individuals have attended my practice. Sex problems are not the prerogative of the less able. And sexual curiosity appears to be universal. Everybody wants to know if they can make sex even better than it already is.

Amongst my clients have been members of parliament, high-ranking police officers, doctors, psychiatrists, opera singers, musicians, and best-selling novelists. There also have been nurses, teachers, a gourmet chef, dentists, accountants, solicitors, factory workers, the unemployed, refuse collectors, men and women with incurable illnesses, and housewives and househusbands.

I have learned a great deal from my clients during this time – not least of which is that sex is fun. It is also restorative, reassuring and provides the underpinning for a loving partnership. It is patently *not* unusual to want to learn more about personal sexuality.

Yet, however hard a therapist works and however many clients she manages to see, there is a limit to the number she can reach. In addition, some men and women have a powerful desire to retain their privacy. This means there are a great many people still longing to know more about their sensual selves and it is for them that I have written this book.

Good sex consists of feeling alive and well in the brain and awake and on fire in the body. It uses technical skills as well as personal preferences. It is an art, not in the sense of being a dead and artificial art-form, but in becoming a unique and creative experience for the two people taking part. Through this book I hope to use my clinical learning to assist such creative experiences. By feeding new thoughts (and occasionally some very old thoughts) to you, I hope you develop a vital, powerful love life. May it provide you with vivid experiences and memories.

CONTENTS

INTRODUCTION

Sex often has been referred to as the poor person's pastime — a reference to the fact you don't need to buy anything in order to do it or to enjoy it. We carry, within ourselves, all the ingredients for ecstasy and even if we don't possess a partner, it is still possible for us to enjoy personally created scenarios of sexual pleasure. But if sex is such a natural resource why should we bother with books such as this one? Why don't we all glide away in a continual stream of orgasmic rapture doing, quite simply, what comes naturally?

SEX IS AN ACQUIRED SKILL

One reason why we often don't make the most of our sexual capacities is because our grasp of them is uncertain. Most of us learn about sex from family and friends and the courting examples of our contemporaries. On a wider level, we learn about sex through the media. And, in our bedrooms, we attempt to put into practice the ideas assimilated. Ideally, this happens spontaneously, re-enacting the antics of childhood.

Life, however, is not ideal. We may not, in our inhibited Western world, get enough information about sex or enough of the right information. Not everyone has enough power of imagination to enable them to use sexual knowledge nor, instinctively, will they know how to do sex, without imagination. Virtually all who reach the heights of bliss do so by accident.

And even if we find we are capable of orgasm it doesn't automatically entitle us to certified bliss. How often have you felt curiously flat after orgasm? As if there should somehow be more to it? There are never, of course, any guarantees we can reach sexual nirvana, but there are methods that get us close. So one purpose of this book is to provide you with a good start and to increase your satisfaction using, in human terms, all natural ingredients.

TOUCH AND SEXUALITY
Touch is the first branch on the tree of stimulation. Through touch we explore our own inner sensation and intimacy with others. As we mature we develop and refine that touch, and sensuality widens into sexuality. This 'growth' is encouraged by curiosity — interest in novelty.

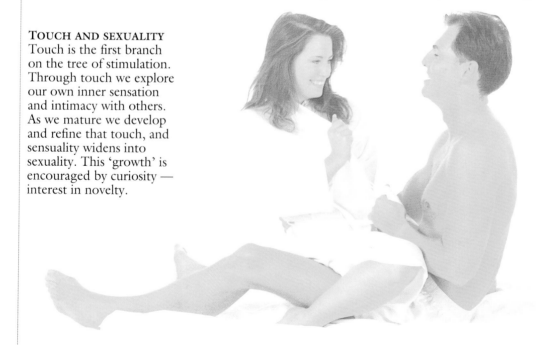

PROBLEMS WITH SEX CAN BE OVERCOME

Being unable to reach one's sexual potential can have long-lasting effects, not only on personal well-being and health but, almost inevitably, on relationships that are the most vital to us. Today, when people seek quality in all aspects of their lives, sexual fulfilment is an area that cannot be overlooked.

Sexual difficulties beset all of us from time to time and, if left unattended, can ruin what would otherwise be a major source of satisfaction. Sexual problems are not usually of a great magnitude; most men are not prevented by impotence from engaging in sex, and most women do not suffer pain on intercourse. But there often does exist an enormous gap between what we imagine our sex lives can be and what we manage to achieve.

Sexual difficulties are not new — they've existed as long as people have been engaging in sexual activities — nor are they particularly unique. On the contrary, they are long-standing, clearly identifiable, and extremely prevalent. They are also 'curable'. Over the years, sexual therapists like myself have perfected techniques to tackle the difficulties that clients relate to us day after day. This book contains the programmes and practices that can do the greatest possible good. Now readers who can't afford the cost of therapy, or who feel reticent about discussing sexual matters, can, in the privacy of their own homes, discover the ways and means of achieving sexual experiences that live up to their expectations.

A NATURAL APPROACH TO SEX

While I cannot guarantee that on perusal of this book you will automatically experience Grade A ecstasy, I can guarantee that by trying some of the sex programmes you will enjoy gorgeous sensuality. Who knows? These items of sex information, fed into your sex play, may trigger a very special erotic experience — the sort that truly feels like rapture. And it is all done by knowing how to stimulate the natural chemicals of the brain and body.

TECHNIQUES IN THIS BOOK You will learn about the reasons to hold back occasionally on orgasm, and ways of enjoying sexuality without intercourse. And although we illustrate intercourse positions for maximum stimulation, we also show positions valuable because they are fun.

VARIETY Men tend to look at many women; women tend to look at one man but seek many qualities within him. To maintain the interest of a partner, keep sex varied.

Few people realize that their bodies are a natural pharmacopoeia. During sex we manufacture chemicals that make us feel wonderful. We produce an amazing substance that floods the tissues, allowing us to experience touch with dreamlike sensuality, and we also create, as a by-product of sexual climax, a substance that sends us to sleep, a pleasurable, natural relaxant. And parts of the sexual response cycle utilize adrenalin surges resulting in powerful bursts of energy. These allow us to take great satisfaction from sustained movement of the body, the naturally aerobic spin-off of the sex act.

In addition, our brains are able to give us journeys into landscape and emotion without anything that acts on our bodies from the inside. We can gain 'other-worldly' experience through guided fantasy or fantasy experiments that bring endless variation to sex and that sharpen up sexual sensation in concentrated fashion.

Children learn about themselves and how to become fully functional human beings through the medium of play, and adults find out about sex in similar fashion. Play isn't just the froth of life, it has purpose. It is a practical way of gaining knowledge and experience, not only of how things work but of how we work. Play is the building block of human experience. Playing, having fun, experimenting, literally messing about, are all methods of learning about sensuality.

The programmes and techniques set out here are based on play and on utilizing the natural resources of our sexuality. They have helped hundreds of people turn their insufficiently rewarding or boring sexual relationships into opportunities for uncovering new and exciting feelings in themselves and their partners. And the only necessary ingredients are imagination, erotic touch and knowledge about our sexual selves.

THE ENDLESS VARIETY OF SEX

One reason why our sex lives stagnate is because the sex act becomes boringly the same every time we do it. The reason for this, ironically, is because when we hit on a good position, or a good combination of fingers and penis, we go back to it increasingly often. After all, we know it works. Yet life often remains interesting because of its uncertainties. Where Sigmund Freud reckoned that sexuality was our motivating life force and Alfred Adler, a drive for integration, I rate the need for survival a more realistic alternative. The drive to survive takes in both sexual urges and social fit but depends most of all on what I have termed the 'anti-boredom' factor or a drive towards stimulation.

Experimenting with different sex positions, or just looking at pictures of them in a book such as this, offers encouragement to those novelty-seeking brain cells. Indeed, it is by forgetting about the possibilities for sexual permutation that many relationships decline sexually. It's not good enough to explain that by knowing someone so intimately you automatically learn everything about them, therefore there is nothing new to discover. There is always something new, but you must use your brain to find it. I hope this book is an aid to such sensual creation.

Even if only one basic sex position is favoured, it can still be varied by the thoughts or dialogue you choose at the time. Physically, there are alterations to your posture or balance that may not seem specially different but, nevertheless, lead to other thoughts and alternative feelings.

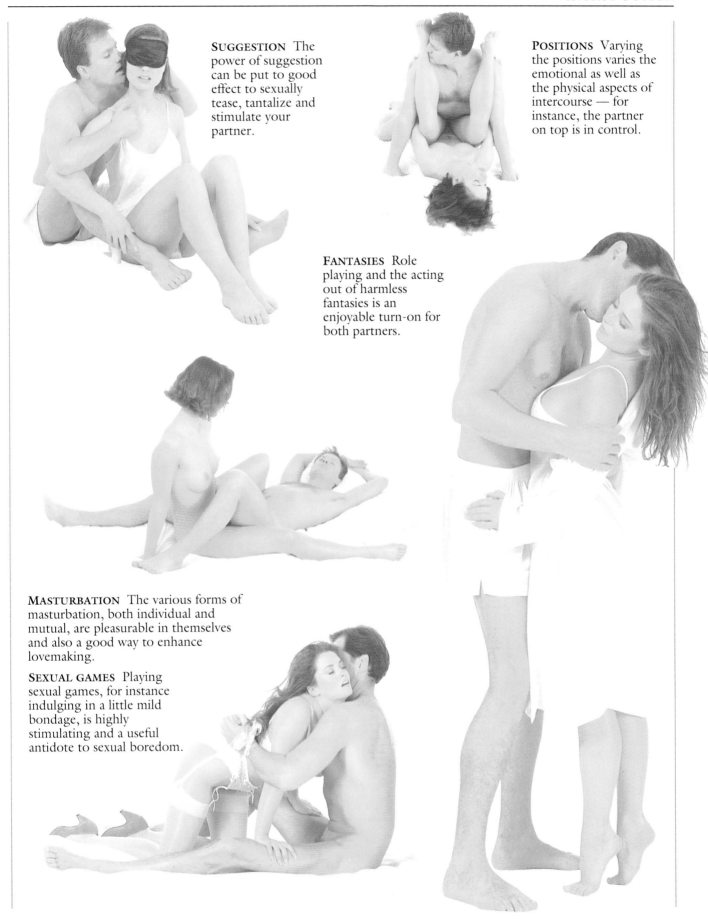

SUGGESTION The power of suggestion can be put to good effect to sexually tease, tantalize and stimulate your partner.

POSITIONS Varying the positions varies the emotional as well as the physical aspects of intercourse — for instance, the partner on top is in control.

FANTASIES Role playing and the acting out of harmless fantasies is an enjoyable turn-on for both partners.

MASTURBATION The various forms of masturbation, both individual and mutual, are pleasurable in themselves and also a good way to enhance lovemaking.

SEXUAL GAMES Playing sexual games, for instance indulging in a little mild bondage, is highly stimulating and a useful antidote to sexual boredom.

THE ACT OF SEX

Becoming adept in the arts of sexual loving requires a clear understanding of the way sex works. Many of the difficulties partners face in their sexual activities can be put down to a lack of information about what happens during sex and, more acutely, how each partner responds, and to what stimuli. Men and women share similarities of sexual response but they see sex and attraction differently and their needs don't always correspond. If taken as a process, the sex act has four distinct phases — arousal, penetration, climax and resolution. Each phase is able to function separately from the other although, at the best of times, the phases flow in a continuum. Unless we understand our readiness for and responses to each phase, our ability to have good sex — and sometimes even sex at all — will be seriously undermined.

AROUSAL

In order to want to have sex, a feeling of desire has to be experienced. Arousal appears to originate in the brain, though the phenomenon is still not completely understood, and hormones play an important part. When a man first experiences arousal his penis hardens and becomes erect; a woman's initial response is a moistening of her vagina. As desire increases, with the exchange of a variety of caresses and the stimulation of each other's erogenous areas, various other changes occur to both internal and external sexual organs. As desire reaches a peak, both partners long for penetration.

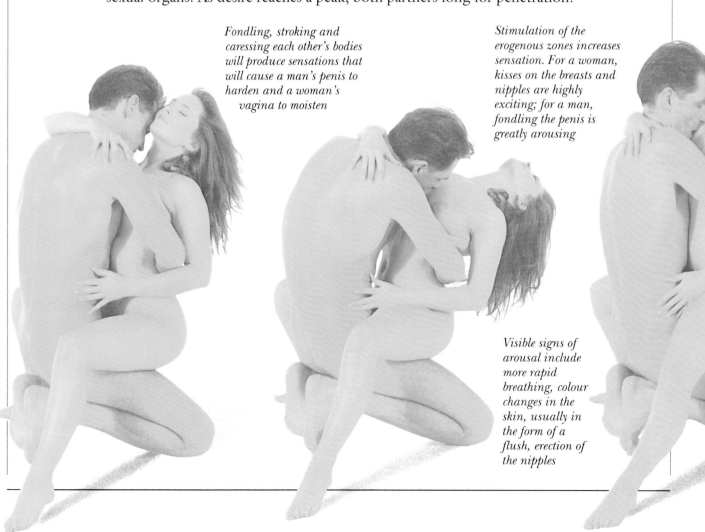

Fondling, stroking and caressing each other's bodies will produce sensations that will cause a man's penis to harden and a woman's vagina to moisten

Stimulation of the erogenous zones increases sensation. For a woman, kisses on the breasts and nipples are highly exciting; for a man, fondling the penis is greatly arousing

Visible signs of arousal include more rapid breathing, colour changes in the skin, usually in the form of a flush, erection of the nipples

PENETRATION

Sex play should have prepared the vagina and penis sufficiently for penetration; the vagina must be lubricated by its secretions in order to receive a fully erect penis without discomfort. The vagina envelops the penis, and thrusting movements of the penis in this confined space produce sensations throughout both partners' bodies that lead to further internal and external changes, most particularly swelling of the genitals and muscular tensions. These, in turn, lead to feelings of such sexual excitement that, particularly for the man, a climax inevitably results.

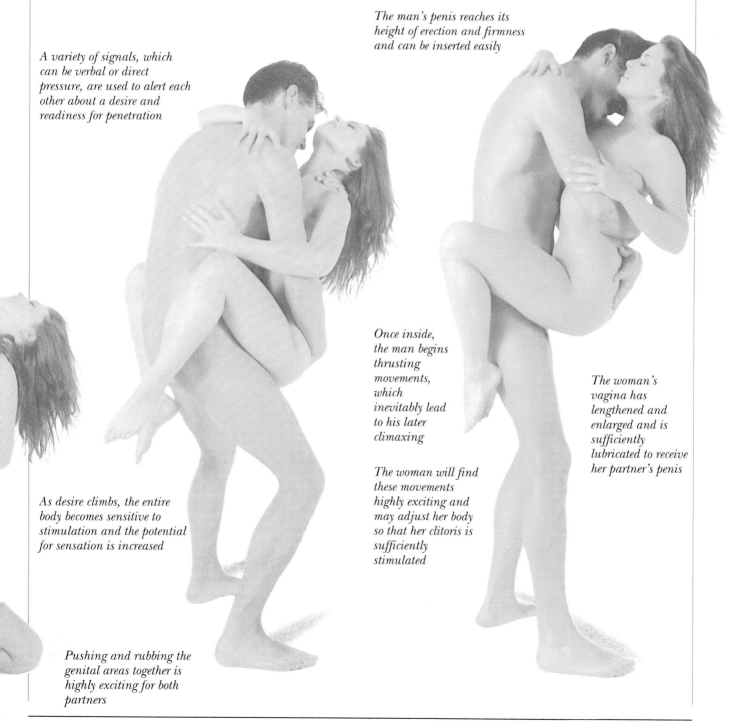

A variety of signals, which can be verbal or direct pressure, are used to alert each other about a desire and readiness for penetration

The man's penis reaches its height of erection and firmness and can be inserted easily

Once inside, the man begins thrusting movements, which inevitably lead to his later climaxing

The woman will find these movements highly exciting and may adjust her body so that her clitoris is sufficiently stimulated

The woman's vagina has lengthened and enlarged and is sufficiently lubricated to receive her partner's penis

As desire climbs, the entire body becomes sensitive to stimulation and the potential for sensation is increased

Pushing and rubbing the genital areas together is highly exciting for both partners

ORGASM

When sensations become overwhelmingly intense, both partners experience a peak of pleasure which, with men, is almost inevitably accompanied by the ejaculation of seminal fluid. A man's orgasm depends almost entirely on having his penis stimulated, manually, orally or by the vaginal walls. A woman's orgasm, whether or not she achieves one, and how long it takes to do so, depends very much on the amount of stimulation her clitoris receives. This is a woman's primary organ of sensation. Again, stimulation can be manual or oral, direct or indirect, but direct clitoral stimulation brings the greatest and quickest response.

Rapid thrusts of the penis lead on to regularly recurring contractions of a man's urethra and this, in turn, produces the highly pleasurable sensations associated with, though not dependent on, ejaculation. As the seminal fluid is spurted out through the engorged penis via the prostate and urethra, most men experience a powerful physical reaction. A man's orgasm is almost always preceded by a feeling of ejaculatory inevitability, and once he ejaculates, his orgasm cannot be delayed until emission has been completed.

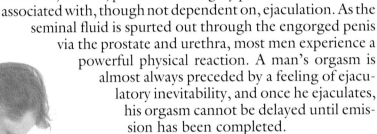

As orgasm approaches, the man's pushing becomes more rhythmic and urgent, and his heart rate and breathing become more rapid

A woman's pleasure proceeds in step-like fashion with that of her partner, her responses keeping time with his thrusting

During the most intense moments of lovemaking the man's sensations are concentrated on being able to thrust deep inside his partner

Just before the emission of the seminal fluid the man passes the point of no return, where he can no longer delay coming

The woman's muscles contract and grip the man, and there is an increased blood supply to the vagina

At the moment of climax, intense sensual feelings flood the vaginal area and spread throughout the woman's body

Like her partner, a woman also experiences orgasmic contractions, similar in number and duration, and at the same intervals. The sensation of orgasm may differ, however, from woman to woman, some experiencing a single peak of pleasure, others having more widespread sensations that can be rekindled, producing more than one orgasm.

RESOLUTION

Once climax occurs, sexual tension falls away. A man experiences an almost immediate falling off of sensation; his penis becomes flaccid, and it will be some time before he can become erect again. This is known as the refractory period. After climax, a man normally feels relaxed and sleepy and often, depending on the circumstances, falls into a deep slumber.

For a woman, the return to normality is much slower. She experiences a slow and gradual decline in the swelling of her breasts and labia, and she remains in a responsive state for much longer, even welcoming further loving attentions from her partner.

It should be apparent, therefore, that although men and women are similar in their responses to sex, significant differences exist particularly as regards arousal and the experience of orgasm. Often, too, we are in such a hurry for orgasm that we lose out on arousal. Yet it is the magic of this stage, that time when we are stimulated to a peak of sexual excitement, that helps the brain leap into a heightened consciousness. It is important that partners are aware of these differences and that they use the techniques shown in this book to give each other the best chance of a totally satisfying sexual life.

After climax, the man's sexual tension falls away rapidly; he soon loses his erection and feels relaxed and sleepy

The woman's sexual tension declines relatively slowly after climax, and because she remains sexually responsive she could be stimulated to further climaxes

Showing warmth and affection to each other will encourage a feeling of closeness that makes the lovemaking complete

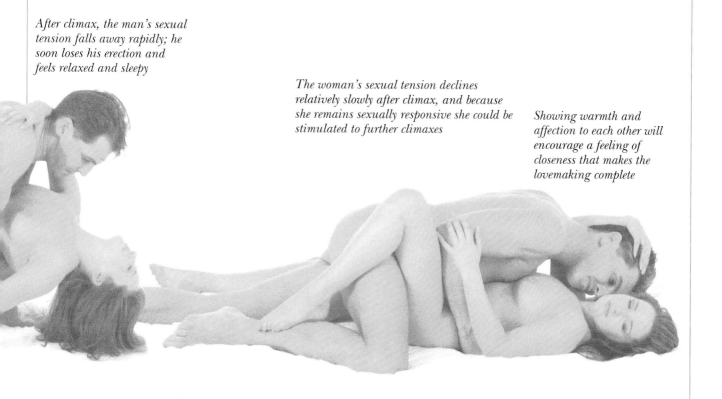

HOW THE BOOK WORKS

Many people express the opinion that sexuality only has value if it is worked out in private, solely between the two people involved. This, however, is faulty reasoning. Sex therapy, far from creating an artificial edge to the rapport between people, assists men and women in experiencing new thoughts and emotions as well as good physical sensations. Here, I offer assistance to all the thousands of people who choose not to meet a therapist face to face but who nevertheless look forward to resolving their sex problems. If you can make full use of the ideas, training methods and therapeutic discussion I have gathered and developed over the years, I sincerely hope you will enhance your loving relationship in every way.

The Ultimate Sex Manual has been compiled to provide you with all the information you need to enhance or improve any sexual relationship. All the areas that are problematical for couples are covered in a similar, easy-to-follow way. Each single question such as "How can I make lovemaking more intimate?" is explored from several angles. For example, in that specific case history, the innermost anxieties and desires that we all may have are communicated safely through the circumstances of one couple in particular. In my assessment of the couple's problem, I explain how emotional intimacy can be fostered, and in the accompanying programme I set out a series of simple exercises that encourage physical intimacy. Finally, the programme is supplemented by the illustrated exercise that follows it and provides detailed pictorial instruction of an enjoyable form of touch therapy that will allow you to develop intimate sensual knowledge of each other.

THE CASE HISTORIES

Throughout the pages of this book are case histories taken from my files, each specifically illustrating the sexual yearning and ambition every individual possesses but few care to admit to. The lovers on these pages are not struggling with premature ejaculation or inability to experience orgasm but they do ask simple questions that sometimes give birth to profound answers. "How can I achieve a deeper orgasm?" provokes, for example, a complicated answer because it concerns stimulating the mind.

The people whose problems I have concentrated on here encompass single men and women as well as those in short, long-term and/or conjugal relationships. The age range is wide, too. This only reinforces the truth that disappointment with sexual experiences affects everyone at some time.

These seemingly personal cases do in fact have implications for us all. I have tried in my assessments to generalize from particular circumstances so that anyone reading the case histories would be able to pick up insights into aspects of their own behaviour, and so perhaps be furnished with ways of adjusting that behaviour for the better.

THE PROGRAMMES

Succeeding each case history are the therapy pages where a sequence of stages are set out to deal with the problem addressed. The different stages include techniques involving specific mood training, factual information and touch manoeuvres.

In the early pages I deal with issues such as self-esteem and assertion, outlining simple confidence-building exercises for men and women. The connection between confidence and sexuality may not be an obvious one but it exists. Having the courage to ask for what you want in lovemaking and the language in which to do it tactfully may, for some couples, be the deciding factor in the rise or fall of a relationship.

The latter pages help expand imagination through assisting couples to explore each other's fantasies and showing how to focus single-mindedly on expanding sensation and consciousness so that the brink of orgasm and orgasm itself become spiritual ecstasy. No-one, of course, can experience ecstasy to order. But by laying the foundations, you have a greater chance of getting there than by leaving it to chance.

Each programme is directed towards a particular aspect of sexuality; some deal with mental attitudes, others with physical improvements through mastering specific, proven techniques. Programmes may be individual or involve a partner. Each programme normally involves several stages. This is part of the philosophy and practice of sexual therapy, that improvements happen over time and as the result of building on previous experiences.

ILLUSTRATED EXERCISES

Each programme is made up of one or more exercises, which are illustrated methods of lovemaking. I have made certain that the techniques are presented in such a way so as to be accessible and helpful to all. The captions and annotation will guide you through the various stages and draw your attention to the finer points of the techniques so that what is on show is achieved.

These illustrated exercises are widely applicable to a variety of situations, and while you will get the most value from the book if you read it through fully you can, should you prefer to, work from it using only the exercises.

I have personally seen hundreds of couples rekindle feelings of love while technically carrying out their sex therapy 'homework' for me. The facts are that some people need help and instruction even for sex and that therapists, like myself, using our expertise and sensitivity, try to give it.

MAKING THE BOOK WORK FOR YOU

In my *Ultimate Sex Guide* I have drawn on my fifteen years of practice as a sex therapist. In creating it I have borne the following three issues clearly in mind and it is extremely important that you do the same.

• It is important to put aside the notions of what you think is allowed between two people in bed, and to embrace the thought that many alternative sex practices may be enjoyed, providing always, of course, you do not cause harm to anyone. *It is possible to change your beliefs.*

• Because of AIDS, it makes a great deal of sense to improve an existing relationship rather than treat it lightly. Bringing warmth, sensuality, and sexual and emotional gratification to lovemaking offers optimum incentive to stay with the same person.

• Focusing simultaneously on sexual *and* emotional issues is a pathway to feeling alive in either an existing or a new relationship. If you can be truly intimate with each other, it's hard to find yourself on 'automatic pilot' in bed and it is far less likely that you will become bored.

YOUR GUIDE TO BETTER SEX

On the simplest level, here you will find an enormous range of mental and physical practices that will expand your repertoire of lovemaking. And that, in itself, is no little thing.

Or, one or more of the questions posed by the case histories may have a particular resonance for you, and may provide a very specific answer. Do not be put off, however, if the individual circumstances do not exactly mirror yours, or if the recommended programmes in their entirety may not, or cannot, be followed as set out. They are there to illustrate the range of the possible, and even in isolation can help to liberate feelings and transform sexual behaviour.

Make sure, however, you involve your partner fully in all these endeavours. In this work, a relationship is any encounter between two people, be it the first one, a casual one or a long-term series of encounters. In case you argue against the feasibility of a first time meeting or casual acquaintance amounting to a relationship, there are undoubtedly people who enjoy great emotional heights of sexuality in precisely these situations.

This is not to argue for the constant pursuit of new partners. While it is true that novelty is a powerful aphrodisiac, so too is that marvellous inspiration between man and woman where you know each other's eroticism so intently you are aroused by merely looking at each other. And AIDS is now such a risk it can no longer be wise to opt for novelty when it may end up by killing you.

Since this is a work about sex, many of the solutions and techniques proposed in the case studies and on the sex programme pages are physical ones. But they are physical solutions that give rise to feelings. The feelings then feed back into lovemaking so that the sex act is enhanced and the relationship itself strengthened.

THE CASE
HISTORIES,
PROGRAMMES
AND
EXERCISES

CHAPTER

HOW CAN I SHOW MY INTEREST IN SEX?

"For some people, meeting potential partners is easy, but developing the relationship is a problem. For others, the difficulty lies in meeting suitable partners in the first place."

A SEX THERAPIST deals with all aspects of relationships, even the initiating of them. Some people find their main problem with sex is a lack of it, due to not being able to attract a partner or, having attracted one, not being able to keep them interested.

Men and women, as you can see from my case notes opposite, often have quite separate 'hang-ups' about their appearance and behaviour that get in the way of successfully communicating their interests and desires. For example, many men erroneously believe that women are attracted by large penis size and a muscular body whereas, in fact, most women are repelled by these attributes but appreciate small but sexy buttocks, a flat stomach, long legs and someone taller or of a similar size and shape to themselves. And while men rate a woman's looks as the most important aspect of her attractiveness, different types of men are attracted to different types of figure.

Of course, physical attraction alone is not enough to sustain a close long-term relationship — there must also be an emotional and intellectual dimension. So someone who wants to find a new partner for a lasting relationship should pay attention not only to their physical appearance, but also to the way in which they behave and the impression of themselves that they convey to other people.

CASE STUDY *Steve & Caroline*

Finding a suitable partner and starting an intimate relationship is difficult for many people. For some, such as Steve, meeting potential partners is easy, but developing the relationship is a problem. For others, such as Caroline, the difficulty lies in meeting suitable partners in the first place.

Name:	STEVE
Age:	31
Marital status:	SEPARATED
Occupation:	ACCOUNTANT

Steve had recently separated from his wife after an eight-year marriage. Although he already possessed many of the physical characteristics that initially appeal to women – he was tall, well-built and in good physical shape – he also projected an air of confident indifference that, in fact, obscured his shyness and relative sexual inexperience. He told me, "I find myself wanting to make love to attractive women but not having too much success. Women usually appear to be quite interested in me when we first meet, but only occasionally do we manage to end up in bed together. Inevitably, however, it seems that somehow I do something to frighten them off.

"What do I have to do to not only get women into bed with me but to help my partners relax, so that we can enjoy some really marvellous sex?"

Name:	CAROLINE
Age:	23
Marital status:	SINGLE
Occupation:	EDITOR

Caroline's one long relationship, which lasted about three years, had ended about a year before she came to see me. Since it ended she had dated several men, none of whom interested her especially. She was a slim, quiet woman, who wore glasses, was efficient in her work, and intelligent. She dressed in well-cut but discreet clothes, and talked easily when addressed but did not volunteer information. She said, "I am impatient with the men who ask me out because most of them don't seem to have a brain. I rarely come across someone who is my intellectual equal but there is one chap at the office whom I find attractive; unfortunately he hardly knows I exist.

"I know my upbringing holds me back from flirting, but I think that underneath I'm really a very sexy person. I have terrible hang-ups about my breasts because they're not very big, but I've got nice long legs and I feel I have a lot to offer the right man."

THERAPIST'S ASSESSMENT

What both Steve and Caroline needed to do was to project themselves in a sexier manner.

ATTRACTIVENESS
We all give off distinct impressions of ourselves, usually quite unconsciously, by the way we use body language and by our lifestyles and how we present ourselves. A zest for life, creativity, sexual interest, curiosity and enjoyment are all extremely attractive. Steve's zest for life certainly wasn't apparent on initial conversations, and he only showed it when talking about his special interest in life, which was gymnastics.

Contrary to what Steve had formerly believed, women are not initially attracted by outstanding looks and physique or even fast-talking ability. The surest way to become attractive to women is to treat them as alluring human beings rather than as convenient sex objects: no woman is the least bit interested in being simply another notch on someone's bedpost.

Caroline was right to target her physical appearance, because this is what men are most attracted to. They respond far more to visual signals than women do, so the value of dressing seductively cannot be underestimated.

LOOKING FOR PARTNERS
My immediate recommendation, therefore, was for Steve to use his sporting enthusiasms for breaking the social ice. His shyness would automatically be lifted, and gymnastics would allow his body language to reflect his more confident feelings about this aspect of his life.

I advised Caroline that she was going to need a partner who could deal with her intelligence rather than be intimidated by it, and to visit places where she was likely to come into contact with such individuals, perhaps putting herself in the path of men several years older than herself. She should display her figure more, too, in particular her long, shapely legs, by wearing tighter-fitting clothes and shorter skirts.

Nor did she have to resort to flirting. Being able to gaze at someone and be genuinely interested in their personal story makes an excellent substitute, and providing information that forms a common ground and facilitates interest is a sensible move to make. Matching a potential partner's story with a similar one would show him that Caroline had emotions and a life experience similar to his, and would let him see that she was being open with him.

My programme for
PROJECTING A SEXY IMAGE

Part of what is conventionally thought of as being 'respectable' behaviour lies in sober dress: if you want to seem discreet and unobtrusive you dress quietly. The trouble with this is that, over the years, you can get used to the idea of yourself as quietly unattractive. However, the opposite is also true — gradually altering your appearance and your body language so that you experience yourself as an erotic individual can be a valuable method of overcoming inhibition. Once you have attracted someone with your appearance, you can use suggestive body language to reinforce the beginnings of sexual attraction, and then use touch to communicate your interest to your prospective partner.

Stage 1 PAY ATTENTION TO YOUR APPEARANCE

Becoming truly sensual is a result of internal changes that alter your attitude to sensuality, but these changes are easier to accommodate and can be speeded up if you tackle your outer sexuality first. Actually putting on a sexier expression as you gaze into a mirror allows you to feel sexier; altering your appearance slowly allows you time to get used to the change. Once you start noticing this change, other people will notice it too. The key to changing outward appearance is to take it gradually. Make one change every couple of weeks or so, and don't be afraid to experiment. But don't let up.

Stage 2 USE BODY LANGUAGE THAT IS SUGGESTIVE

Watch yourself the next time you meet someone new. The odds are that your arms will be folded, or your hands clasped in front of you. If seated, you may have swivelled sideways to avoid directly facing your acquaintance. If you are anxious, one leg may be draped over the other, maybe even wrapped around it. Or you may be huddled back in a corner looking as though you are trying to get as far away from people as possible.

BARRIER SIGNALS All these postures are barrier signals indicating that you feel tense or nervous or even under attack. To the person you are with, they show that you don't welcome them and you don't want them to come near. And even though we don't usually analyze the body language of the person opposite, and may in fact be unaware of it on a conscious level, our subconscious still takes in the messages being given and makes us respond accordingly.

If you want to make someone feel welcome you need to be open to them. Avoid barrier signals. If standing, put your arms at your sides. Keeping your shoulders back and leaning forward slightly can indicate that someone has all your attention but that you want them

WARMTH MOVES

• Look longer than usual into a partner's eyes

• Move towards the other person rather more than you would normally

• Smile more than usual, looking in turn at various parts of the body

• Nod your head in vigorous agreement

• Sit using open body signals

• When talking, use hand gestures that manage to take in the partner or that indicate an appreciation of him or her

• Take fast glances at the other person and while doing so, moisten your lips with your tongue, widening your eyes a little

• Make small touching movements. For example, when standing together, stand behind your partner cuddling lightly against his or her body, with both arms around the waist; put an arm around your partner; caress and massage your partner's back

to notice you. If you know someone slightly, don't be afraid of hugging them or even casually resting an arm across their shoulders. These are displays of warmth.

If you are seated, resting your arms on the arms of the chair or extending your arms along the back of a sofa are indications that you are open to the person opposite. If you want them to feel in charge of the situation, ensure that they sit in a chair slightly higher than yours. If you want them to feel vulnerable, direct them to a chair lower than yours.

EYE CONTACT Part of a show of personal interest is an intent gaze focused on your partner's eyes. This makes the person feel special since research has shown that sexual interest is demonstrated by enlargement of the pupils and that this, in itself, is arousing. Men and women, judging photographs where one of a pair has had the pupils of the eyes enlarged by retouching, always rated that picture as the more attractive. (But don't overdo the gazing, or you will just look silly.)

EMULATION Body language can be used to emulate that of a person you are talking to, and reinforces the sense of matching. When a person shifts position, you can copy that shift. Once tuned in to the other person's body movements you can start altering your own, slowly, so that your body becomes open and receptive. The object of your attentions is likely to copy you unconsciously, and assimilate the new feeling of intimacy this creates.

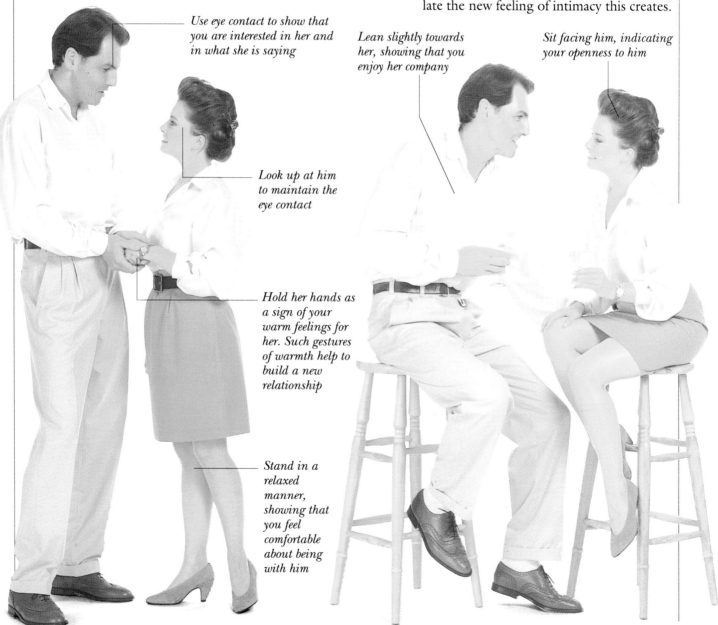

Use eye contact to show that you are interested in her and in what she is saying

Look up at him to maintain the eye contact

Hold her hands as a sign of your warm feelings for her. Such gestures of warmth help to build a new relationship

Stand in a relaxed manner, showing that you feel comfortable about being with him

Lean slightly towards her, showing that you enjoy her company

Sit facing him, indicating your openness to him

Stage 3 USE TOUCH TO SUGGEST INTIMACY

There are a number of occasions and opportunities when you can indulge in deliberate touches that charge your meetings with eroticism. It is important, though, that you deliberately hold back for a while from anything overtly sexual so that you lay the groundwork for a buildup of sexual tension: a mild withdrawal can seem tantalizingly provoking. Because your behaviour will arouse mild anxiety, your partner's entire arousal level will be raised, thus readying him or her to be erotically receptive.

CONVEY WARMTH Hold hands on introduction a little longer than necessary. Look directly into your friend's eyes while talking, but don't stare at them. Use touch to convey warmth; for example, when you feel good about something give him or her a hug. If you feel concerned about something that the other is worried about, display your sympathy by covering his or her hand with yours. When walking, demonstrate your concern for that person's well-being by slipping your hand under his or her arm.

If you accompany a friend to a party or dance where you are standing together much of the time, stand close. When in crowds, put a protective arm around him or her.

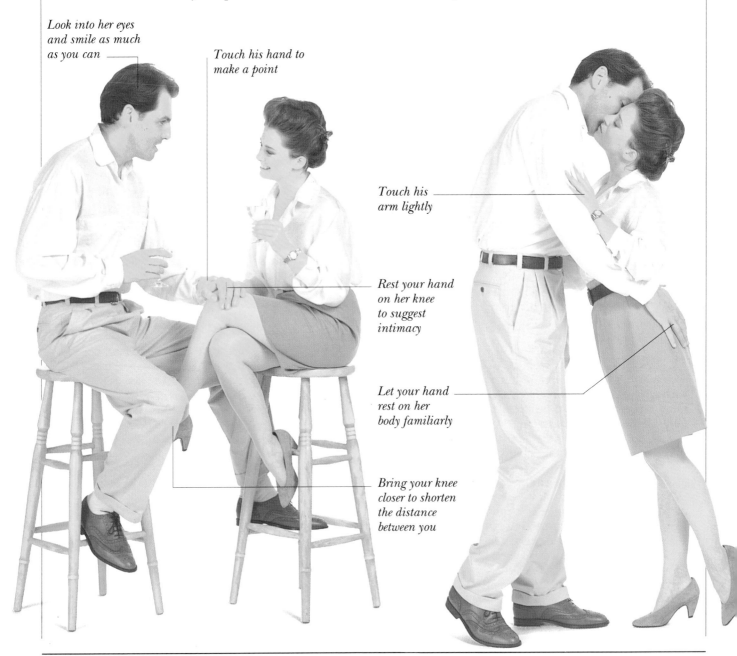

Look into her eyes and smile as much as you can

Touch his hand to make a point

Touch his arm lightly

Rest your hand on her knee to suggest intimacy

Let your hand rest on her body familiarly

Bring your knee closer to shorten the distance between you

INTRIGUING TOUCH   As you get to know each other more, put an arm around your partner as you walk and instead of resting a hand on his or her waist, place it farther down the side of the hip. If your hand reaches round near the pubis, even though this is still a casual touch, it begins to feel suggestive to the person experiencing it. But because they don't know whether or not you mean it suggestively, it also becomes intriguing. A variation on this move is to rest your hand on your partner's waist, and then let it slip a little lower so that it is on the small of the back or even resting on the top of the buttocks.

KISSING   Kiss as a greeting: kiss your partner lightly at first, but as time goes by and you get to know each other better, make the kiss more direct and more lingering. Don't oblit-

Sensual erotic touch p28

erate your partner with the first kiss but make it light and exploratory, rather than fevered and oppressive. This may sound very basic advice, but by following it you are setting the scene for truly sensual lovemaking.

By creating unhurried but sensual beginnings, in which your partner receives a sense of choice without feeling under any pressure, you are creating important foundations upon which to build a happy and successful sexual relationship. And when you get to know your partner better, and you begin to spend more time alone together, you will find that you have many opportunities to make everyday situations more sensual by the use of erotic touch. This will build up the sense of intimacy between you and deepen the feelings you have for each other.

IMPROVING YOUR APPEARANCE

POINTERS FOR MEN

• FACIAL APPEARANCE If you have a beard, consider altering the shape of it to allow your more sensual facial features, such as your lips and cheekbones, to show through more clearly. Your hair should, of course, be clean and tidy, but it may also benefit from trimming or even a total restyling, preferably by a good hairdresser

---

• GLASSES If you wear glasses, are they as flattering to your facial shape as possible? If not, invest in some that are — the range of frame shapes and colours now available means that practically everyone can find a style that suits them — or consider a change to contact lenses

---

• UNDERCLOTHES Many women prefer the appearance of boxer shorts to that of briefs, but whatever your personal preference is, the important thing is that they should be clean, tidy and a good fit. Old-fashioned cotton vests may be practical but the new coloured thermal underwear that clings suggestively to the form is sexier

---

• CLOTHES Smart casual clothes, starting with basic jackets and trousers, can slowly be acquired to replace old drab garments. Beware of bright colours, if you wouldn't normally use them, but concentrate your attention on the style and cut of your clothes: for example, blouson-style jackets team well with classic jeans or with casual trousers. If you are plump, beware of buying trousers that are pleated in front. Trousers with straight panels at the waist invariably look slim and sexy

POINTERS FOR WOMEN

• FACIAL APPEARANCE Emphasize your facial features to bring out the best in them — outline your eyes and lips to accentuate them and highlight your cheek contours with blusher. Pay attention to your hair; have it cut or restyled if it doesn't really suit you the way it is, and if it is a dull colour, brighten or colour it. Don't forget to adapt the colour of your make-up to match your new hair tones

---

• GLASSES If you wear glasses, are they as flattering to your facial shape as possible? If they are not, invest in some with frames that are a better shape or colour, or consider a change to contact lenses

---

• UNDERCLOTHES Throw away old-fashioned, boring underwear and invest in lacy briefs, bras and body suits — knowing that you are wearing sexy underwear, and the sensation of it against your skin, will make you feel sexier and more self-confident. Wear discreetly-patterned tights that show off the shape of your legs, and alternate these with lacy suspenders and sheer stockings

---

• SHOES Start buying shoes with higher heels than you normally wear

---

• CLOTHES Invest in dresses, skirts and trousers that cling and are made of sensual materials. Focus gradually on showing off the shape of your body

---

• SCENT When you take a shower or bath, use body and lotions and spend time in selecting a light but fragrant perfume that enhances your natural scents

SENSUAL EROTIC TOUCH

A variety of situations, including casual everyday experiences, lend themselves to becoming more sensual and erotic by the use of deliberate touch. Close body contact and gentle movements will not only relax your partner, but make him or her aware of your presence at a level deeper than conscious sensation.

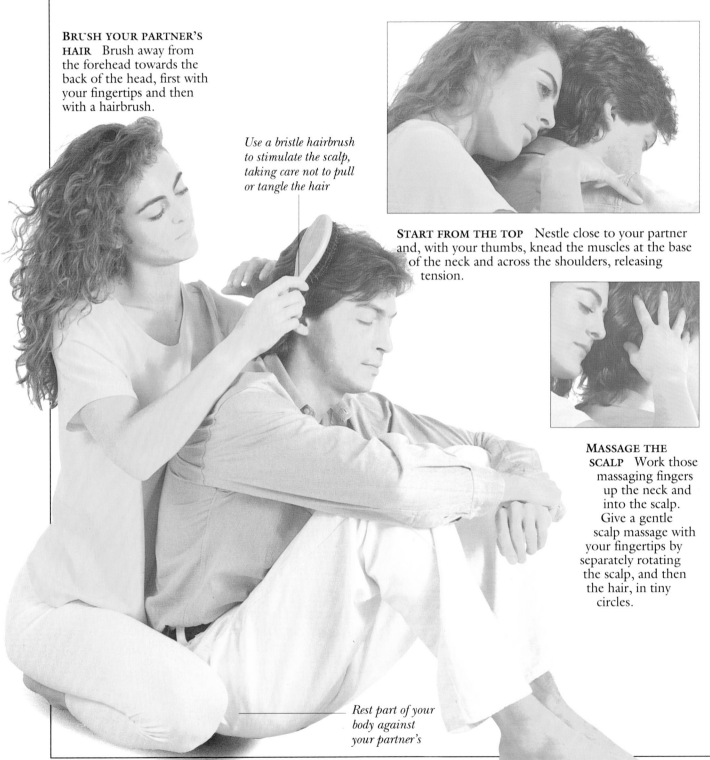

BRUSH YOUR PARTNER'S HAIR Brush away from the forehead towards the back of the head, first with your fingertips and then with a hairbrush.

Use a bristle hairbrush to stimulate the scalp, taking care not to pull or tangle the hair

START FROM THE TOP Nestle close to your partner and, with your thumbs, knead the muscles at the base of the neck and across the shoulders, releasing tension.

MASSAGE THE SCALP Work those massaging fingers up the neck and into the scalp. Give a gentle scalp massage with your fingertips by separately rotating the scalp, and then the hair, in tiny circles.

Rest part of your body against your partner's

TRAIL YOUR NAILS ALONG THE ARMS Lightly draw your fingernails from the crook of the elbow down to the wrist. Repeat this several times in different areas of the inner arms.

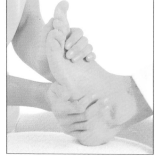

MASSAGE THE SOLES With both hands, and with thumb and forefinger then your whole hand, massage the sole of each foot with a circling movement.

WORK ON THE TOES Gently push a slippery forefinger in and out between each of your partner's toes, turning it from side to side.

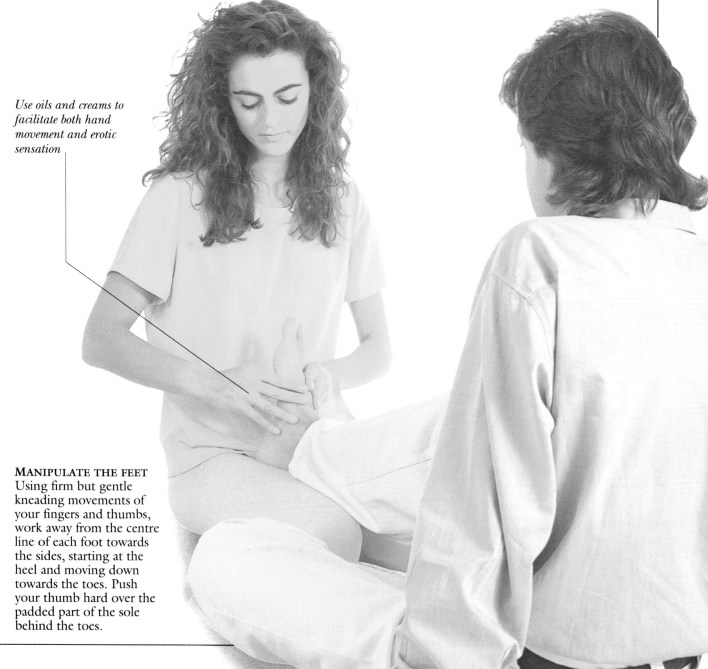

Use oils and creams to facilitate both hand movement and erotic sensation

MANIPULATE THE FEET Using firm but gentle kneading movements of your fingers and thumbs, work away from the centre line of each foot towards the sides, starting at the heel and moving down towards the toes. Push your thumb hard over the padded part of the sole behind the toes.

BASIC LOVEMAKING POSITIONS

There are many different positions in which you can make love, and these simple and straightforward ones are generally recommended when starting a new relationship. They offer opportunities for intimacy as well as satisfying each partner's need to take control. However, because it is possible to make love in so many ways, trying new positions can be great fun and will help to stop your lovemaking settling into a predictable routine, which can lead to the boredom that so often destroys relationships.

THE MISSIONARY POSITION   The missionary is so called because, allegedly, missionaries sent out to 'civilize' the colonies of the old European empires thought that it was the only respectable position for decent people, and insisted that their new converts use it when making love. Despite its staid image, however, it is an enjoyable position with many variations.

You should support your weight on one or both of your hands or elbows to make the most of this position

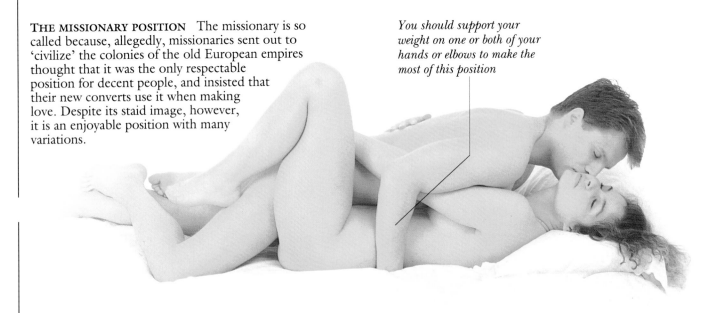

SIDE-BY-SIDE POSITION   As with the missionary, the side-by-side, face-to-face position has many possible variations. In that shown here, she has wrapped both her legs around him; this is fine if he is not too heavy, but if he is, she might find that his weight bears uncomfortably on the thigh that is beneath him.

In this face-to-face position you can kiss on the lips and caress each other easily while making love

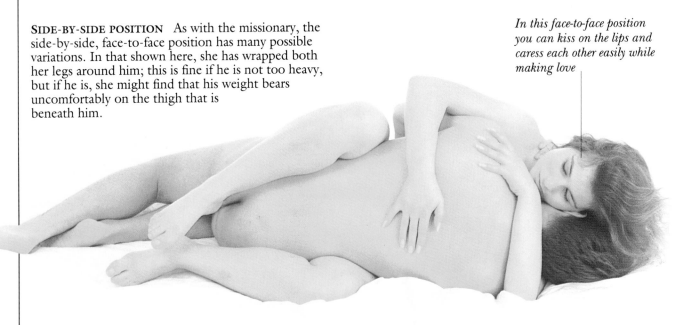

You can use your fingers and hands to stroke and stimulate your partner's genitals and other erogenous zones

THE SPOONS POSITION The spoons is a rear-entry position in which the couple snuggle up together, forming a shape said to be like a pair of spoons nestled together. Pleasant variations on this position include her pushing one leg right back between his after penetration, him leaning backwards away from her, and her bending forward from the waist. The last two variations usually allow greater penetration.

REAR ENTRY There are many rear-entry positions in addition to the spoons and its variations. These include the well-known kneeling (or 'doggy') position shown here, as well as standing, lying and sitting positions and those where she sits astride and facing away from him.

When you are on top, you can control the movements and the depth of penetration

WOMAN ON TOP There are many different woman-on-top variations. For instance, she can kneel astride him and then sit upright, lean forwards or lean backwards, she can lie on top of him with her legs outside his or between them, and he can sit up with her on his lap.

SELF-STIMULATION When the woman is on top she can use her fingers on her clitoris to give herself greater stimulation.

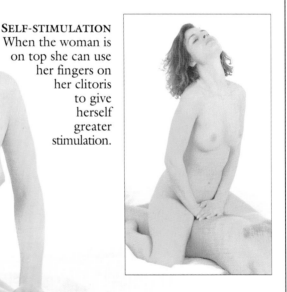

As well as being able to stimulate yourself, you can use your hands to give your partner extra stimulation, too

CHAPTER

2

HOW CAN I TUNE IN WITH WHAT MY PARTNER WANTS?

"There is no harm in saying to your partner, on hearing the question 'What do you like?' the words 'I'm really not sure but I'd certainly love the opportunity of finding out.' It gives both of you, after all, glorious carte blanche."

MANY A MAN subscribes to the myth that he ought to know everything about his woman's sexual needs and that he should be able to read her mind. This is a leftover from the time when the male was traditionally expected to be active in the sexual relationship and the woman passive. And many women, too, suffer from not knowing what it is their male partners would like. These worries can be an especially heavy load if you don't happen to be sexually experienced.

In addition, there are nearly always situations when we feel uncomfortable. New ideas about men's and women's changing roles question sexual as well as social values and place us in situations our upbringing has not equipped us for. For example, a man, dining with a woman friend, may find it hard to cope if she propositions him directly. He may, quite simply, not know how to respond, because she will have stepped outside an age-old formula of dating and mating. If he says "Yes", does that mean he is somehow too easy and therefore weak? If he says "No", will he seem a prude, or a coward who can't deal with the modern woman?

CASE STUDY *Jon & Nora*

Jon and Nora were both sexually inexperienced, and neither knew how to go about finding out what the other enjoyed. Jon thought that asking for sexual information would reflect badly on him while Nora asked, rightly, how you can become experienced without being sexual in the first place.

Name:	JON
Age:	24
Marital status:	SINGLE
Occupation:	SOUND ENGINEER

Jon was tall, slim and blond, and full of nervous energy that made him very extrovert yet inwardly anxious where forming new sexual relationships was concerned.

"I so badly want a girlfriend to love me," he said. "I'm dying to wake up in the morning with someone's arms around me and to feel love for her and know she cares about me. For me, falling in love and making a relationship are based on sex. If the sex part of the relationship isn't right, then I can't love someone.

"The two women I really cared for gave me up, not vice-versa. This means I'm feeling very uncertain of myself. I'm just getting into a new relationship but now I'm scared that I'm somehow going to miss what she really wants, both from the relationship and from sex. How can I find out what my partner really wants?"

Name:	NORA
Age:	29
Marital status:	SINGLE
Occupation:	COMPUTER OPERATOR

Nora had almost waist-length blonde hair, and because she was so beautifully groomed she looked like a model. Yet she was, in fact, shy and retiring, having lived all her life in her parents' home and had only one former man friend, who was a colleague by the name of Bobby.

"I know I've a lot to learn sexually," she told me. "I never had an orgasm with Bobby and he used to tell me I was full of inhibitions and probably frigid. I'm not frigid because I can have orgasms on my own, through masturbation, but when I meet a new man who interests me, and there's one on the scene now, I really feel confused.

"I'm honestly not sure what I want of him. Getting on to his wavelength seems fraught with difficulty. He keeps asking me how I like to make love. The trouble is, I don't really know. But you feel such a wimp saying that. Yet how can I find out what I want without making love with him in the first place? And what happens if I want things he doesn't seem to be offering? I want to please him. How can I reply when he asks me what I want?"

THERAPIST'S ASSESSMENT

Jon was worried that asking his new partner what she wanted in their lovemaking would show up his inexperience and make him seem unattractive. In reality, by enquiring about his partner's likes and dislikes, Jon would be showing that he was interested in her as an individual, and not as a sexual machine off an assembly line.

ASKING QUESTIONS
One way of getting comfortable with asking sexual questions is to think through a phase of lovemaking in your mind. For example, if a man in Jon's situation wants to know if his lover really enjoys her breasts being touched, before he actually asks her he can imagine himself lying naked in bed with her in his arms. In his thoughts, he slowly runs his fingers around her breasts, gently pinching and rubbing her nipples a little. As he does so he says to her, "Does that feel good?" Then, running his fingertips along the sides of her breasts from her armpits down to her waist, he asks, "Or does this feel better?" By giving her options for her answer he is less likely to bulldoze her into saying it was good when it wasn't. He will also provide himself with accurate information. Carrying on from there, in his fantasy, he could say to her, "I'd like it if you would tell me if I do anything you dislike."

I suggested that Jon rehearse such scenes mentally, so that the real event would be much easier to handle and then both he and his woman friend would feel more confident about discussing their likes and dislikes.

FINDING OUT WHAT YOU PREFER
Nora's problem lay in finding out what she herself would like, so that she could tell her partner about it. Once again, I recommended rehearsing various sexual situations mentally, in Nora's case to enable her to predict the emotions that such situations would arouse in her were they to happen in real life.

We all experience a variety of reactions on considering these situations, such as arousal, discomfort or dislike. Arousal and dislike speak for themselves. Discomfort, however, does not indicate unsuitability of, but rather unfamiliarity with, an activity we might like to try. We feel discomfort when we are faced with something new that we are unprepared for. Rehearsing some of these scenes will help give you confidence should you find yourself choosing one of them in reality.

My programme for
IMPROVING SEXUAL
COMMUNICATION

This programme is intended to make both partners in a relationship aware of each other's sexual likes and needs. Discussing and/or actually demonstrating sexual proclivities is essential for a relationship to succeed. Don't worry if you feel inhibited or embarrassed at first, or if your partner does. If you each mentally rehearse the parts that you find awkward, and then take those rehearsals into real life, you will end up knowing a great deal about each other's erotic response. You will also have knocked down walls of inhibition and have fostered an invaluable intimacy between you. Like all the best therapy exercises, however, this programme for improving sexual communication is deceptively simple.

Stage I — INITIATING COMMUNICATION

It is just as important for your partner to know what you like as it is for you to know what your partner likes. But not all of us are good at expressing in words what it is that we do like, and some of us find it especially difficult to express what it is that we like to do in lovemaking. Sometimes, therefore, the

INTIMACY Good communication between yourself and your partner will promote a warm intimacy.

partners in a relationship find that communication about sexual likes is best done with actions and demonstrations as well as through conversation.

TAKE IT IN TURNS If that is the case for you or your partner, you might find it useful to

take turns at demonstrating what each of you likes, sharing the experience as much as possible. Even if you are both quite happy to discuss your sexual needs and desires, you might still find it useful (as well as pleasurable) to demonstrate to each other what it is that you like to do or have done to you.

Showing what you like p38

SEXUAL AWARENESS Of course, you may not be sure exactly what it is that you want from sex, or you may know what you want but find it hard to discuss the subject. This often happens when we are sexually inexperienced and relatively unaware of our own sexual responses, and it is something that happens to us all when we first become sexually active.

Many people find that a programme of self-pleasuring (see pages 226 and 228) helps them to develop an awareness of their own sexual responses, and that this awareness provides them with useful knowledge to bring to their sexual relationships.

And if you are shy about discussing such intimately personal matters as your sexual preferences, the sexual assertiveness programme on page 72 will show you how to overcome your reticence so that you can discuss your sexual likes and dislikes openly.

Stage 2 SHARING A SEXUAL BIOGRAPHY

One of the results of living in a culture where discussions about sex are still partly taboo is that we do not normally share sexual information about ourselves. But even when we are willing to disclose such information, some of us don't consider ourselves to have been particularly sexual in the past, and so feel that we have little to say on the subject. Yet we are all sexual beings from the minute we are born, and our very earliest experiences have a bearing on how we relate to a partner in the here and now.

Thinking back to our early days, asking ourselves a few pertinent questions and then sharing the information with a new partner, is a wonderful way to give that partner a full picture of who we are today. Even if we have never been to bed with anyone, it is still possible to work out, from our life experience, just what is going to matter to us (and therefore to our new lover).

The questionnaire on the right is designed to stimulate your sexual memories. Set aside periods of time in which you can talk through these memories with your partner, and corresponding periods for your partner to talk through his or her memories with you. You will need at least a couple of hours each. If you turn out to be really interested and interesting, the sex talk could go on for days.

MEMORIES Sharing sexual memories with your partner helps you to get to know each other better.

SEXUAL BIOGRAPHY QUESTIONNAIRE

• What was your parents' background? What was their class, religion and culture?

• What were their moral attitudes and their views on enjoyment and play?

• Were your parents affectionate towards each other or were they tense and aggressive towards each other?

• What do you remember of incidents that may relate to your parents' sex life?

• What was their attitude towards nudity?

• Looking back, how successful would you rate your parents' marriage both sexually and socially?

• What kind of hidden messages do you think you received from your parents with regard to sex?

• What kind of attitudes to sex do you consider you acquired during childhood?

• When and how did you first learn about sex?

• Were there any early sexual experiences that were embarrassing or humiliating for you?

• When did you first masturbate?

• Do you have sexual fantasies? And, if so, at what age did they begin?

• Did you or do you have crushes on people of the same sex as yourself?

• If you are a man, at what age did you have wet dreams? If you are a woman, at what age did you start menstruation?

• What was your earliest sexual experience? Was it with someone of the same sex as you, or someone of the opposite sex?

• What have your subsequent sexual experiences and relationships consisted of?

DEMONSTRATING WHAT YOU LIKE

Unless your partner knows what you like or how you become aroused, you can easily be turned off sexually. Demonstration is often the best way of communicating. Take turns at stimulating yourselves and at touching each other's pleasurable areas, so that each of you shows the other what it is that really turns you on. Encourage your partner when he or she is doing something that is particularly arousing for you.

DEMONSTRATE EROGENOUS ZONES
Put your hand over your partner's while they caress you, and guide their hand to your favourite erogenous zones. These might include — apart from your genitals — your nipples, the insides of your thighs, your perineum and your anus, and any other area of your body that, when touched or stroked, arouses you sexually.

Watch your partner's reactions to being touched in a certain spot; this will tell you a lot about its sensitivity

Guide your partner's hand gently, letting it caress you rather than using it to stimulate yourself

DEMONSTRATE SELF-STIMULATION While your partner watches, demonstrate how you like to caress yourself. Explain what you do and how it feels, and include all your favourite erogenous zones.

HAND-ON-HAND STIMULATION With your partner's hand lightly covering the back of yours, caress, stroke and stimulate yourself. Show your partner how best to touch and arouse you, and demonstrate the kind of pressure, motion and rhythm that is most effective. Describe your preferences, for example whether you prefer your nipples to be stimulated by gentle massage of their tips or by having a fingertip circle their sides.

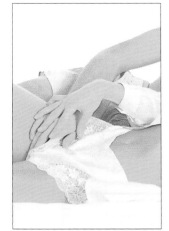

GUIDE YOUR PARTNER Take hold of your partner's hand and use it as you would your own to stimulate your genitals and the area around them, including your pubic region, the insides of your thighs and your perineum.

LET YOUR PARTNER STIMULATE YOU When you have shown where your erogenous zones are and how you like them to be touched, let your partner stimulate them. Keep a hand lightly on your partner's, so that you can apply any guidance that might be necessary, but let your partner do the actual stimulation and so learn how best to turn you on.

Give your partner feedback and encouragement, and when you are getting turned on, let it show

When arousing a partner by hand, a gentle and loving touch is usually what is needed

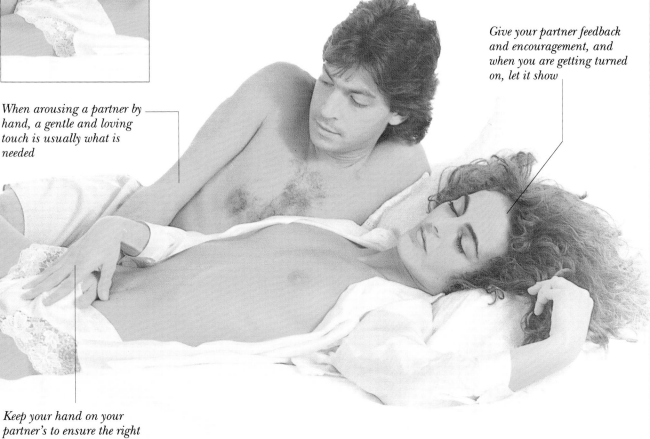

Keep your hand on your partner's to ensure the right areas are stimulated

CHAPTER 3

HOW CAN I OVERCOME MY PARTNER'S INHIBIT~ IONS?

"You can make the break for your generation's sexual freedom in the privacy of your own bedroom."

MANY PEOPLE COME to me because they feel inhibited in their sexual responses. Often, this problem is a result of difficult personal experiences that they have had at some time in the past, or of their being influenced too greatly by societal attitudes. But sometimes the cause of the problem is simply that the individuals involved are being rushed by their partners.

Personal counselling can help where family members or other inhibiting persons are creating problems, and it is important that we recognize that some inhibitions stem from attitudes in society that have been handed down from generation to generation to keep control of our sexual behaviour.

However, if a person's sexual inhibitions are the result of feeling rushed, the guidelines in my programme can be used by everyone to combat this. Personal sexual exploration, for example, which teaches individuals about their own sexual response patterns and, equally importantly, how to enjoy sexual pleasure without feeling guilty, is often a great help in dealing with inhibitions.

CASE STUDY *Louis & Charlotte*

Charlotte's sexual inhibitions, largely the result of the influence of her domineering and moralistic father, were aggravated by the impatience of her partner, Louis. Charlotte wanted to shed her inhibitions, and in order to help her Louis had to learn to take life at a gentler pace.

Name:	LOUIS
Age:	29
Marital status:	SINGLE
Occupation:	FINANCE BROKER

Louis was a busy young executive. Immaculately suited and complete with furled umbrella he gave the impression of being in a continual rush.

"I've been dating Charlotte for a month and find her very attractive," he told me. "She is gorgeous to look at and very bright. Frankly, because of that I expected her to be hot stuff in bed. Maybe she is. I don't know. She never has been when she's with me.

"I've rarely met a girl so inhibited. When we make love she just lies there, completely frozen. But she is quite obviously attracted to me, because when we're not in a sexual situation she winds herself around me and she seems to be tremendously turned on. What I want to know is this: is there really any point in us continuing with the relationship if the sexual side isn't working?"

Name:	CHARLOTTE
Age:	25
Marital status:	SINGLE
Occupation:	LIBRARIAN

Charlotte had huge, dark eyes, bubbly black curls and an engaging, lively personality. Her entire appearance seemed seductive, yet when she talked about her difficulty in making sexual relationships her confidence deserted her and she rapidly became distressed.

"I'm only really attracted to men who are high-flyers," she confessed. "But I know I need a lot of time in which to unwind sexually and high-flyers like Louis rarely have that to spare. I can already sense his impatience with me. I've only had two other serious love affairs. Neither lasted more than a year and only one of them really worked sexually. Even then I didn't have a climax. I know I need time in which to relax and get to know someone before I can start to be sexual. How can I get Louis to take things more slowly?

"My father was strictly religious and extremely moral, and although I don't agree with his views on sex, I do find myself remembering them at the most inconvenient of times. In fact, as soon as I find myself in a sexual situation, I actually feel that I can see his face looking at me."

THERAPIST'S ASSESSMENT

Charlotte was a textbook case of someone trying to live up to her difficult and demanding father all over again in her adult life, only for 'father', read 'lover'. Trained by her father's volatile temper, she was continually tense and awaiting impatient explosion, so it was hardly surprising that she couldn't relax with Louis, who barely disguised his need to get her cured quickly. Charlotte had a double burden because she had also taken in, at a deep level, binding moral messages, so much so that when she found herself getting turned on she instantly imagined her father's face judging her.

PERSONAL SEXUAL EXPLORATION
Charlotte needed to do some personal work, with a therapist, on understanding the effect her father had had on her. This helped her to substitute pleasurable mental images for thoughts of her inhibiting father. She also needed to do some personal sexual exploration of herself (page 232) as she revealed that not only had she never experienced climax, she also had never attempted masturbation. Finding out about her sexuality, discovering its pleasures and the fact that retribution did not fall on her if she enjoyed it, went a long way to improving her chances with a man friend.

Whether Louis is the right man friend for her remains to be seen. Unless he can learn to change his rushed behaviour, he probably isn't. But the fact that he was willing to seek help was a positive sign and meant that it was certainly worth the couple trying a sexual enhancement programme together (page 60).

SEXUAL ENHANCEMENT
Louis also needed some help, because he saw women as objects to consume, or to facilitate his life in his rush for the top of the career ladder. What he hadn't yet worked out for himself was the fact that haste has its price. In his case, the price was that of immense pressure, a sense that he had to carry everything and everybody on his shoulders, Charlotte's sex problem included. Through practising joint sexual enhancement exercises together with Charlotte, Louis learned that she was an individual with responsibility for herself, rather than a fellow lemming. He also received the opportunity to create spaces in his life in which to relax, calm down and enjoy himself.

My programme for
LOSING INHIBITIONS

There are many factors that can affect mental and physical sexual expression. Tension, for example, is a component of sexual response, but too much of it can block excitement and arousal. Sexual repression is another inhibitor of successful lovemaking, and many of us are embarrassed by sex. We find it hard to let go, fearing we will appear primitive or animalistic if we give vent to cries or spontaneous sexual movements. Spending time discovering what makes us feel good, and being able to express those feelings, will make our sexual experiences more satisfying.

Stage PROJECT A SEXIER IMAGE

If you look inhibited, you will probably feel inhibited, and thus narrow your opportunities for joyful sexual expression. By making changes to your outward appearance so that you project a sexier image (see pages 24-27), you can begin to alter your inner responses.

LEARN TO RELAX
Relaxation exercises can help to dispel the tension that often fuels inhibitions.

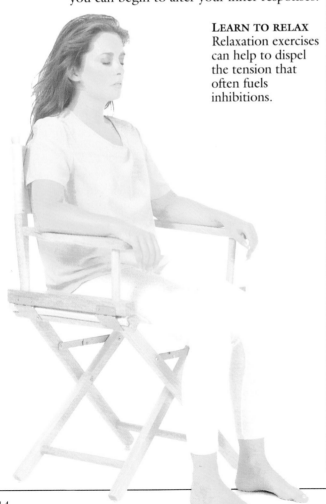

Stage USE RELAXATION EXERCISES

Deliberately practising relaxation exercises before lovemaking can dispel tension and make the difference between eroticism and despair. Neither partner should feel rushed in their responses, and being relaxed means that you can more quickly attune yourself with not only what your partner finds pleasurable but also what you yourself are experiencing.

As a general rule, relaxation exercises are best carried out when lying flat on your back. But because this may not always be practical, the relaxation exercises that are described on the facing page have been chosen because they can be practised in a sitting position, on a comfortable chair.

PREPARATION Before you begin your relaxation exercises, prepare your surroundings. Make sure that you are not going to be disturbed and that the room is warm and comfortable. Then, as a prelude to your relaxation exercises, take a long, warm bath, which will itself help you to relax.

Stage GIVE VENT TO SEXUAL EXPRESSION

An effective way to keep in tune with your sexual responses is to practise self-pleasuring routines (see pages 226-229). Give yourself an hour of privacy, and relax on your bed in a warm room. Caress your body where you know it feels good, moving down towards your genitals. If you usually lie on your back when you masturbate, try it from some other position, such as lying on your side.

RESPOND TO YOUR AROUSAL Let out gasps of breath and make yourself moan when you begin to feel aroused. Try moving your legs around and stroke the rest of your body with the hand that isn't massaging your genitals.

Self-stimulation p230

Start off by making slow body movements but deliberately exaggerate them as you become aroused, and move your pubis against your fingers so that your whole body is active.

As you get aroused, practise saying a few sexual words, quietly but deliberately. As you near orgasm allow your breathing to sound in the room, let yourself gasp and sigh, allow those breaths to become heavier and louder. If you want to scream when you reach orgasm, don't stifle it — let it go.

EXAMINE YOUR FEELINGS If there are aspects of this exercise that make you embarrassed or ashamed, think back into your family history. Where did those attitudes come from? Practise the exercise again a few days later, and compare the moments that embarrassed you the first time with what discomforted you the second time. Are they different? Are you growing more comfortable with noise and movement? As you survive the uncomfortable moments is it getting a little easier to do the exercise? It's important to practise this somewhat exaggerated behaviour slowly, and you may need to do the exercise at least twice a week for some time before you really feel comfortable about it.

Stage DRESS TO STIMULATE EROTIC TOUCH

At the beginning of a sexual relationship we often feel hesitant about taking our clothes off. Meeting up with a partner who actually enjoys making love while clothed can not only be a relief to the inhibited, it can be deliberately piquant to those people who would normally only make love when naked.

Playing the temptress p46

Erotic touch, combined with sensual clothing, very definitely enhances lovemaking. The ways of doing this are as varied as is the imagination and the wardrobe. For instance, a woman could play the temptress — while wearing a bodysuit and refusing to take it off, she could strip her partner and use her hands and her clothed body to stimulate his naked skin. Then she could either leave him aroused but unfulfilled, promising intercourse later, or strip off and make love to him.

RELAXATION EXERCISES

This simple but effective relaxation exercise routine includes deep breathing, mental relaxation and an exercise to release the muscular tension from your body. As well as using these exercises as a prelude to exploring your own sexual responses, you can practise them whenever you want to relax and unwind, for instance at the end of a busy day.

• **HEEL PRESSURE** Sit on a firm but comfortable chair, with your feet about a foot apart from each other on the floor, and push down with your heels for a count of ten. As you do so, enjoy the feeling of being connected to the ground through your heels. When you stop pushing down with your heels, try to retain that feeling of connectedness with the ground. Then start to pay attention to your breathing — get into a steady rhythm of breathing in slowly through your nose and letting go through your mouth

• **DEEP BREATHING** To begin with, you will probably be breathing shallowly from the chest. But as you continue, grow aware of your breathing moving deeper within your body until it is originating from the diaphragm. Once you have reached what feels like a comfortable rhythm, continue automatically while concentrating on your thoughts

• **THOUGHTS** Close your eyes and try to focus your thoughts on one thing, such as a tiny, imaginary pinpoint of light in the darkness. Let your body relax into the most comfortable sitting position you can find, and clear your mind of any intrusive thoughts that may arise (this will become easier after a few sessions, when you no longer have to give much thought to what you are supposed to be doing next in the routine)

• **TENSE AND RELAX** Pay attention to your limbs: some of them may remain tense. Starting with your left foot, deliberately clench it in as tight a muscle spasm as you can manage. Hold this for a count of five and then let go. Repeat the tense-and-relax routine with the whole of your left leg, your right foot and right leg, and then your buttocks, first one side and then the other, then both together. Give your stomach, shoulders, left hand, left arm, right hand and right arm the same treatment, and then screw up your face for a count of five

• **RELEASING TENSION** By exaggerating the tension and then letting it go, you end up by ridding your body of tension altogether. Spend fifteen minutes on working through your body, searching out the trouble spots and applying the tense-and-relax pattern. Once you feel relaxed, sit back and enjoy the lack of tension for a while, perhaps for an extra five or ten minutes if circumstances allow

PLAYING THE TEMPTRESS

Dress can be used to stimulate erotic feeling. In this arousing scenario you wear a form-fitting but seemingly irremovable body suit, and gradually strip your partner of more and more of his clothes while making him intensely aware of your clad body. Whether or not you bring him to climax is optional, but you can increase the tension by deliberately leaving him at the peak of his arousal and making it clear that he has to wait for a follow-up session.

1 UNDRESS HIM Undo his clothing to get at his bare skin, but don't strip him completely.

Press your clothed limbs against his bare skin

2 BE TEASING Use teasing movements of your gloved hands against his naked skin to make him aware of his bare body and your clothed one.

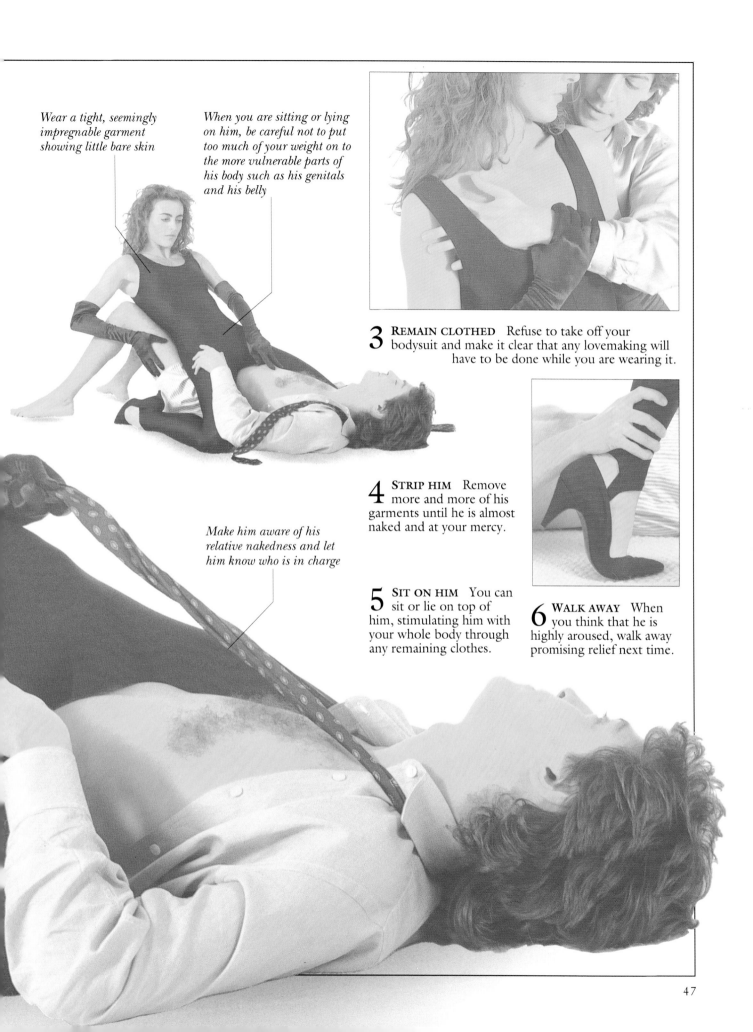

Wear a tight, seemingly impregnable garment showing little bare skin

When you are sitting or lying on him, be careful not to put too much of your weight on to the more vulnerable parts of his body such as his genitals and his belly

3 REMAIN CLOTHED Refuse to take off your bodysuit and make it clear that any lovemaking will have to be done while you are wearing it.

Make him aware of his relative nakedness and let him know who is in charge

4 STRIP HIM Remove more and more of his garments until he is almost naked and at your mercy.

5 SIT ON HIM You can sit or lie on top of him, stimulating him with your whole body through any remaining clothes.

6 WALK AWAY When you think that he is highly aroused, walk away promising relief next time.

CHAPTER 4

HOW CAN I FULLY AROUSE MY PARTNER?

"Since good sex has always been supposed to be spontaneous, it has been unacceptable to consider the idea of planning. And yet, if we truly want to increase our sexual options, that's what we need to do."

HOWEVER DIFFICULT a relationship may have been, men and women grow accustomed to the pattern of certain activities, lovemaking being a prime example. It is possible to have sex with a husband or wife, year in year out, with very little love involved and yet for the mechanics of the sex act to work perfectly.

Take away the feeling of familiarity, substitute a new partner, and a load of insecurities rear their insinuating heads in the subconscious. Sometimes it simply feels wrong to be making love to another, however irrational you know that feeling to be. Sometimes it is the pattern of lovemaking itself that traps you. Only the old one will work, but the partner who provided it is no longer in your life.

Sometimes, the problem is one of trust. You can't fully trust somebody until they have fulfilled certain psychological criteria. Within lovemaking this can include the feeling that a person cares so much about you that your sex problems won't matter; that giving you the necessary time for lovemaking is not only not a bore but a positive joy; that it is the human being who really counts, not just the sex act he or she takes part in.

CASE STUDY *Kathryn & Martin*

Kathryn and Martin were both experienced lovers. Each of them knew exactly what they were doing when it came to lovemaking, but over the years Martin had grown so used to making love in a certain way that he found it difficult to climax when he made love with Kathryn.

Name:	KATHRYN
Age:	31
Marital status:	SINGLE
Occupation:	TEACHER

Kathryn was a 31-year-old teacher who had fallen in love with an older colleague after having had several lovers, including one long-term relationship of six years. She regarded herself as sexually experienced and felt surprised that she didn't know how to deal with the situation she found herself in.

"Martin is a very special man," she said. "He makes me feel beautiful, dynamic and sexy, but we have a problem in bed. Everything's fine for me. He's a gorgeous, imaginative lover, knows exactly what to do and brings me to orgasm in just about any and every way imaginable. The trouble is, he only manages to climax with the greatest difficulty, and we can spend hours on having intercourse before he can come. By the time we finish, I'm tired, sore and dare I say it, bored? Is there any way I could speed him up?"

Name:	MARTIN
Age:	50
Marital status:	SEPARATED
Occupation:	TEACHER

Martin had thick, grey hair and an attractive, tanned face, but an air of fatigue. He had recently separated from his wife, and revealed that there had been little sex in his marriage for many years. Kathryn was the first woman he had made love to, other than his wife, in twenty years.

"I didn't have a very active sex life during my marriage but when we did get it together I had no trouble at all in coming. Now, though, it's as if the sensation in my penis is blunted. When we start off I do feel very aroused, but turning her on takes time, and by the time she has climaxed my first impetus seems to have vanished. Of course, I've been used to lovemaking in a certain pattern with my wife and I suppose not doing this is impeding me.

"Did my wife do anything differently from Kathryn? Well yes, of course she did. One of the things I miss is that she used her hands on me a lot. For instance, she was quite rough with my penis."

THERAPIST'S ASSESSMENT

Both Kathryn and Martin were saying, independently of each other, that they wished the other would speed up a bit. Unfortunately for Kathryn, Martin was experiencing a period of readjustment after the end of his marriage, and he was finding it difficult to adjust to new lovemaking routines. Moreover, he, like many other older men, had difficulties with stimulation: it is perfectly common for men to need more stimulation as they grow older.

EXTRA STIMULATION
The extra stimulation that an older man often needs may take the form of additional visual stimulation, such as the use of blue movies or books, or it may involve physical stimulation such as very firm or vigorous handling of his genitals. Many a man likes attention paid to his penis and genitals by his partner's hand during intercourse, while others also need some anal and prostate gland stimulation in order to climax.

MUTUAL TRUST
Then, too, Martin and Kathryn may not have learned to trust one another sufficiently. Martin hadn't liked to suggest that he should go ahead and climax first during lovemaking, instead of taking time to stimulate Kathryn, because he felt it would prevent him from satisfying her. It hadn't occurred to him that Kathryn might not mind this, or that she might love him enough to tolerate a lack of satisfaction occasionally. Another thing that didn't occur to him was that even if he no longer had an erection, there are many enjoyable ways of satisfying a partner other than by intercourse.

SPEEDIER RESPONSE
Once all these new scenarios had been explored in counselling, Martin did allow more feeling to seep through into his consciousness and ultimately his penis. He managed to be upfront about the methods he preferred: like many men, he favoured very rough handling of his penis, and once Kathryn understood this his response speeded up remarkably.

USING A VIBRATOR
Martin welcomed the suggestion of occasionally using a vibrator to give Kathryn an especially intense arousal. He liked the option this gave him, namely that if, on these occasions, she climaxed quickly, he could remain spontaneous with his early excitement.

My programme for
INCREASING YOUR OPTIONS

Most of us enter into sexual relationships with little thought about what we want from them. One result is that often we don't end up doing what we want, nor do we get the sort of lover we really desire. Part of increasing your options is to know yourself, your own responses and those of your partner. And by slowly becoming more daring, either on your own or with a partner, you will gain more confidence, become more assertive, will learn to cope with rejection better and will go on to initiate sexual acts that you may have wanted to do but didn't have the confidence to suggest.

Stage   LEARN MORE ABOUT EACH OTHER

Deliberately exploring yourself and your partner is the first step in learning what sexual options may exist for you. Self-pleasuring that leads to self-knowledge is vital, as is learning your partner's erogenous zones. Only by widening your knowledge of yourself and your partner can you give yourself choices.

EROGENOUS ZONES When you explore your partner's erogenous zones, start with the obvious ones such as nipples and genitals and try out different ways of stimulating them. Then ask your partner what other erogenous zones they are aware of, and find out how he or she likes them to be stimulated.

After you have explored the erogenous zones that your partner is aware of, look for others: most people have more erogenous zones than they ever imagined.

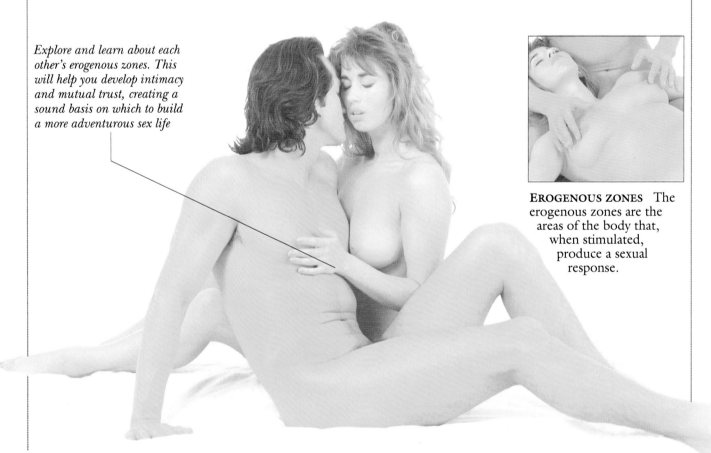

Explore and learn about each other's erogenous zones. This will help you develop intimacy and mutual trust, creating a sound basis on which to build a more adventurous sex life

EROGENOUS ZONES The erogenous zones are the areas of the body that, when stimulated, produce a sexual response.

Stage DISCOVER YOUR OPTIONS

There are a number of activities you can begin to experiment with to increase your sensuality and explore possibilities that may not have occurred to you before.

Sensual touch p28

STROKING Touching and stroking yourself and your partner are among the more obvious sources of sensual pleasure. Touch yourself slowly and sensuously after a hot bath, using sweet smelling body lotions or oils and discovering your hidden erogenous zones. Stroke your partner from time to time, and in addition give 'mental stroking' by regularly telling your partner that you love them and find them attractive and sexy. Explain to your partner that you, too, would like to be touched and stroked, and share your feelings about this openly and freely.

MASTURBATION Learn to masturbate freely and with no guilt, and have sex only when you want to, not when you don't. Be choosy and seek the sort of sex experience that you desire, and don't be afraid to indulge in fantasy. Try expanding on your existing fantasies, and bring in new ideas; if possible, find a fantasy that you can act out with your partner, remembering that you may have to adapt it slightly in order to cater to your partner's sexual preferences.

Be frank with your partner about what you would like to do, but be willing to drop the idea if your partner isn't keen on it, and to consider any ideas and suggestions that your partner may have.

SEX WITHOUT INTERCOURSE Don't forget that there are plenty of non-intercourse sexual activities that you and your partner can share. These range from simply looking at and admiring each other's naked bodies to mutual masturbation and oral sex.

You can, of course, combine any or even all of these activities with intercourse. You might want to do this simply for the pleasure of it, or perhaps as a means of introducing an element of variety into your lovemaking so that you don't slip into a predictable routine that will inevitably become boring.

Either way, you will find that the sharing of non-intercourse sexual activities will add a new dimension of sensuality and intimacy to your relationship.

Stage ADD MORE OPTIONS

Even when you and your partner have learned to discover your options, there is still room for expanding what the two of you have found possible to do in bed so far. Taking what you have already discovered as your starting point, you will find it easy to build up a wide variety of loving sexual practices.

INCREASE EROTICISM Every day, tell your lover what you love about him or her, and also tell yourself what it is you love about you. Add to the eroticism of your lovemaking by putting mirrors alongside your bed, so that you and your partner can watch yourselves making love. An extension of this idea is to record the sounds of your lovemaking on tape, or even to set up a camcorder or a video camera and recorder and make a movie of it.

SHARE SENSUAL EXPERIENCES Masturbate in front of your lover, and try a new sex position every few weeks. When you have time, take a shower or bath together, then massage each other with scented oils and give each other a foot massage. Other shared sensual experiences you might like to try include brushing and washing each other's hair, eating dinner together in the nude, fingerpainting each other's bodies, reading erotica together or out loud to each other, and sharing a vibrator.

MENTAL EROTICISM Eroticism is, of course, a mental as well as a physical phenomenon, and there are plenty of ways in which you and your partner can show your love for and attraction to each other without physical contact. For instance, you could send each other love letters or leave love notes in unexpected places, or describe sexual fantasies to each other in explicit detail. You could even arrange to meet in a bar or at some other suitable venue and pick each other up.

Fantasies pp138-143

SHEDDING INHIBITIONS Perhaps the main difficulty confronting people who are convinced that they are ineffective, and therefore couldn't carry out any of the suggestions mentioned above, is that of breaking away from their inhibitions. However, someone who is going through any experience of making overtures to a partner (or possible partner) is already making that essential breakthrough, even though they may not realize it.

SEXY UNDRESSING

Visual stimulation is extremely important to a man's arousal. A normal sex drive can be given an extra boost and a depressed one awakened by the sight of a female removing her clothes in a provocative way. A professional stripper will have had plenty of experience, and while no-one expects you to be as good, you can improve your undressing technique enormously by regular practice in private in front of a full-length mirror.

Let a strap slip over your shoulder to hint at further disarray

Wear an underwired uplift bra to emphasize your breasts and cleavage

Rub your hand seductively up and down your thigh before removing your slip

Let some thigh show between the tops of your stockings and the bottom of your panties

SLIP OR CHEMISE Your order of undressing, once the outer layers have been removed, might focus on your slip. One that you can drop and step out of, while still wearing your high heels, is preferable to one that is pulled off over your head.

HIGH HEELS These are often a turn-on for men, because they make a woman's legs look longer and tend to push her buttocks to a sexier angle. (Try walking around the room in your underwear and heels, and see what effect it has on him.)

Keep hold of your slip as you step out of it, so that you can then throw it aside with the kind of dramatic gesture that a stripper would use

FEIGN MODESTY
Keep your eyes facing downwards, feigning modesty. This false modesty will heighten his excitement by making him feel, subconsciously, that he shouldn't really be watching

PANTIES Pulling your panties off using only one hand looks more graceful than bending over and using both.

STOCKINGS AND SUSPENDERS Stockings and suspenders are always sexier than panty-hose, and cutaway briefs or French knickers, preferably silk ones, are sexier than ordinary cotton panties.

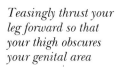

Teasingly thrust your leg forward so that your thigh obscures your genital area

STOCKING REMOVAL
Undoing suspenders allows you great opportunities for making delicious shapes with your legs, and slowly peeling the stocking away from a perfectly groomed limb is extremely erotic.

Adopt positions that you know are a turn-on

TAKING YOUR BRA OFF
Being reluctant to disclose your breasts, and teasing a little about whether you really are going to take your upper garment away or not before finally daring to do so, will be far more erotic than if you just suddenly whip it off.

Use your fingers and hands to stroke your legs seductively as you slip your stockings off

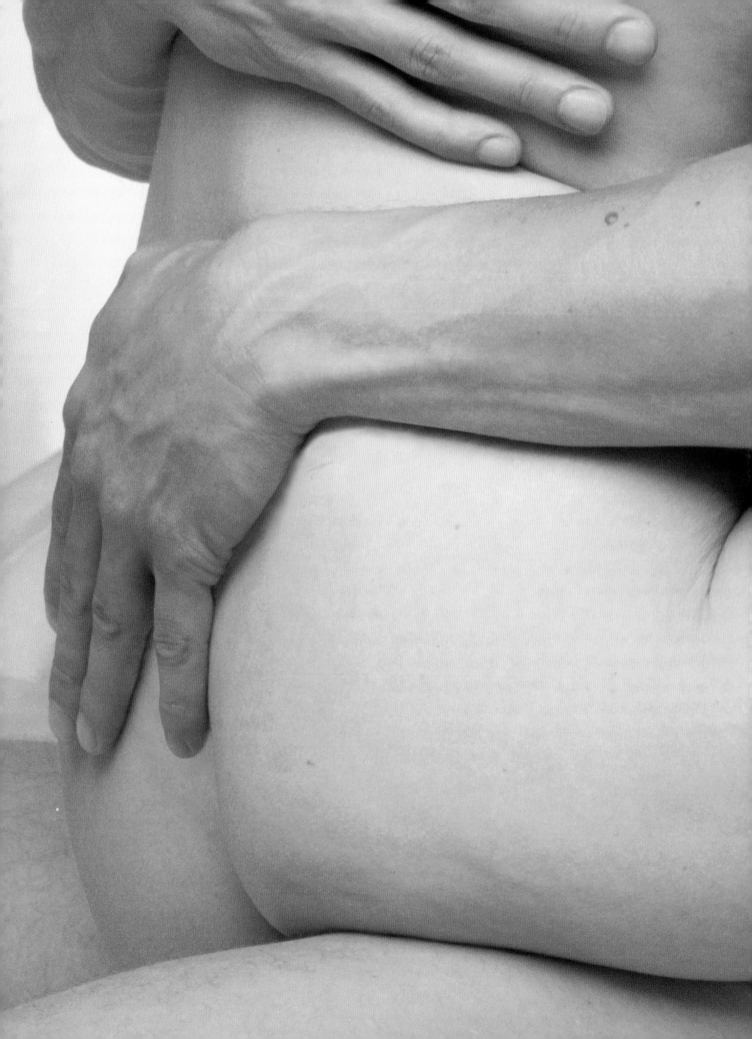

CHAPTER

5

HOW CAN WE PROLONG THE SEXUAL EXPERI~ENCE?

"Some men complain that they come too quickly, but when questioned they admit to lasting for over half an hour. The question then has to be asked, too quickly for whom?"

EJACULATION control is one of the main causes of anxiety among men, particularly among younger men with relatively little sexual experience, and it is often coupled with a lack of self-confidence about sexual activities. Many men with a tendency to come too fast have anxious, over-tense natures. They may hurry over many ordinary aspects of their daily lives, their eating habits being a prime example.

But there are many different versions of rapid ejaculation, ejaculation that occurs too soon for the couple concerned but is not, technically speaking, premature. Some men come too quickly with certain women, but have no problem at all with others. Such selective rapid ejaculation usually indicates something problematic about the relationship rather than about the sex act.

Also, some men come quickly when they are making love, but they can last out for hours during solitary masturbation. This is probably because they do not feel that they are under pressure to perform when they are masturbating.

CASE STUDY *Alan & Maya*

Alan and Maya each had what they saw as a difficulty, and in combination these difficulties turned into a problem. The problem was not one of premature ejaculation on Alan's part, nor one of an inability of Maya to reach a climax. It was simply that Maya took longer to climax than Alan did.

Name:	ALAN
Age:	31
Marital status:	SINGLE
Occupation:	BANK CLERK

Alan was a bank clerk and meticulous but anxious by nature. He came from a divorced home and was needy for a steady partner. He had been dating since he was 14, and had had two steady girlfriends.

"I was really depressed after Annette, my last girlfriend, chucked me," he confessed. "But now I've met another lovely woman. I think she's amazing but I'm terrified I'm going to mess up this relationship, too. One of the things that's on my mind, and this is because I think it was partly to blame for Annette ending with me, is that I'm worried I come too fast. It's not that I'm a premature ejaculator, I'm not, but my new girlfriend, Maya, takes a long time to reach orgasm. By the time she's there, either I've lost interest because I've had to keep going for so long or I come before she's had her climax, even though we've been making love for half an hour. I really want this relationship to work. How can I get her more stimulated, and how can I last out long enough to do this?"

Name:	MAYA
Age:	33
Marital status:	DIVORCED
Occupation:	BANK CLERK

Maya was Alan's colleague. She had had a number of menfriends in the past, including a brief marriage, and was quite surprised to hear what Alan was saying.

"I hadn't realized he was so anxious about our lovemaking," she said "He disguises it very well. But I've never been able to climax quickly. It's faster when I masturbate, of course, but I do wish I could find a man who somehow seemed to know what is right for me sexually. I think I'm asking for the impossible, though. I'm also aware that some of this is to do with trust. I do feel a great deal of this for Alan. In fact, that's the reason I've managed to climax with him at all. I've had very good feelings about him. I have been able to open up to him. And the more I trust him, the easier it gets for me to climax, but if there is any way in which I can speed up my arousal then obviously I'd like to know about it."

THERAPIST'S ASSESSMENT

It's important to stress that needing to ejaculate after half an hour's lovemaking is not a sex problem, nor is climaxing only after about three-quarters of an hour's stimulation. But for this couple, the difference in timing constituted a relationship problem.

EJACULATION CONTROL
To improve his ejaculation control, I advised Alan to practise the squeeze technique with Maya. This technique is a method of learning to control the ejaculatory reflex. The woman masturbates her partner until he tells her that he is just about to ejaculate. At that point she squeezes his penis firmly, with her thumb on the frenulum and her fingers on top of the penis just below the glans, until his urge to ejaculate has gone. Then she continues to masturbate him, applying the squeeze each time he is about to ejaculate. By practising the technique patiently and regularly, and trying to hold back without his partner needing to apply the squeeze, a man can learn how to control his urge to ejaculate.

STIMULATION
Alan also greeted Maya's statement, that she didn't mind in the least if he came first, with profound relief. How then to stimulate her after he had climaxed became an urgent concern. For the first time the couple talked about Maya's needs. "How is it different, when you do it to yourself?" Alan asked. In subsequent lovemaking sessions he asked her to show him and to help him do the same. Although all this accelerated Maya's response, the couple needed encouragement since the improvement, on both sides, took time. To begin with, it was easy to lose heart.

NON-GENITAL SEXUALITY
In addition to explaining ejaculation control and ways to give stimulation, I recommended that Alan should learn to focus on aspects of sexuality other than the purely genital. He then appreciated, almost for the first time, the touching, stroking, caressing and cuddling side of sex. With Maya, he took it in turns to do the sexual enhancement programme (see page 60). Apart from giving him good sensual experience it taught him to relax and enjoy pleasure which his anxious feelings had previously ruled out. Alan had, in effect, needed permission to enjoy lovemaking, and Maya, too, needed permission, in her case to use a vibrator (see page 238). This turned out to be something she had wanted to experiment with for years, but she hadn't allowed herself to do so.

My programme for SEXUAL ENHANCEMENT

Our mutual lovemaking routines tend to develop into certain specially rewarding patterns. There is every good reason for this, for the patterns we adopt are those that give us maximum pleasure, but meanwhile the alternative routes to sensuality are dropped by the wayside. This is a pity because, however marvellously a couple may embrace each other, it is always fun to have alternatives.

In addition to the benefits of having alternative routes to sensuality, it is stimulating to encounter feelings of newness; but these are difficult to manage in a long-standing relationship. Regaining freshness in lovemaking involves using a sexual enhancement programme that takes you back to basics, doing things together that you may not have done since the earliest days and developing a kind of touch therapy that restores your belief in each other and evokes delight. A good sexual enhancement programme also helps to improve sexual communication (see pages 36-37) by asking you to share your feelings and reactions with each other, and by encouraging a return to the days of 'petting'.

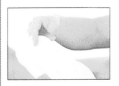

Tactile erotism p64

THE IMPORTANCE OF TOUCH Touch is possibly the most important and enhancing aspect of any relationship. Good touch takes us back to our earliest days when we were touched all over by the enclosure of our mothers' wombs, and to when, as little children, we found comfort and security in being cradled in our mothers' arms, and fun in playing touching and tickling games with our parents and our brothers and sisters. In later life, we in effect recreate these childish experiences with our lovers. But not all of us are good at touching, maybe because we received very little of it as babies, or because our partners are reluctant to be touched, or perhaps because we believe that touch is only acceptable when it is directly linked with sex.

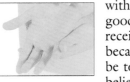

Erotic touch p28

BACK TO BASICS What follows here is a programme designed to introduce you to the sensuality of the skin. It allows you and your partner to get back to basics and to rediscover hitherto forgotten delights by the use of massage and mutual caressing.

Stage GIVE EACH OTHER
A MASSAGE

Comfortable surroundings, privacy, warmth and a firm surface (preferably covered in a large, soft towel) to lie on are prerequisites for a successful massage session, as are warm hands and warm massage oil. When using the oil, rub it into your hands first before applying it to your partner's skin. Do *not* drop it directly on to your partner's skin because this often gives a distracting shock.

Your partner lies face-down while you are giving this massage, which concentrates on the back, shoulders and buttocks. During your massage sessions, don't forget both to ask for and to give feedback. You are learning what feels good for each other, rediscovering forgotten sensations and creating new ones. Let each other know where touch feels especially marvellous.

A general rule of massage is to make it *slow*, using the following basic massage strokes.

CIRCLING The first and most basic stroke, which can also be used to link other strokes, is to place the palms of your hands on your partner's shoulders and move them in circles. Move both hands in the same direction, working firmly outwards and away from the backbone and progressing down the back and along the sides of the body until you reach the buttocks.

Continue the circling on down the buttocks until you reach the upper part of your partner's legs, and then reverse the process and work your way back up the body again. The circling stroke can be used in this routine and in any other you want to invent. On the last circling session, finish below the buttocks. From there, you can carry out the next movement, which is the glide.

THE GLIDE The glide is the most spectacular part of any massage. Place your hands on the lowest part of your partner's bottom with the palms flat and the fingers pointing towards the head. Then, with the weight of your body directed from your solar plexus, start pushing both hands up along the spine, taking as long as you like. This is a heavy stroke, as you are actually leaning on your partner, who experiences it as a wave that flows along his or her back and threatens to engulf the head. After the glide, continue the massage by using swimming and thumb strokes.

SWIMMING The swimming action is similar to circling, but your hands circle close together in opposite directions instead of in the same direction, moving in the sort of way that

SWIMMING The action of the swimming massage stroke involves moving your hands close together in opposite circles, rather you would if you were swimming the breast stroke. This stroke is best suited to massage of the back, especially the more fleshy areas of it, and the buttocks. As with all massage strokes, this one calls for the use of plenty of warm massage oil.

they would if you were swimming using the breast stroke. You can do this stroke up and down all the fleshy parts of your partner's back, including the buttocks.

THUMB STROKES Working with both thumbs on your partner's lower back, make short, rapid, alternate strokes with each thumb, moving up the buttocks towards the waist. Carry this on up the right-hand side of the body to the shoulders, then repeat on the left-hand side. Finish off by concentrating again on the buttocks.

FEATHERING The light, skimming touch of feathering has a soothing and calming effect, and your partner will find that apart from relaxing the mind it enhances the effects of

CIRCLING Circling is a basic stroke in which both hands move in circles in the same direction, unlike in the swimming stroke where they move in opposite directions.

FEATHERING One of the most playful of strokes for a massage is feathering. You skim your fingertips across your partner's skin, using both hands or just one hand at a time.

Give your massage on a bed or, if your bed is too soft, on a mattress, duvet or folded blankets placed on the floor

Use warmed massage oil to make your hands and your partner's skin slippery and sensuous

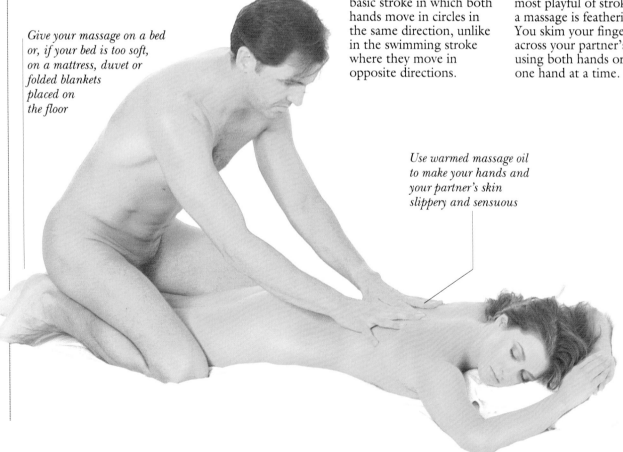

the whole massage session. It feels good after the firmer types of massage such as circling, kneading and thumb strokes, and you can use it at any point (and any number of times) during your massage session. You can also use a variation of it at the start of the session, before you begin the circling, as a pleasurable and relaxing way of applying the warmed massage oil to your partner's body.

Begin by giving your partner a series of gentle, flowing hand strokes. Using the palm and fingers, draw your hand as lightly as possible down your partner's back from shoulders to buttocks. Just as your hand reaches your partner's buttocks and you are about to lift it away, begin a second stroke with your other hand.

Continue in this fashion for about a dozen such overlapping strokes, so that the sensation your partner feels is of one long, continuous stroke. Repeat the stroking down the back of each leg, and then repeat the back and leg strokes all over again, using only the tips of your fingers and touching your partner's skin as lightly as you can.

KNUCKLING You can apply firm, localized pressure to areas such as the shoulders, chest, hands, legs and feet by using your thumbs, either by simply pressing with them to apply static pressure for a few seconds or by moving them in small circles to create rippling, circular waves of pressure. An alternative to this thumb pressure is to use knuckling strokes.

PRESSURE Use your thumbs to exert localized pressure — either static pressure, where you press for a few seconds before moving to a new position, or circular pressure, where you move your thumbs in small circles.

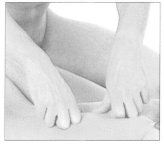

Always take your time when giving a massage — make your strokes slow and sensuous

KNUCKLING Use your knuckles to massage your partner's shoulders, chest, palms and soles. Use small, circular movements to create a rippling effect.

KNEADING The kneading massage stroke is, as its name implies, the sort of action you use when kneading dough. It is particularly useful for massaging the fleshier areas of your partner's body, such as the buttocks and thighs, and also for the shoulders and the base of the neck.

Your partner will be more comfortable with a pillow for head support

As the name suggests, this involves using your knuckles, moving them in small, circular strokes to create a rippling effect on your partner's skin and the underlying flesh.

Use the middle sections of your fingers for these strokes, with the fingers curled back so that their tips are lightly pressing against your palms. Like kneading, knuckling is especially suitable for massaging the upper chest, the shoulders and the base of the neck, and for the hands and feet and the tops and outer sides of the thighs.

To massage a hand by using knuckling, first support it palm-up in one of your own hands. Then work the knuckles of your other hand into the palm with small, circular movements, covering the whole palm and using pressure that varies from light to firm. Use this stroke in conjunction with thumb pressure — applied to the palm and to the back of the hand — to loosen up and relax the muscles and tendons. Use a similar combination of knuckles and thumb to massage your partner's feet.

KNEADING   Kneading is a massage stroke that employs the same sort of action as you would use when kneading dough— you take an area of flesh between your fingers and thumb and alternately squeeze and release it. Light kneading will stretch and relax the skin and the muscles that lie just beneath it; to massage the deeper muscles the kneading action must be firmer.

Kneading is especially useful for massaging and relaxing the fleshier parts of your partner's body, such as his or her buttocks, hips and thighs, and for dispelling the tension from the shoulders and the base of the neck. It can, however, be used on any part of the body where there is sufficient flesh to make the stroke effective and pleasurable.

The basic kneading action involves both hands, which you place flat on your partner's skin, side by side with thumbs extended sideways. Press the palm of one hand down so that a bulge of your partner's flesh is squeezed up into the area between your thumb and forefinger. Grasp the flesh with that hand and gently squeeze it, then as you release it grasp it with the other hand. Repeat this action several times, rhythmically squeezing and releasing the flesh with alternate hands.

When you become practised at this stroke, you will be able to squeeze the flesh so that it appears to travel from one hand to the other with a short, wave-like motion. Use a firm, deep kneading action on particularly fleshy parts of the body such as the buttocks and the outer sides of the thighs and hips. To make the kneading action even more deep and stimulating when you are massaging these areas, give each handful of flesh a firm but gentle twisting motion in addition to the basic squeezing action.

Less fleshy areas (such as the inner thighs and the calves, abdomen, chest, back, shoulders, neck and arms) require a relatively light kneading.

Stage USE MASSAGE FOR SEXUAL ENHANCEMENT

Begin with a warm bath, preferably shared. Soap each other's body lingeringly, and let your slippery fingers glide around each other's curves. Lie back and luxuriate in the warmth, and enjoy the sensation of skin on skin. Take your time.

Once out of the bath, wrap each other in warm, fluffy towels, and move to a warm bedroom (all this heating-up needs to have been organized in advance). You are now going to take it in turns to give each other a massage, but you should agree not to have intercourse (this removes any performance demands) and for half an hour each of you massages the other. The one being massaged tells the other exactly how it feels to be touched in every part of the body — except the genitals, which you may not touch at this stage — and describes in turn how he or she would like to be touched. You are just trying to give and receive pleasure at this stage, and you should repeat this procedure at two or three one-hour sessions a week, at times when you are ensured privacy.

Stage GENITAL PLEASURING

Begin with the warm bath as before, and then move to the bedroom. Once again, you should agree not to have intercourse. Continue with

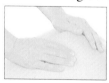

Sensual massage p128

the massages, but this time include the genitals. The purpose of this is to provide information about response to touch and to give good sensual feeling. The man should explain how he likes to be touched on his penis and the woman how she likes to be touched on, at or near the vagina and clitoris. You should both be trying to give pleasure, but not trying to give orgasm.

TACTILE EROTICISM

Exploring the erotic delights of touching and being touched is not only great fun, it also encourages trust and intimacy and helps to develop good sexual communication between you and your partner. In addition, by making you more aware of your own responses to touch and by teaching you more about your partner's responses, it is a useful technique for enhancing or rejuvenating your sex life.

A TOUCH OF SILK Silk has long been prized for its sensual delicacy, and you can use it to stroke and tantalize your partner to great effect. Use a silk scarf or handkerchief, trailing one end of it lightly and teasingly across your partner's naked skin.

Draw the silk across her skin as slowly as possible to maximize the eroticism of the sensation

One effect of being blindfolded is a dramatic heightening of your sensitivity to touch

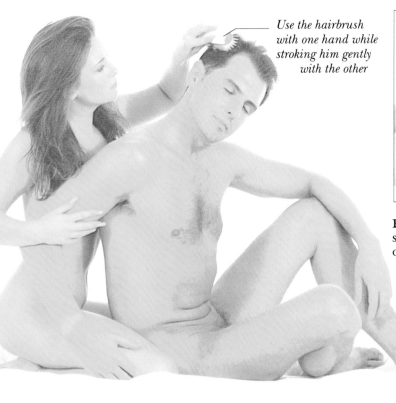

Use the hairbrush with one hand while stroking him gently with the other

BRUSH STROKES An altogether different sensation from that provided by silk can be obtained by the gentle use of brushes. Use a soft-bristled brush, such as a baby's hairbrush, to tickle and stimulate your partner's bare skin (above), and a harder-bristled brush to groom your partner's hair and massage his or her scalp (left).

He will find that the tingling feeling created by the scalp massage is pleasantly relaxing and soothing

PAINT YOUR BODIES
Using your fingertips to apply body paints to each other is sensual on a variety of levels — there is the pleasure of dipping your fingers into the paint and smearing it on to your partner's skin, the enjoyable sensation of having it applied to your own skin, and the sheer playful fun of creating coloured patterns on each other's body.

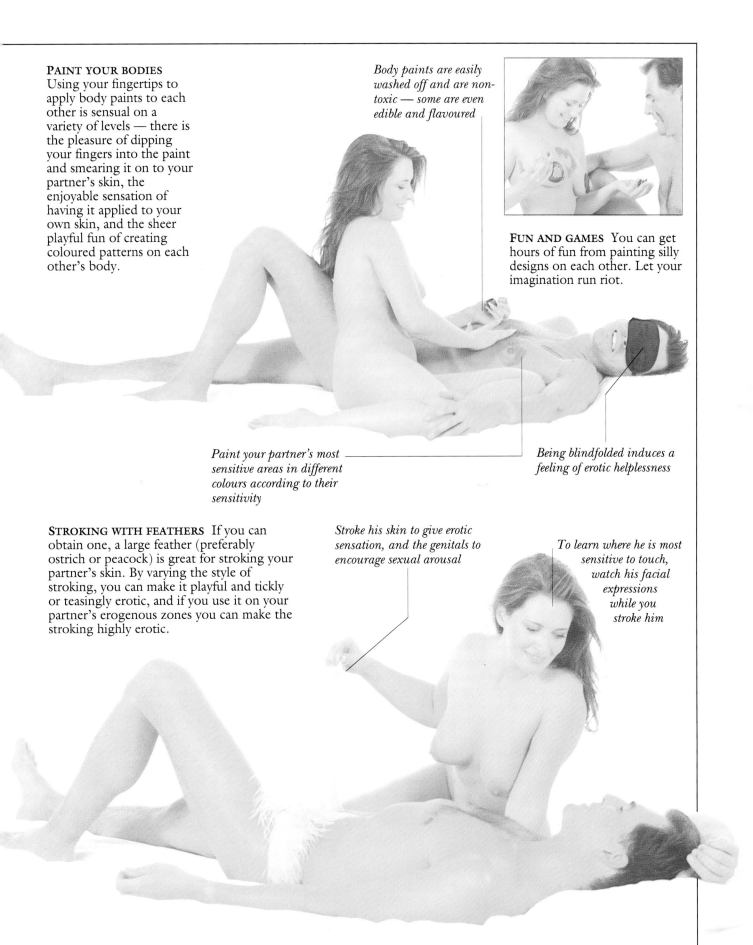

Body paints are easily washed off and are non-toxic — some are even edible and flavoured

FUN AND GAMES You can get hours of fun from painting silly designs on each other. Let your imagination run riot.

Paint your partner's most sensitive areas in different colours according to their sensitivity

Being blindfolded induces a feeling of erotic helplessness

STROKING WITH FEATHERS
If you can obtain one, a large feather (preferably ostrich or peacock) is great for stroking your partner's skin. By varying the style of stroking, you can make it playful and tickly or teasingly erotic, and if you use it on your partner's erogenous zones you can make the stroking highly erotic.

Stroke his skin to give erotic sensation, and the genitals to encourage sexual arousal

To learn where he is most sensitive to touch, watch his facial expressions while you stroke him

A SEXUAL BANQUET

Eating and making love are two of life's great sensual activities. The mouth, one of the most versatile parts of the body, is capable of giving and experiencing pleasure in a variety of ways. To create a sexual banquet, the kissing, sucking on, nibbling and gentle biting of a lover's body can be imaginatively combined with the erotic application of specially selected foods to create an experience that is tasty in every sense. This touch of the exotic should help to widen one's sexual horizons in a most enjoyable way.

TREAT YOUR PARTNER
As a special sensual surprise, say when your partner has just emerged from a relaxing bath, prepare a dish of fruits and other delicious fare, and serve with some chilled wine.

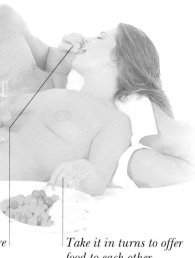

Make the experience more erotic by feeding your partner

Take it in turns to offer food to each other

POUR ON THE PLEASURE
A little honey, syrup, or some champagne feels good going on over the breasts and navel.

Use bath towels to protect your sheets and bedding

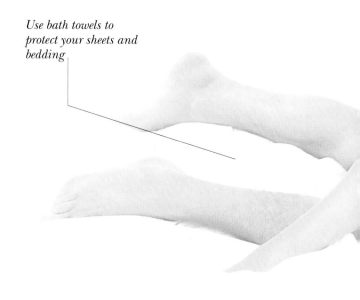

USE YOUR MOUTH CREATIVELY   Lick and suck up the honey, syrup or wine from your partner's body, making exaggerated gestures with your tongue. Long sweeps of your tongue's rough surface will feel incredibly sensuous and are bound to make your partner feel good.

APPLY BODY 'PAINT'
Cream can be dabbed onto your partner's nipples using slow circular movements, and can be sucked off afterwards.

Let her know she looks good enough to eat

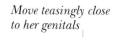
Move teasingly close to her genitals

STRATEGIC POSITIONING
Place some fruit close to your partner's genitals and eat it off him or her in a provocative way.

NO HOLDS BARRED Smear your partner all over with soft fruit, crushing it against his or her naked body and rubbing it slowly and sensuously up and down and round in circles (see left). You can even heighten the feelings of erotic intimacy by feeding each other mouth-to-mouth while continuing to caress each other through the fruit. When you are both thoroughly aroused and ready, bring your sexual banquet to a glorious climax by making love while continuing to massage each other with the crushed fruit (see below).

Seductively press the fruit against your partner's body

Let your partner see how much you are enjoying this novel experience

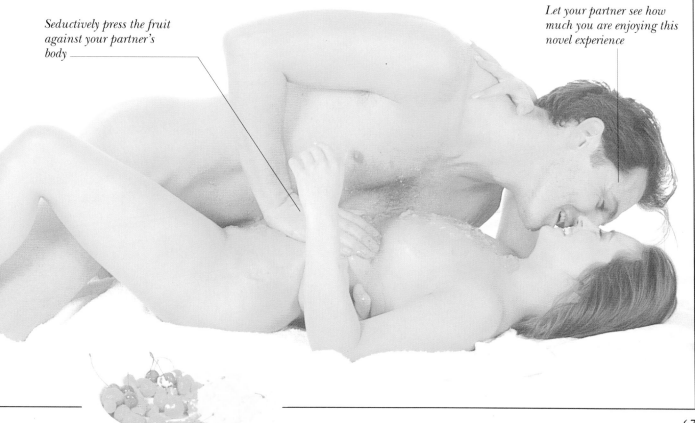

CHAPTER

6

HOW CAN I ASK FOR WHAT I WANT IN BED?

"How can the more timid reach the level of self-confidence that allows us to ask for exactly what we want? The secret is to start in small ways, tackling easier tasks first and harder ones later once our confidence has begun to rise."

ONE OF THE common sources of problems within relationships is a lack of communication between the two partners, and this failure to communicate is especially rife when it comes to sexual matters. Many women have unsatisfactory sex lives because they cannot bring themselves to discuss with their partners the subject of what they need in bed.

In an ideal world, men would recognize and be sensitive to the sexual needs of their partners and would do their best to ensure that these needs were met. But men are often unaware that their partners are not getting proper sexual fulfilment. They don't notice it, and their partners are too shy, or for some reason reluctant, to raise the subject.

The best way to overcome these difficulties in a relationship is for the woman to take the initiative and learn how to express her needs clearly but tactfully, and to explain to her man what her needs are and what he can do to meet them.

The first step is for her to become more assertive and to learn how to feel comfortable discussing the subject. Once she is able to talk freely to her partner about sex she will find it easier to take a more active role in their lovemaking, and that will increase the pleasure for both of them.

CASE STUDY *Irene & Tom*

Tom was a hurried lover, and never quite got Irene to orgasm. She was pretty certain that if only he would continue stimulating her with his fingers for a little longer she could come. But once he had reached his orgasm she never liked to ask him, and the result of this was that he never knew that she was physically capable of climax, and so he didn't learn how to get her there.

Name:	IRENE
Age:	22
Marital status:	SINGLE
Occupation:	RECEPTIONIST

Irene, who was in her second sexual relationship, felt strongly that she wasn't getting as much physical pleasure out of her love affair as she would have liked to.

"I've never had an orgasm," she said. "But I've read enough about it to know I'm missing something. Tom's a lovely man but he's always in a hurry. Not just with sex but with the whole of life. He's a salesman, and very ambitious – he's off to work early, and he telephones people half the evenings we spend together, which since we don't even live together is a bit much. I've hardly started in bed before he's all over. I think I could have a climax with him if only he'd slow down a bit, but I find it terribly hard to ask for any changes. I'm scared he'll think it'll mean he's no good in bed, and then he'll reject me. It's not that. I need a different pace. But I can't face asking for it."

Name:	TOM
Age:	26
Marital status:	SINGLE
Occupation:	SALESMAN

Tom was dressed in a business suit and carrying both a briefcase and a sample case. On several occasions he glanced at his watch. "I'm here because Irene asked me to come. She seems to have quite a sex problem which obviously I'd like to help her with. Naturally I'd prefer her to have orgasms with me but to be quite fair she's always seemed to enjoy sex anyway. Yes, I'm pretty serious about her. I wouldn't be here if I wasn't. We're intending to get engaged in four months' time. Two of her brothers are great mates of mine and I think a lot of her family.

"I've had several girlfriends before, none of whom had this difficulty. But I never felt serious about any of them. Irene may be quiet but she's an extremely bright girl. I find her really interesting to talk to and I get good feelings from being with her. Yes, I want to do well. I'm trying to make as many sales now as possible in order to get enough money to serve as a deposit on a house. I want my wife and kids to have as high a standard of living as possible."

THERAPIST'S ASSESSMENT

There were two issues to deal with here. One was that Irene needed to learn how to ask difficult questions when she feared the outcome. The second was that, from the sound of it, Tom was not only not paying enough attention to Irene's needs, he was also rushing his climax.

LEARNING TO SLOW DOWN
Tom's hurry with life generally, with his career, with sex and with answering questions on Irene's behalf in particular, was pointed out. Perhaps because his hurry had already been touched on in the session, he quickly grasped the point — he needed to give Irene more space to be herself. In answering for Irene he had, he felt, been protecting her.

It was pointed out that the person he was really protecting, when doing this, was his childhood self. Since the original family set-up no longer existed, except in his own head, this was no longer necessary. Tom visibly relaxed as this was recognized and Irene voiced her sympathy for him with warmth.

Tom swore to turn over a new leaf and a private code word was worked out between the couple for Irene to say, should Tom fall into his old habits. In addition, Tom agreed to try to prolong his orgasm, if necessary using sex therapy methods such as the squeeze (see page 59) in order to do so.

BECOMING HEALTHILY SELFISH
Irene's first task was to learn how to have orgasms through self-stimulation (see page 232). Once she had discovered what her sexual response consisted of, she was then in a much better position to take this information into the relationship and share it with Tom. The second was to learn the basic principles of assertion training by using simple exercises that helped her to ask for what she wanted, even in situations she found difficult, and to apply these when in bed with her partner.

Tom still needed a bit of restraining through the following months, but he learned to slow himself down enough to give Irene opportunity to start being herself, instead of a pale shade of him. He also learned to enjoy stimulating her and discovered that this could be highly arousing for himself. The sex improved enormously as did the general level of communication between them, and in a few months' time it was a much happier couple who announced their engagement without the least hesitation.

My programme for SEXUAL ASSERTIVENESS

Assertiveness helps us deal with tricky situations. It establishes feelings of self-value and importance, and assures us that it's alright to change our minds and normal to make mistakes. Becoming sexually assertive means coping with situations that are uncomfortable to you, knowing what you are allowed to have or do, and finally putting your assertiveness into action.

Stage 1 DEALING WITH WHAT MAKES YOU UNEASY

The first thing to do is to clarify in your own mind what your problem situations are. Make a list of the situations (they don't all have to be sexual ones) with which you find it hard to cope. Then shuffle the list into an order of priority with the most difficult situations at the top and the least difficult at the bottom. Starting at the bottom, practise acting through each situation with a friend. If, because it is intimate, there is a particular situation you do not want to rehearse with someone else, practise alone in front of your mirror and tape-record your voice to make sure you express yourself clearly and convincingly.

When you have gained confidence in this way, you will be ready to cope with the real thing. Take a deep breath and try to deal with it in the way that you handled it when you were practising, bearing in mind the 'assertiveness bill of rights'.

Stage 2 SAYING DIRTY WORDS OUT LOUD

There is a famous training technique, used to get professional counsellors comfortable with talking about sex, that consists of showing a blitz of films about sexuality, which are then discussed. One of the first movies is of an actor simply reading through a list; the list goes on and on. Any film of a man reading a list would be bizarre, but this one is particularly so because the list consists of dirty words.

Your first reaction at the start of the movie is incredulity and shock, but what happens as you hear so much foul language formally presented is that in the end, as you sit there and listen, none of it affects you any more.

You've simply got used to the experience. The process of being exposed to something for so long that it no longer affects you is called desensitization.

DIRTY WORDS Dirty words carry with them negative connotations — a sort of negative charge. If you should hear one or more of these words you may well immediately think with condemnation of the object described. But the fact is that these so-called 'dirty' words are almost invariably words that describe

THE ASSERTIVENESS BILL OF RIGHTS

• I have the right to judge my own behaviour, thoughts and emotions and to take responsibility for their initiation and consequences

• I have the right to offer no reasons or excuses for justifying my behaviour

• I have the right to decide whether or not I am, or should be, responsible for finding a solution to other people's problems

• I have the right to change my mind

• I have the right to make mistakes and be responsible for them

• I have the right to say "I don't know"

• I have the right to be independent of the goodwill of other people while I am dealing with a tricky situation or problem

• I have the right to be illogical in making decisions

• I have the right to say "I don't understand" and to ask for information

genitalia and sexual activity. Small wonder, perhaps, that we tend to look upon sex as a negative experience to be kept very private indeed. The harm in that is that if we are inhibited, we remain that way because we never dare talk about the problems.

TALKING EXPLICITLY   The logic behind desensitization is that it reduces the negative charge of the words to a point where we can think objectively about the subject described by them. It is obviously desirable to be able to talk about sex without negative feelings.

If you find it hard to talk explicitly about sex without extreme self-consciousness, that might inhibit you from talking frankly about what you want in bed. To make it easier for you to talk freely about sex, draw up a check-list of 'loaded' words and practise saying them out loud in front of a mirror. When you can say them without cringing you are going to find it a whole lot easier to discuss sex.

Stage 3 DEMONSTRATING YOUR ASSERTIVENESS

A woman can demonstrate her assertiveness in many ways, including the way in which she undresses. For example, the body language of a good professional stripper will in-

Sexy un-dressing p54

dicate self-love, and she will often fondle herself, with no apparent self-consciousness, as she looks over her shoulder at her audience. She will not use body language that cringes, or attempt to hide parts of herself. No-one is suggesting, of course, that you should bump and grind, but gaining a clear idea of a smooth way in which to disrobe, and of the body language that will make this most pro-vocative to your partner, can't hurt.

It is definitely more erotic to be undressed by someone than to do it yourself, and un-dressing your partner demonstrates your assertiveness as well as being very stimulating for him. If you are going to be effective at disrobing your partner, you need first to have had practice in undoing things and second to know the right order in which to undo them. For example, your man won't thank you if you get his trousers and briefs off first and then leave him exposed while you work on the upper half.

TAKING THE LEAD   Another sign of assertive-ness is taking the lead during sex. Many men don't expect their women to want to do anything other than be passive. It can be a surprise when she turns to him after they have made love and says, "That was lovely. Now I want to make love to you." However, many men are so conditioned to be active that they find it almost impossible to lie back and accept pleasure. To overcome this, turn the lovemaking session into a sort of sensual massage. It is also worth being assertive if your partner climaxes before you, leaving you un-fulfilled. If you are confident in bed you could, at a discreet interval after his climax, say simply, "Would you rub my clitoris again like you were doing before? It felt wonderful and I'd like a climax now." The result would be that he would then learn something im-portant about satisfying you sexually, and you would feel good both for asking for pleasure and for receiving it.

Taking the lead p74

COMMUNICATION If your partner doesn't know what it is you want or need, it is up to you to ask for it.

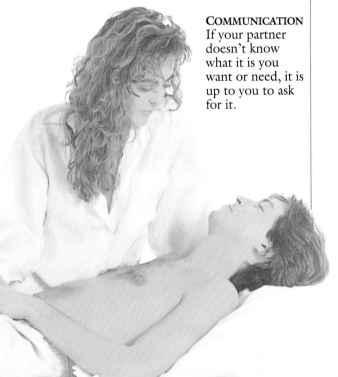

TAKING THE LEAD IN LOVEMAKING

Many men don't expect their women to want to do anything other than be passive, and are so conditioned to be active that they find it almost impossible to lie back and accept pleasure. The best way of overcoming this is to confront it openly and turn the session into a version of "Me, Jane; you, Tarzan."

1 MAKE THE FIRST MOVE Slide playfully on top of your man, stroking him erotically and rubbing your body sensually against his.

2 START TO AROUSE HIM Before he gets a chance to heave you off him, move sensuously down his naked body, kissing and stroking his torso.

3 TICKLE HIM If you have longish hair you can sweep across his genitals with it, dragging your mane across his abdomen and down over his penis.

Press the length of your body against his so that he feels surrounded by you

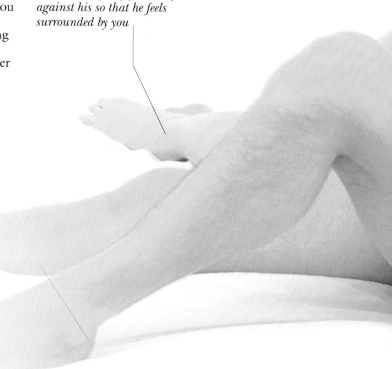

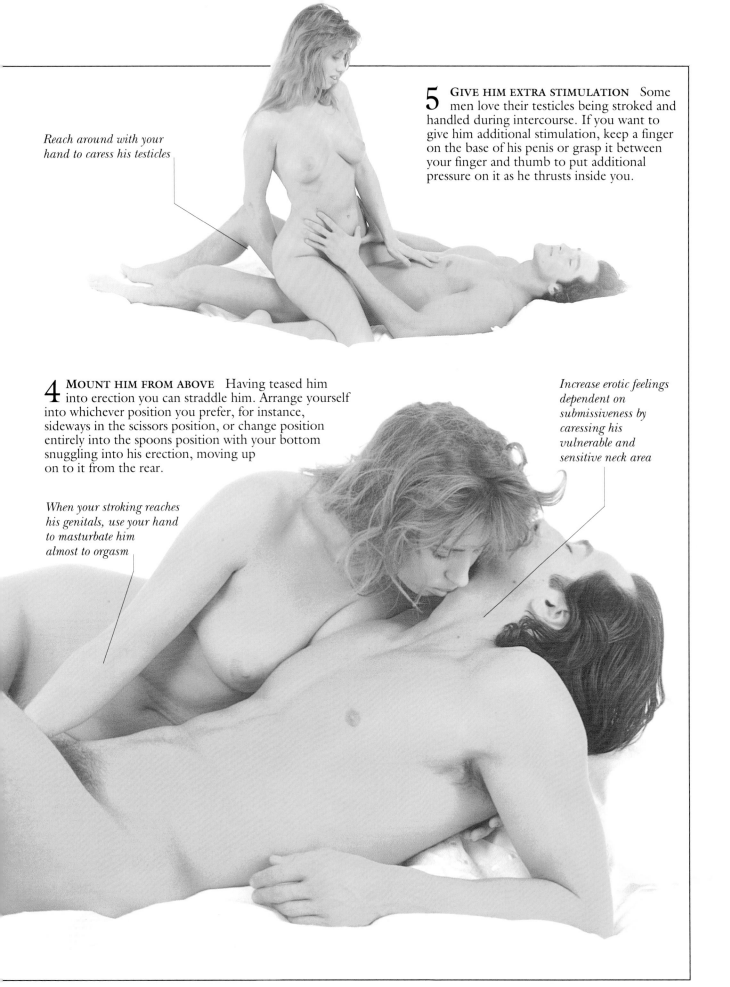

Reach around with your hand to caress his testicles

5 **GIVE HIM EXTRA STIMULATION** Some men love their testicles being stroked and handled during intercourse. If you want to give him additional stimulation, keep a finger on the base of his penis or grasp it between your finger and thumb to put additional pressure on it as he thrusts inside you.

4 **MOUNT HIM FROM ABOVE** Having teased him into erection you can straddle him. Arrange yourself into whichever position you prefer, for instance, sideways in the scissors position, or change position entirely into the spoons position with your bottom snuggling into his erection, moving up on to it from the rear.

Increase erotic feelings dependent on submissiveness by caressing his vulnerable and sensitive neck area

When your stroking reaches his genitals, use your hand to masturbate him almost to orgasm

CHAPTER 7

HOW CAN I MAKE LOVE~ MAKING MORE INTIMATE?

"Opening your innermost self to your partner can be difficult, but it is essential if you want your relationship to flourish and grow."

JUST BECAUSE two people make love does not, surprisingly enough, guarantee that they are intimate. Intimacy is a quality that grows through a sharing of feelings; it heightens all aspects of the relationship and is the main ingredient responsible for turning sex into an ecstatic experience as opposed to a pleasurable but uninspiring one.

In order to achieve intimacy we need to be brave enough to reveal our innermost selves to our partners, which is something that many people find difficult to do.

This difficulty may arise for many people because they worry that their inner selves might be unacceptable, or because they feel that revealing too much about themselves to another person (even though that person may be someone who is very close to them) will make them vulnerable in some way.

Creating the conditions in which your lover feels safe enough to talk about deep, inner feelings helps him or her to overcome such fears, and so does the ability to open up and share your own feelings.

CASE STUDY *Maria & Jack*

Although Maria and Jack had not known each other for long, they got on very well together, both in bed and out of it. But they found it difficult to be truly intimate with each other and to confide their innermost thoughts and feelings, and that left them both dissatisfied.

Name:	MARIA
Age:	28
Marital status:	SINGLE
Occupation:	HAIRDRESSER

Maria was from an Anglo-Italian family, and her brother, two sisters and most of her cousins were already married. She had some strongly independent ideas about life, though, and owned her own car and house.

"I don't have any difficulty in attracting men," she said, "I'm dating an extremely interesting guy at the moment. He's ambitious and bright and I've got a lot to learn from him. He'd be an extremely suitable husband but, as happened with the last couple of menfriends I had, I can't really be myself with him when we go to bed.

"It's not that I'm afraid of talking about sex or of making sexual suggestions, but there is a feeling, at the end of lovemaking, that things aren't quite right. I don't feel really relaxed, even though I've climaxed. Afterwards, I feel a million miles away from him. I look at him and wonder what he's thinking. And because he never opens up to me, I don't really reveal my interior self to him. I'd like to. But I'm not quite sure how to."

Name:	JACK
Age:	37
Marital status:	SINGLE
Occupation:	TRANSPORT MANAGER

Jack was brisk and confident, excellent at managing staff and working for one of the most efficient companies in his field. His career record was excellent, but his record with girlfriends was not so good. There had been several live-in partners in the past and Jack was unsure about why these affairs had not lasted.

"I do like Maria a great deal," he told me. "And I know what she's talking about. I'd love to feel really relaxed with someone, too, but it's not easy for me. I seriously want to marry and have children but I don't believe in divorce. My parents got divorced when I was twelve, and my mother was devastated by it.

"For me, living with someone is one thing, but marriage is for life. And since that's the case, it's really got to work out, right from the start."

THERAPIST'S ASSESSMENT

Both Maria and Jack were complaining about a lack of intimacy. Sex, for them, was pleasant, but each of them felt that it would have to provide them with something more than simple physical satisfaction if their partnership was going to be other than temporary.

Their anxieties were brought to a head by the needs of each of them to make a permanent relationship. But since both were highly assertive and capable, their sense of helplessness was accentuated because this was one of the few situations in their lives where neither of them had a clue how to proceed.

FOSTERING INTIMACY
Intimacy is fostered both by the romance of the surroundings and by the ability of those involved to be open and self-disclosing. Because Maria and Jack were busy, capable individuals they had learned to compartmentalize their lives. This worked excellently as a method of getting efficiently through their workloads, but it also meant that they were poor at sharing their feelings and their experiences with each other.

Since Maria and Jack were both also highly competitive they had learned, early on, not to reveal anything that might make them vulnerable, for fear that it would be used against them. During my individual discussions with them, I learned that there were, in fact, many things about both of them that, if they were revealed, would make them feel vulnerable.

SELF-DISCLOSURE
In order to open themselves to each other, reaching to their vulnerable inside selves, the couple needed to learn how to self-disclose. I warned them that it was going to feel extremely risky trying to do this, since it meant exposing soft parts of the ego, and that if they were going to succeed, each would have to give a great deal of reassurance to the other.

REASSURANCE
Maria and Jack learned how to give reassurance to each other by using comforting, loving words and touch, and how to get each other to self-disclose and express deeply personal thoughts and emotions. Maria and Jack followed through these suggestions and ended up with a deeper and tender relationship, a good basis for marriage.

My programme for INCREASING THE PHYSICAL SIDE OF INTIMACY

On the previous pages I've suggested methods of reassuring and opening up to each other in the sharing of feelings. On these pages I suggest you play doctors, using a therapy sequence called the Sexological Exam, which I first learned about in America. This brings a couple firmly into the picture with regards to their genital sensuality and, in the course of doing so, produces a sometimes extraordinary experience of discovery that draws them closer together. If you need an excuse, so as to make it easier to get started, pretend it's a game — you are the doctor, he is your patient, and he lies on a bed in a warm room while you examine him.

Stage 1   BREASTS AND NIPPLES

Sexological Exam p82

In the Sexological Exam, either partner can examine the other: on these two pages we show how she can examine him. Begin by finding out how his breasts and nipples respond to touching and stroking. Gently stroke each breast, then stroke or lightly press around the area of each nipple, using your fingertips. If his nipples become firm and erect, that shows that they are sensitive to stimulation. And if small pale spots appear on his erect nipples, this indicates high arousal.

Stage 2   PUBIC HAIR PATTERN

After examining your partner's breasts and nipples, transfer your attention to his pubic hair. Examine the hair's abundance and texture, and the area that it covers. Pubic hair patterns and thicknesses vary greatly from one man to another, taking a variety of shapes ranging from a sparse amount of hair just above the penis to a luxuriant growth stretching from the abdomen down to the genitals and on to the upper leg.

Pubic hair growth is commonly associated with the amount of free-ranging testosterone (a sex hormone) circulating in the body, and large amounts of testosterone may result in an abundance of body and pubic hair, while also causing baldness on the head.

Stage 3   THE PENIS

Hold your partner's penis in one hand and ask him to point out the areas that are most sensitive. Note where these are and ask what stimulation works best for him in these areas. Let him show you, then repeat the stimulation yourself. Please note, however, that the intention is not to bring him to orgasm, but to clarify for both of you his penile sensitivity.

PENIS SHAPE   Note the shape of his penis. Contrary to what many people believe, the appearance of a man's penis is as individual as the appearance of his face: penises don't look all the same. Ask him on which side he prefers to wear his penis when dressed, and ask if one side feels more sensitive than the other.

THE FORESKIN   If he is uncircumcised, ask him to show you how far back he can comfortably move his foreskin. If he is circumcised, look carefully at the exposed penis where the foreskin would have been and check this for scarring. If there is scarring, ask him what kind of sensation he feels in this area.

THE URETHRA   Look at the head of the penis. The urethra, the tiny slit from which your partner urinates and ejaculates, should be a healthy red colour. On the underside of the penis, at the head, is a central ridge of skin called the frenulum. See if this is unbroken or if it is broken or scarred, and ask your partner what kind of sensation he experiences here.

THE PERINEUM   Ring the base of the penis with your fingers and ask your partner what specific sensation there is here, if any. Trace your fingers lightly down his testicles and underneath them, where you should encounter the perineum. The perineum is the area between the testicles and the anus (on a woman, the perineum is the area between the vagina and anus), and it is often rich in nerve endings and so may be very sensitive to being touched or stroked. Gently run your fingers along the ridge of the perineum, and ask him how it feels to be stroked there.

Stage 4   THE ANUS

Imagine his anus to be a clock and press gently but firmly at the hour positions around it. Ask him if any of the areas feel sensitive: if they do, remember them when stimulating your partner during later lovemaking.

Finally, ask your partner to help you practise the squeeze technique on him (page 59), so that both of you can learn thorough control over his erection and ejaculation.

ANAL REGION   Check the response of your partner's anal region by pressing gently but firmly at the 'hour' positions around his anus. Imagine the point on the rim of his anus that is nearest his penis is at the 12 o'clock position. The most sensitive parts of his anus — those that produce the most sensation when they are pressed — will probably be the 10 o'clock and 2 o'clock positions.

BREASTS AND NIPPLES   The exam begins with a check on how your partner's breasts and nipples respond to stimulation. Stroke or lightly press around the area of the nipples to see if they erect.

GENITAL STROKES   Get your partner to show you where the most sensitive parts of his penis are and to demonstrate to you how best to stimulate them, but remember that the object of the exercise is to gain information, not to bring him to orgasm.

Use a gentle touch when you are probing your partner's most sensitive parts

PRIVACY AND COMFORT
To do the Sexological Exam in comfort you need privacy and a warm, draught-free room

Ask him for information and in return tell him what your own impressions are

THE SEXOLOGICAL EXAM

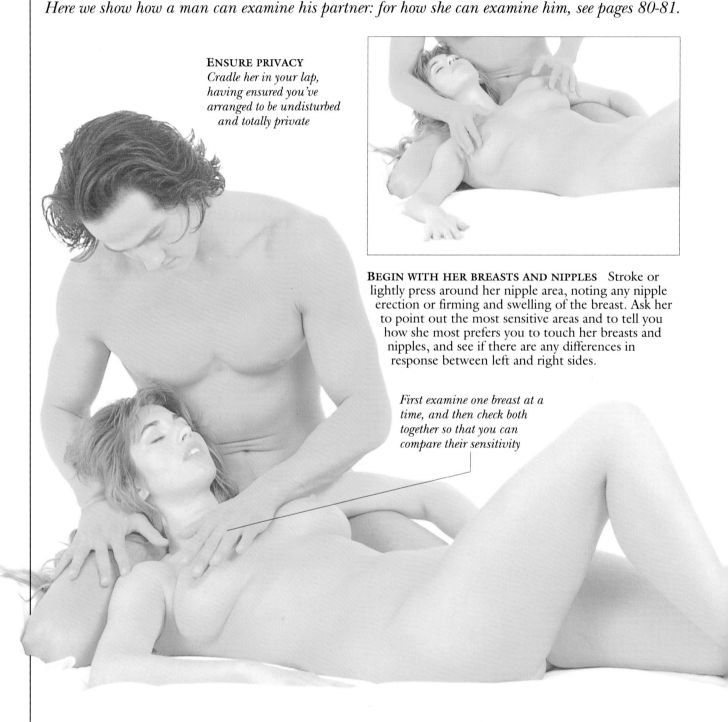

Exploring each other's 'private parts' will bring you and your partner a new awareness of your genital sensuality, helping you to open up to each other and share your feelings more easily. You each in turn play the role of 'doctor', examining your partner's body to get to know it intimately, and asking questions about how your partner responds to being touched and caressed in his or her most sensitive areas. Here we show how a man can examine his partner: for how she can examine him, see pages 80-81.

ENSURE PRIVACY
Cradle her in your lap, having ensured you've arranged to be undisturbed and totally private

BEGIN WITH HER BREASTS AND NIPPLES   Stroke or lightly press around her nipple area, noting any nipple erection or firming and swelling of the breast. Ask her to point out the most sensitive areas and to tell you how she most prefers you to touch her breasts and nipples, and see if there are any differences in response between left and right sides.

First examine one breast at a time, and then check both together so that you can compare their sensitivity

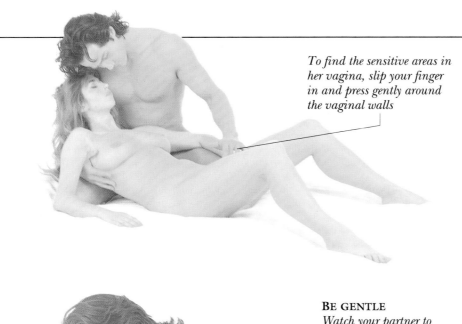

To find the sensitive areas in her vagina, slip your finger in and press gently around the vaginal walls

EXAMINE HER GENITALS
First place your fingers deliberately but gently on the outside of her labia, then at the opening of the vagina and just inside the vagina, and then on the base, the middle and top of the pubococcygeus muscle (which is located on the floor of her vagina when she is lying on her back). At each point, ask her how much she would like it if your penis could hit that particular spot during intercourse.

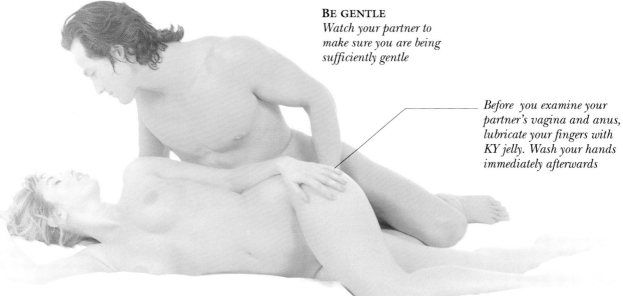

BE GENTLE
Watch your partner to make sure you are being sufficiently gentle

Before you examine your partner's vagina and anus, lubricate your fingers with KY jelly. Wash your hands immediately afterwards

PROBE AROUND HER ANUS Imagine her anus to be a clock and press gently but firmly at the hour positions around it, asking her which feel the most sensitive: the 10 o'clock and 2 o'clock positions are often the areas of greatest sexual stimulation (12 o'clock is the point closest to the vagina). The perineum, between the anus and vagina, is rich in nerve endings and so is always sensitive to stimulation.

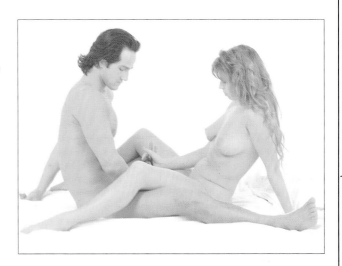

USING A MIRROR Give your partner a mirror so that she can see her genitals. Point out to her the outer and inner labia, and part them to reveal her clitoris and urethra and the entrance to her vagina.

ORAL SEX

There are basically two types of oral sex — licking and sucking of the penis (fellatio) and licking and sucking of the vagina (cunnilingus) — and both are capable of producing ecstatic orgasms. Some members of both sexes find that, for them, oral sex is the most powerful form of sexual stimulation.

FELLATIO   Licking the penis as if it were a delicious ice cream is the starting point for fellatio. Hold the base of the penis in one hand and then, using the blade of your tongue, lick up from the base of the penis, first on one side and then on the other. After you have repeated this a few times, move on to the famous butterfly flick.

USING YOUR HANDS
When you are reasonably skilled at fellatio you will not need to hold your partner's penis while you do it, which will leave both your hands free to caress him.

Take the penis between your lips, and slide your mouth gradually down to the base of it and back again. You should cover your teeth with your lips

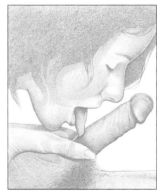

THE BUTTERFLY FLICK
This consists of flicking your tongue lightly across and along the ridge on the underside of the penis.

CUNNILINGUS For really sensational cunnilingus your head needs to be right between her thighs and preferably slightly below them so that you can stroke your tongue upwards against the shaft of her clitoris. From here you can also occasionally insert your tongue into her vagina. Experiment with the tip of the tongue, then the blade of the tongue. Try stimulating one side of the clitoris, and then the other, always from underneath. Ask her for feedback so that you learn which she likes best.

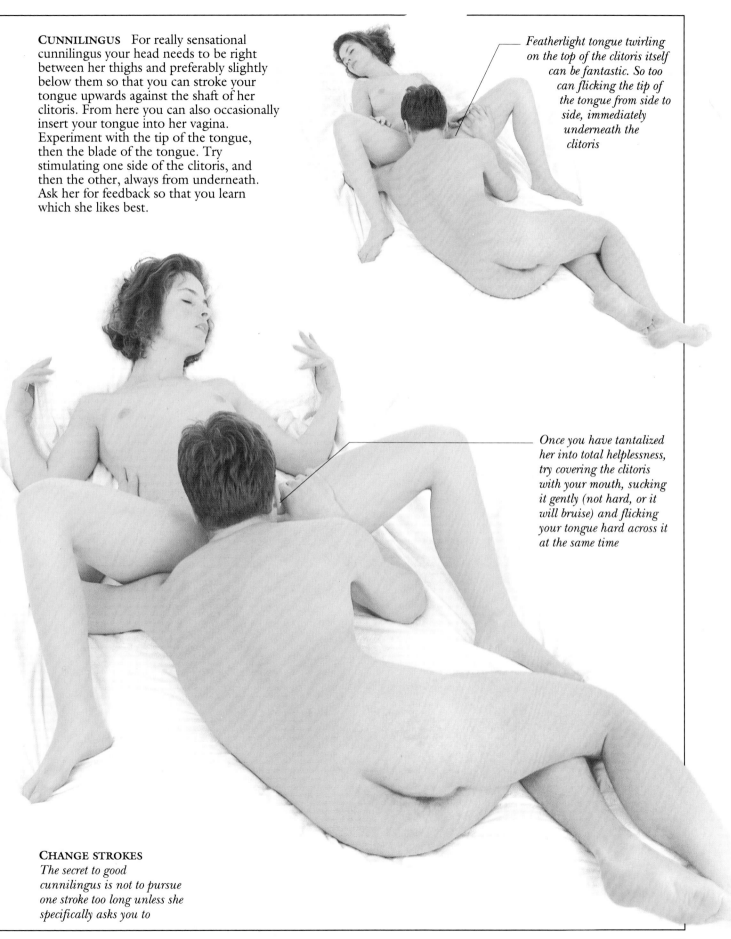

Featherlight tongue twirling on the top of the clitoris itself can be fantastic. So too can flicking the tip of the tongue from side to side, immediately underneath the clitoris

Once you have tantalized her into total helplessness, try covering the clitoris with your mouth, sucking it gently (not hard, or it will bruise) and flicking your tongue hard across it at the same time

CHANGE STROKES
The secret to good cunnilingus is not to pursue one stroke too long unless she specifically asks you to

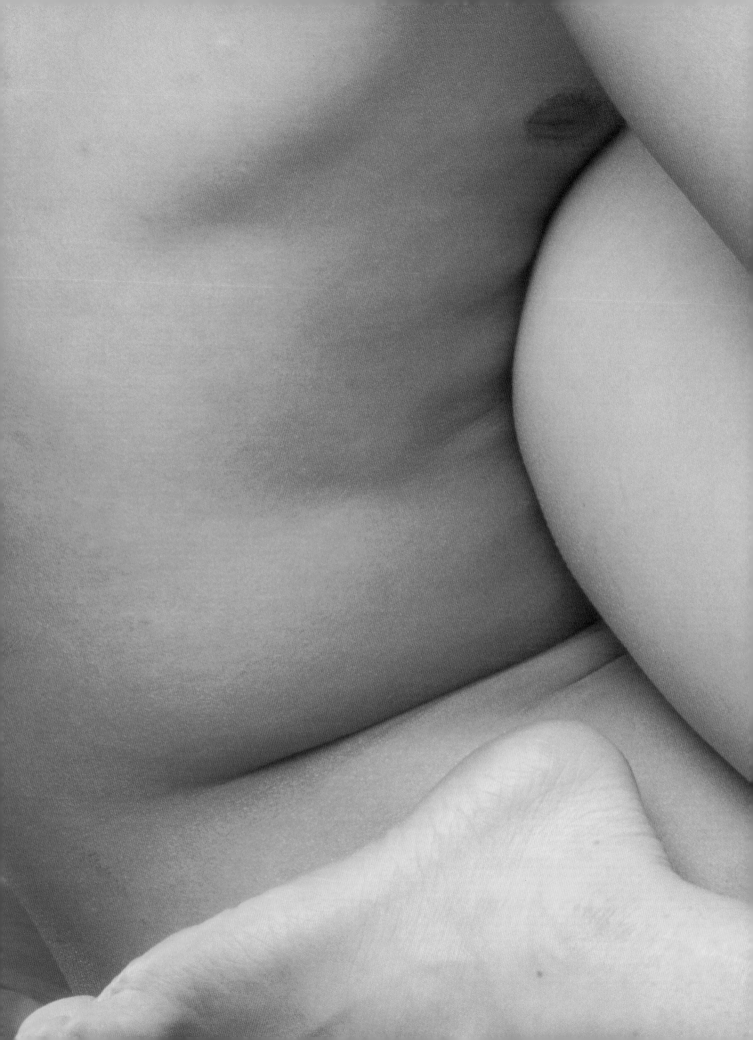

CHAPTER 8

HOW CAN I EXTEND SEX PLAY?

"Taking the time and trouble to get to know your partner really well can pay dividends in terms of increased sexual fulfilment."

SOME MEN AND women are slow starters when it comes to sex, despite wanting sex to be important in their lives because it represents the height of joyful physical love and pleasure.

Although they have no trouble in becoming physically aroused when making love, they find it more difficult to be mentally and emotionally involved in it. A quickie isn't an alternative for these people because, even if they can achieve orgasm under these conditions, they very often find it to be emotionally unsatisfactory.

Being able to draw out lovemaking so that desire is communicated intelligently by both body and mind is crucial to a sexual experience that allows us to go 'right over the top'. This does not mean that intercourse itself has to last as long as possible, but that the whole lovemaking process should be extended.

Sex play — literally just playing around together in bed — has a lot to recommend it, both as a fun prelude to intercourse and as a way of getting to know each other better. It also encourages a more relaxed approach to sex, and it helps to remove any performance anxieties.

CASE STUDY *Jody*

Jody suspected that she was missing out on something in her sexual relationship with her partner, Rod. She was sure that sex should and could be more fulfilling for her than it was, but she didn't know how to find out what it was that would make her properly satisfied.

Name:	JODY
Age:	34
Marital status:	SINGLE
Occupation:	BEAUTICIAN

Jody was a former model with a chameleon-like ability to change her appearance. She was excellent at striking up friendships, but although she enjoyed a happy relationship with her partner, Rod, she was shy and inexperienced in her love life.

"I never feel as though I have entirely 'let go' with Rod," she said. "I always end up thinking, 'Surely there is more to it than this?' I don't actually know too much about sex, let alone about suggesting new things for us to do in bed. In fact, I find it hard to instigate things at all, although I do try. And yet, I obviously need to bring some of this to Rod in order to inspire him.

"I suppose some of this is a communication problem. I'm wary of asking Rod if sex feels OK for him. Scared of the reply, I suppose. If he says it's ace, it'll be impossible to let him know it's not for me. It would spoil good sex for him and would also indicate that his sexual imagination doesn't go much further. If he said that sex was boring, that, strangely enough, would be easier, but nevertheless I would then worry that he was finding me boring. So I can't even start the conversation, let alone work on the answers.

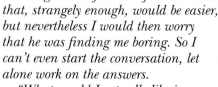
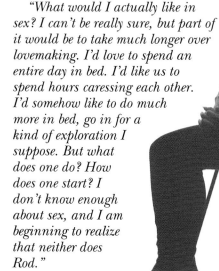

"What would I actually like in sex? I can't be really sure, but part of it would be to take much longer over lovemaking. I'd love to spend an entire day in bed. I'd like us to spend hours caressing each other. I'd somehow like to do much more in bed, go in for a kind of exploration I suppose. But what does one do? How does one start? I don't know enough about sex, and I am beginning to realize that neither does Rod."

THERAPIST'S ASSESSMENT

Probably the ideal way to find out about good lovemaking is by taking a very long time in which to get to know one's first lover. The old-fashioned idea of courtship — 'walking out' — where a couple would just make conversation for many months and where sexual familiarity was frowned upon, was frustrating for some. But it afforded most people time and space in which to get comfortable with a partner, and in which to get to know their frame of mind, how they thought, how quick or slow they were and how their special brand of intelligence worked.

NERVOUSNESS
We are deprived, these days, of this long period of getting to know our partners before we begin to have sex with them. The effects of this show up in our nervousness in asking for what we want, in the fact that we don't know how a partner will react if some special sexual activity is offered, and in the lack of any spontaneous evolution of sex play, which is what we are really talking about.

Although a sex manual can describe how to do oral sex, mutual masturbation and all the other varieties of sexual activity, we still need to find the right frame of mind in which doing these things becomes not just a curious experiment but something that feels natural to us and provides excitement and meaning.

SEX PLAY
Jody's desire to spend a day in bed makes sense in this context, and I recommended trying it. It would be the sensual equivalent of 'walking out' and would give her the opportunity to find out more about sex play. Sex play is not foreplay, because it doesn't necessarily end in intercourse or orgasm, although sometimes it involves both.

Sex play means literally messing around together in bed, having fun, being silly, being carried away. Why bother with this infantile activity? Because it is the most enjoyable kind of learning process, and it can encourage two people to progress to a more relaxed sensuality.

SEXUAL IGNORANCE
Jody's perception that sexual ignorance makes the finding-out process harder was a correct one. I advised her to find out more about the subject so that she was aware of all the possibilities that might appeal to her.

My programme for
MUTUAL SEXUAL DISCOVERY

Among the great sexual myths is the belief that we all function sexually in exactly the same way, and in a way documented by works of romantic fiction. Many men, therefore, expect all women to have nipples that instantly erect on touch, and vaginas super-responsive to the thrusting of a penis. And many women, in turn, believe that all men have little body-sensation because of muscular coverage, and that male sensuality is focused entirely on the penis. These mental body-maps are, of course, totally inadequate and unrealistic, as our programme for mutual sexual discovery will show.

The biggest sex organ of all is probably the mind. There are some who dispute this, however, and give that accolade to the skin. Whichever one you favour, each offers a great variety of erotic charge. The mind is the subject of our section on fantasies (see pages 134-143), but if you want to find out just how wide is the scope of our bodies' erotic sensitivity, you might like to try our Map Test. This will enable you to discover each other's erogenous zones, and you can give each one a 'score' according to how much erotic sensation it produces when stimulated. Then you can go on to explore the sensitivity and response of her G-spot and his prostate.

Fantasies p138

HOW TO SCORE   After each stroke, the partner who is doing the stroking stops and the other one rates the eroticism of the touch on, for example, a plus three/minus three scale. If, for example, strokes along the forearm felt pleasant but not very special, they might rate as zero. If strokes on the elbow were uninteresting, they might rate as minus two, while if strokes on the back of the hand felt surprisingly good, you might rate them at plus two — and if strokes across the nipple felt especially arousing you might score those as plus three. Of course, should something feel outrageously good, you might even want to make an exception to your scoring rules and whizz the score up to plus ten.

Stage   THE MAP TEST

In this exercise, one partner sits nude in a comfortable chair, while the other stands, then later kneels, in front. The object is to discover, through touching the body all over, which parts of it are sexually responsive. What is more, the person being touched is asked to rate the pleasure of his or her response by scoring either high or low. In this manner you can virtually build up a contour map of that person's body responses, which includes the peaks and troughs of sensation the person feels. (For a more intimate mutual examination, try the Sexological Exam.)

Sexological Exam p82

The partner doing the 'mapping' strokes specific areas of his or her partner's skin. These areas should be not more than five centimetres (two inches) in diameter, and should be stroked once or twice with one finger (see the box on the facing page).

Stage   STIMULATE HER G-SPOT

The G-spot (or Grafenburg spot), named after its discoverer, German gynaecologist Ernst Grafenburg, is a small area inside the vagina, on its anterior (front) wall, that when pressed in the right way can trigger orgasm. Grafenburg himself related the sensitive area to the point where the urethra runs closest to the top of the vaginal wall. The American researchers Perry and Whipple assert that the area is located higher up along the vagina, while Dr Zwi Hoch, an Israeli sexologist, claims that the entire area of the anterior wall of the vagina, rather than one particular area, is richly endowed with nerve endings that will readily produce arousal when stimulated.

When you are searching for the G-spot it is probably safest to assume it could be anywhere from the urethral opening to the back of the vagina. Research also seems to show that not all women possess this sensitive area.

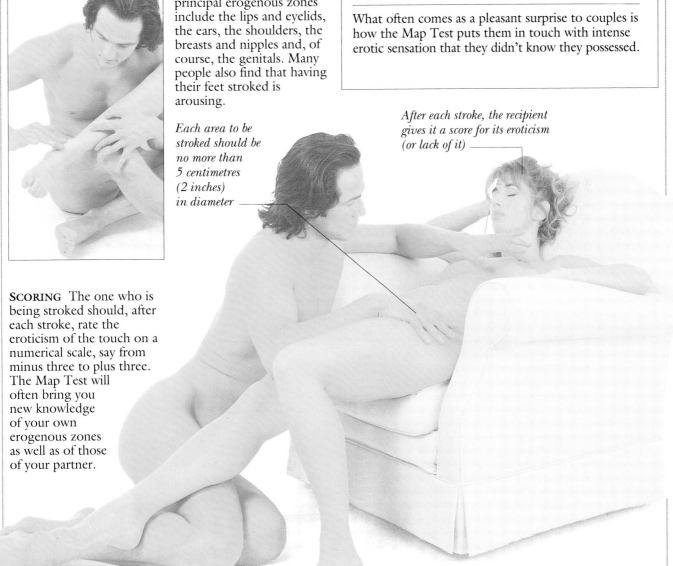

THE MAP TEST The Map Test is designed to be an enjoyable way for you and your partner to discover each other's erogenous zones. Begin at your partner's head then work your way, slowly, right down to the toes.

EROGENOUS ZONES The principal erogenous zones include the lips and eyelids, the ears, the shoulders, the breasts and nipples and, of course, the genitals. Many people also find that having their feet stroked is arousing.

Each area to be stroked should be no more than 5 centimetres (2 inches) in diameter

DOING THE MAP TEST

When you do the Map Test, touch your partner's body all over to discover which parts are sexually responsive and those which are not. The parts of the body to be stroked should include:

• The head, including the scalp and ears

• The neck

• The face, including the lips, nose and eyelids

• The shoulders

• The breasts or chest, including the nipples

• The arms, not forgetting the insides of the elbows

• The hands and fingers and so on, right down to the little toes

What often comes as a pleasant surprise to couples is how the Map Test puts them in touch with intense erotic sensation that they didn't know they possessed.

After each stroke, the recipient gives it a score for its eroticism (or lack of it)

SCORING The one who is being stroked should, after each stroke, rate the eroticism of the touch on a numerical scale, say from minus three to plus three. The Map Test will often bring you new knowledge of your own erogenous zones as well as of those of your partner.

EJACULATION The G-spot response consists of extreme erotic sensitivity, resulting in orgasm and accompanied, in a few women, by what looks like ejaculation. The women who took part in Perry and Whipple's laboratory tests sent out a fine spurt of fluid from their urethra during orgasm. (This is documented on film.) What this 'ejaculation' consists of is subject to debate. Some researchers claim that it is urine, but others, including Perry and Whipple, insist it is not urine but a substance corresponding to the seminal fluid produced by men (but without the sperm).

Other researchers, notably Daniel Goldberg who has analyzed the fluid and insists it is urine, dismiss this claim. However, not all women with a G-spot response do ejaculate, while some women admit to doing it but report that out of five G-spot orgasms only one may include ejaculation.

G-SPOT STIMULATION To locate your G-spot, insert your forefinger into your vagina and rest the fingertip on the front wall, about two-thirds of the way along the vagina towards the cervix. If you have a G-spot area, you will be able to feel it like a kind of muscular crossroads, a small configuration of vaginal muscles that are able to resist firm but gentle pressure from your fingertip.

Press into this, but be careful because too little pressure will do nothing for you and too much will simply hurt. Gently increase the pressure until it feels erotic. Maybe you will be able to climax simply as a result of this pressure, or maybe the sensation will just act as a form of additional buildup to your overall feeling of eroticism.

However, stimulating your own G-spot can be difficult to do, because it may be the case that your own fingers are not long enough, and cannot stretch so far back as to allow you to reach the spot and still exert an adequate pressure. If your fingers are not long enough to reach your G-spot, you might find that stimulation is easier and more successful if your partner does it, thanks to the (generally) longer fingers of the male.

G-SPOT STIMULATION
A woman can, in theory, stimulate her own G-spot by using her fingers, but many women find that their fingers are not long enough to reach it. If that is the case for you, ask your partner to do it for you if he has longer fingers, or ask him to use penile pressure on your G-spot when you have intercourse.

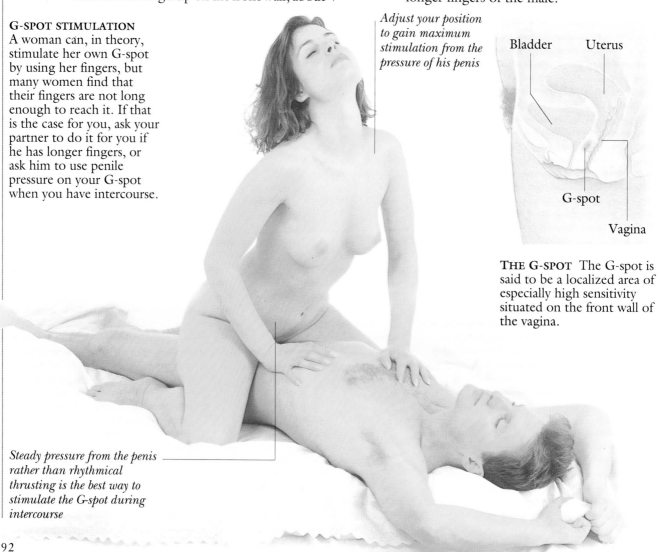

Adjust your position to gain maximum stimulation from the pressure of his penis

Bladder   Uterus

G-spot

Vagina

THE G-SPOT The G-spot is said to be a localized area of especially high sensitivity situated on the front wall of the vagina.

Steady pressure from the penis rather than rhythmical thrusting is the best way to stimulate the G-spot during intercourse

STIMULATING YOUR PARTNER To stimulate your partner's G-spot with your fingers, gently insert your forefinger into her vagina and search for the G-spot area on the upper vaginal wall, as described earlier. Take it easy when giving her finger pressure, and ask her to tell you how it feels so that you don't press too hard and hurt her.

You can also stimulate the G-spot with your penis during intercourse. However, since the G-spot needs an intense and quite localized pressure, penile thrusting in the normal way is not really the best medium for this, steady and prolonged pressure being much more effective.

Start off in the missionary position and then, once you have penetrated, kneel up. Maintain penetration by putting your hands beneath your partner's buttocks to lift and support her. Then lean back so that your penis is thrust against the uppermost side of her vagina, and thus against the G-spot, and without having to move you can simply press long enough to bring her to orgasm.

Stage STIMULATE HIS PROSTATE

The male equivalent of the woman's G-spot is the prostate gland, which encircles the urethra at the exit from the bladder and when stimulated will produce deep feelings of sexual excitement. One of the gland's functions is the production of seminal fluid, and if it is stimulated before or during intercourse, orgasm can be very intense.

A man can locate and stimulate his prostate by putting his thumb into his anus and pressing against its front wall, that is, the side of the anus nearest his penis. If you do this (after first lubricating your thumb with KY jelly), you will feel the prostate as a firm, walnut-sized mass that produces highly arousing feelings when pressed and stroked. However, you may find that your prostate is awkward to reach, and if so it will be easier if your partner gently stimulates it for you by inserting a well-lubricated finger into your anus.

STIMULATING YOUR PARTNER Stimulating the prostate isn't as messy as some people expect, because the lower rectum is normally empty, but you should wash your hands immediately afterwards and not touch your vagina until you have done so, otherwise there is a risk of transferring bacteria there from his anus.

Stage SPEND A DAY IN BED TOGETHER

Extending your mutual sexual knowledge naturally means that you are each discovering what is unique about the other's body. A good way for you and your partner to learn about each other is to spend a day in bed together, exploring each other's bodies, experimenting with different ways of caressing each other, and generally playing around and enjoying yourselves.

When you are doing this, take the opportunity to discover where her G-spot is and how to stimulate it to trigger orgasms, and to discover his prostate and the arousing effects it produces when it is stimulated.

Try the following six-point plan, which provides a good framework for mutual sexual discovery and could be pleasantly translated into a day in bed.

A SIX-POINT PLAN FOR SEXUAL DISCOVERY

1 Lie side-by-side in bed and mutually caress each other, without touching the genitals, for at least fifteen minutes

2 Give each other a body massage (see page 60)

3 Stimulate each other's erogenous zones, for instance by kissing and biting the ears, sucking the toes, giving a foot massage, stimulating the nipples and massaging and rimming the anal entrance. He should pay special attention to her vagina, finding and stimulating the G-spot, and she should lick and rub his penis and massage his prostate

4 Give body stimulus to his penis: try thrusting the penis in and out of her armpit, between her breasts if they are big enough to hold on and around it, between the thighs, or hard against her pubis

5 Give body stimulus to her vagina: try thrusting the vagina against his thigh, his elbow or his penis (but not with penetration), and even against his nose

6 Try having intercourse without climax, avoiding intercourse positions known to lead rapidly to orgasm. This means that both the ordinary missionary and woman-on-top positions probably need to be avoided. Try instead the side-by-side position, the scissors, the spoons, her legs over his shoulders while he kneels up thrusting into her, and her sitting on him both forwards and backwards

DELAYED GRATIFICATION

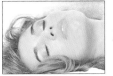

Since sexual response is susceptible to conditioning, the more unlikely the position you use, the harder it will be to get highly aroused sexually, and the longer it will take you to reach a climax. That can be a great advantage should you want to delay the 'point of no return' so as to prolong your lovemaking, particularly if there are problems with premature or early ejaculation. The positions shown here are all fairly easy to get into and will help you to delay your climaxes; some also have the benefit of being good for G-spot stimulation, an important component of some women's sexual satisfaction.

THE SCISSORS POSITION   This position is so called because, seen from above, the man's head and shoulders naturally rest to the side of his partner's and the couple forms a scissors shape. In the version shown here, his left leg is between her legs and his right is on the outside of her left; he is half-kneeling, and she has her right leg raised, but the position also works if both keep their legs straight.

You can reach down and kiss and/or nibble her neck

Teasingly stroke his back, alternating between feathery and more insistent touches

Use your thigh to press up and against your partner to vary her sensations

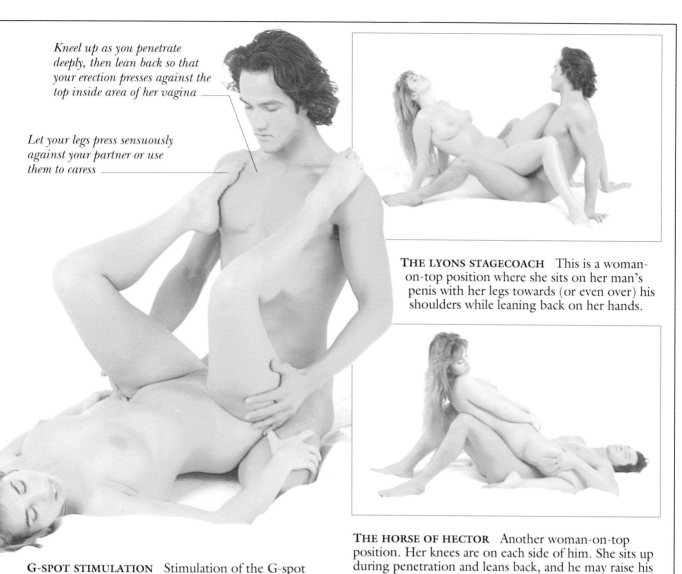

Kneel up as you penetrate deeply, then lean back so that your erection presses against the top inside area of her vagina

Let your legs press sensuously against your partner or use them to caress

THE LYONS STAGECOACH This is a woman-on-top position where she sits on her man's penis with her legs towards (or even over) his shoulders while leaning back on her hands.

G-SPOT STIMULATION Stimulation of the G-spot requires fairly intense and localized pressure, and penile thrusting is not particularly effective. But in this position, once the man has penetrated, he can lean back so that his penis is pressed firmly against the uppermost side of his partner's vagina, which includes the G-spot, and without moving he simply can press long enough to bring her to orgasm.

THE HORSE OF HECTOR Another woman-on-top position. Her knees are on each side of him. She sits up during penetration and leans back, and he may raise his knees to give support. It is good for deep penetration.

BACK-TO-FRONT In this woman-on-top position, he lies on his back, with his knees raised. She sits astride him upon his penis, facing towards his feet and leaning forward against his thighs and knees. One drawback of this position is that mutual masturbation is difficult.

MUTUAL MASTURBATION WITHOUT INTERCOURSE

*Intercourse is not the only means to sexual excitement and satisfaction —
skilled and loving mutual masturbation will also do the trick. Back in the days
before contraception, young people went in for 'heavy petting', which consisted of
sex without intercourse. Most of the sexual stimulation was done by hand, and it
took many sessions to get familiar with a partner. This was a bonus because it meant there was
time to develop trust and to build up knowledge of each other's body and responses.*

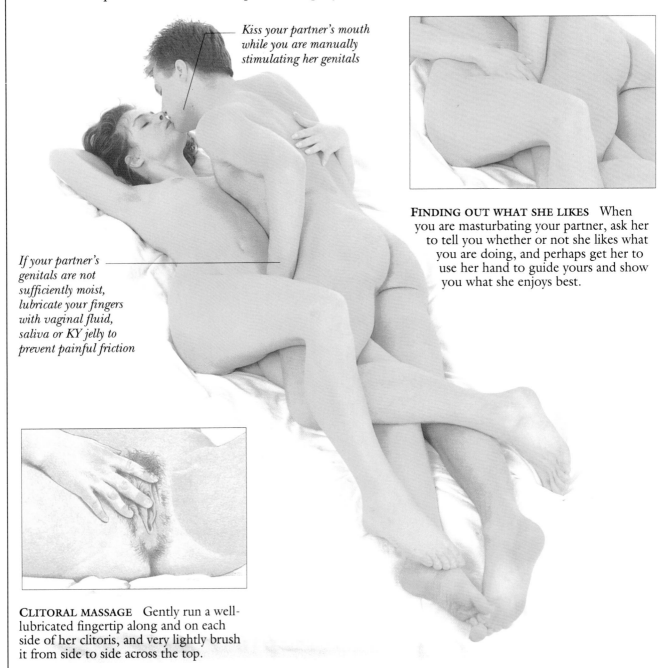

*Kiss your partner's mouth
while you are manually
stimulating her genitals*

*If your partner's
genitals are not
sufficiently moist,
lubricate your fingers
with vaginal fluid,
saliva or KY jelly to
prevent painful friction*

FINDING OUT WHAT SHE LIKES   When
you are masturbating your partner, ask her
to tell you whether or not she likes what
you are doing, and perhaps get her to
use her hand to guide yours and show
you what she enjoys best.

CLITORAL MASSAGE   Gently run a well-
lubricated fingertip along and on each
side of her clitoris, and very lightly brush
it from side to side across the top.

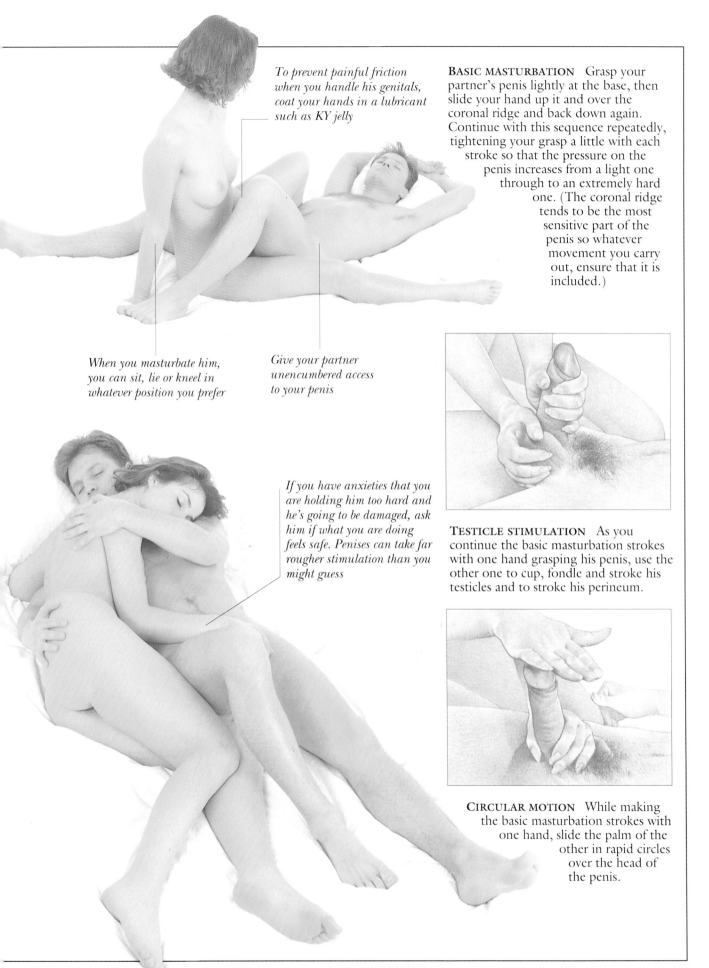

To prevent painful friction when you handle his genitals, coat your hands in a lubricant such as KY jelly

BASIC MASTURBATION Grasp your partner's penis lightly at the base, then slide your hand up it and over the coronal ridge and back down again. Continue with this sequence repeatedly, tightening your grasp a little with each stroke so that the pressure on the penis increases from a light one through to an extremely hard one. (The coronal ridge tends to be the most sensitive part of the penis so whatever movement you carry out, ensure that it is included.)

When you masturbate him, you can sit, lie or kneel in whatever position you prefer

Give your partner unencumbered access to your penis

If you have anxieties that you are holding him too hard and he's going to be damaged, ask him if what you are doing feels safe. Penises can take far rougher stimulation than you might guess

TESTICLE STIMULATION As you continue the basic masturbation strokes with one hand grasping his penis, use the other one to cup, fondle and stroke his testicles and to stroke his perineum.

CIRCULAR MOTION While making the basic masturbation strokes with one hand, slide the palm of the other in rapid circles over the head of the penis.

CHAPTER 9

HOW CAN WE REACH THE HEIGHTS OF SEXUAL ECSTASY?

"As is the case with many activities, the excitement of lovemaking is often heightened if there is a certain amount of novelty or risk involved."

AS WE GET OLDER and possibly experience love affairs with several partners, we get to learn about our sexual abilities and acquire glimpses of our sexual potential. But combining a loving and secure relationship with ecstatic sex is not always easy, since the heights of sexual passion often (although not always) depend on an edge of uncertainty and feelings of anxiety.

Many couples find that even though their sexual relationships are working well in most respects, there is a sense that something is missing, something that could add an extra, almost indefinable, element of excitement to their lovemaking.

By finding out what that extra ingredient is, they can often greatly enhance their sex lives. There are many ways in which a couple can achieve this enhancement, including introducing elements of novelty into their lovemaking and finding ways of heightening the sexual tension between them.

But what works for one couple may not work for another, and so imagination and possibly some experimentation are usually called for if a couple want to put the spark back into their relationship.

CASE STUDY *Gaby*

Gaby was highly experienced sexually, having started her sex life in her early teens. She knew the kind of ecstatic joy that sex can bring if the circumstances are right, but she was unsure about how to find it in the context of her relationship with Richard, her future husband.

Name:	GABY
Age:	24
Marital status:	ENGAGED
Occupation:	FASHION BUYER

Gaby was short and sparkling, with curly hair and a plump figure. At 21 she was engaged to Richard, had already bought her own apartment and had been working in the fashion business for over four years.

"My parents have got what seems to me the ideal marriage," she said. "And I'd like the same for myself. I was sexually precocious, started my sex life at 13, and I'd made out with a lot of boyfriends by the time I was 16. But suddenly, I stopped. I think now that I was looking for some kind of closeness that sex alone didn't provide. I didn't go out with anyone for two years.

"Then I met this chap who worked in the antiques business, and after having just spent two years with no-one I'm afraid I rather threw myself at him. I was terribly passionate, but he really didn't care about me at all and I just fell apart. It was Richard who picked up the pieces. He was kind and patient, and I shall always be eternally grateful. He restored my belief in myself. We've been together for three years now, we're getting married shortly and we're deeply attached. My only query, and it's not a problem, only a query, is how could we make what is already good sex really amazing? The only time I've ever felt as though champagne corks were popping and fireworks exploding was with this awful man who didn't care a toss for me. And that was despite the fact that the sex with him was awful. I'd like to marry up the excitement with the good sex and produce something even more wonderful. How do you think we could do it?"

THERAPIST'S ASSESSMENT

There are undoubtedly special circumstances that influence the quality of a sexual encounter. If there is an element of risk or anxiety, sex acquires a special edge, giving it an almost addictive sense of excitement. If we come to a love affair very needy for love (perhaps having been starved of it for a long time), our nerves may be on edge and our adrenalin levels high. If we have recently had a row, again those adrenalin levels may be raised. When a relationship is new, the excitement of novelty often leads to sexual ecstasy.

Security and familiarity, on the other hand, make for a different sexual experience, and it's important to emphasize that this is not an inferior one. But while you can reach the heights of passion, it often takes some out-of-the-ordinary situations or settings to enable you to manage it.

NOVELTY AND ANXIETY
In Gaby's case, it's worth noting that she was at her most passionate when she had not had a sexual relationship for two years, when the relationship was a new one and when her boyfriend's behaviour was such as to create feelings of extreme anxiety mingled with desire (he was a very charismatic individual). None of these factors were going to be available with Richard (which, all things considered, was generally all to the good).

ALTERING YOUR CIRCUMSTANCES
But, as I explained to Gaby, there are ways in which, by altering your circumstances, you can also alter how you feel within them. Gaby had worked out for herself that sexual abstinence, novelty of situation and an edge of anxiety were ingredients likely to give her less feeling of control and, therefore, more spontaneous sexual enjoyment. How to get this with the man she knew very well and was about to live with permanently was the question. It's hard to make yourself feel insecure deliberately, and not necessarily sensible.

HEIGHTENING SEXUAL TENSION
Other options that heighten sexual tension are: to spend fifteen minutes on kissing only; to take the risk of confiding a particular sexual desire in the hope that your partner will act upon it; and to focus on kissing and biting specific parts of the body such as ears, neck and shoulders. In addition, many men have extremely sensitive nipples and perineal areas, which react strongly to stimulation.

My programme for
EXTENDING YOUR SEXUAL BOUNDARIES

One of the reasons that many couples' sex lives become boring and deteriorate is because one or both partners are too inhibited to ask the other to experiment sexually. If you or your partner feel, for example, that the missionary position and the woman-on-top position are part of the natural order of things, but that oral sex, wanting to stimulate your partner's anus, or wanting to masturbate either yourself or your partner during intercourse are somehow 'different', then it can be surprisingly difficult for you to ask for these things. So instead of rushing things and asking bluntly for something new, try edging your sexual activities gently towards what it is that you want.

Stage | INTRODUCING ORAL SEX

As with any new activity, when you are trying some new sexual technique it's a good idea to take things slowly and by degrees. If your desire is to give your lover oral sex but you aren't sure of what their reaction will be, here's how you could slowly work towards it.

TONGUE BATHING Making certain that your bodies are scrupulously clean beforehand, kiss and lick your partner all over. Start at the face, the mouth and the lips, and then travel on down the neck to the shoulders, across the chest and down the arms, bathing and tonguing every inch and scrap of their skin. Don't forget to include the crook of the elbow. A little gentle biting or tugging with the teeth at the hairier areas also feels good.

Move on to the curves of the abdomen, allowing your face to pass suspiciously near the genitals, perhaps allowing your hot breath to tickle them into the beginnings of interest. Follow this with a long, sensual exploration of the inner thighs, those grooves on the inside leg, and carry on licking right down to the tips of the toes. The toes themselves are a highly sensual area and some people climax solely from having their toes sucked.

Tongue bathing p104

Then, having driven your mate delirious with excitement from your travelling tongue, lick your way up the legs again and once more

around the stomach, finally ending at the genitals. One of the most erotic of all sensations with tongue bathing can be when every inch of the body, bar the genitals, has been stimulated this way, and you 'accidentally' brush across those aroused and expectant

Kissing and licking your partner all over is a great way to encourage him or her to try oral sex for the first time

parts. They will be so longing to be licked and caressed at this stage that your introductory tonguings just won't be enough. When that happens, treat the genitals in the same way as you did the rest of the body, with lavish, exciting kissing and licking.

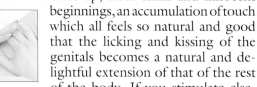

ORAL SEX There will be few objections at this stage to your oral intimacy. What you have done is built up, from small and innocent beginnings, an accumulation of touch which all feels so natural and good that the licking and kissing of the genitals becomes a natural and delightful extension of that of the rest of the body. If you stimulate else-

Oral sex p84

where but leave out the sexual areas, those feel starved. Yet this is precisely what you need to do on the first occasions, so that the need to be tongued on the genitals becomes so urgent your partner no longer pays attention to the warning messages of inhibition.

This is plenty for an introductory journey in tongue techniques. But the next time you do it, take in a little less of the body and a little more of the genitals.

Stage BEGINNING ANAL STIMULATION

Just as you may tempt your partner towards greater sexual sensation and new experiences with oral sex, so too can you use this gradual building technique for introducing other sexual activities. To introduce anal stimulation, for example, you might begin by caressing and stroking your partner's genitals and slowly and delicately working your way from front to back. Just letting your fingers brush across the anus the first few times serves as a taste of things to come.

FINGERING AND RIMMING Next, you might try following the overall caresses by deliberately stroking around the outside of the anus but withdrawing soon to other caresses. On a later occasion, the stroking might last longer, and subsequently this fingering could slowly turn to rimming.

Rimming is where you gently draw the pad of one of your fingers in circles around the outside of your partner's anal passage. You need to facilitate your progress by moistening both your fingertip and your partner's anus with a suitable lubricant, such as KY jelly. As your partner becomes relaxed about this, insert the tip of the finger a half inch and

continue to rim in circles, but on the inside. If all goes well, make the rimming firmer and use the fingertip actually to stretch the entrance to the anus.

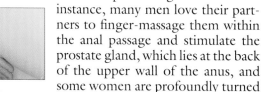

Many people are quite happy for this to be the limit of their anal stimulation, but some adore it if their partners go further. For instance, many men love their partners to finger-massage them within the anal passage and stimulate the prostate gland, which lies at the back of the upper wall of the anus, and some women are profoundly turned on by a simultaneous combination of fingering of the anus and stimulation of the clitoris.

Anal stimulation p105

DEALING WITH OBJECTIONS What if, at any stage of these activities, your partner objects? First, it's important to be clear that they are entitled to object. It is their body, and if they don't want any part of it to be available to you that is their choice, not yours. If, however, your partner is worried or panicky rather than actually disliking these activities, it could be because he or she no longer feels in control of the situation.

FEELING IN CONTROL The way to allow someone to feel in control of a sexual situation, should they become anxious, is to go back a step. This should be accompanied by discussion about the specific area of anxiety, because if your partner is anxious about what you have been doing, then he or she is going to need your reassurance that it is all quite safe and natural. To trust you, your partner needs to know that you will stop any time they ask, and that you will be careful and sensitive.

Stage EXTENDING YOUR ACTIVITIES

Once you have begun to experiment with oral sex and anal stimulation, you can use the technique of gradually introducing new ideas

to open up by using these methods of gentle exploration are mutual masturbation without intercourse, individual or mutual masturbation

Fantasies p138

during intercourse, the use of sex aids and the acting out of fantasies, all of which are described elsewhere in this book.

Always remember, however, that when you want to try some new sexual activity you should only do so if your partner agrees to it.

TONGUE BATHING

Using your tongues and licking and kissing each other all over will give you and your partner an unforgettable sensual experience and can also serve as a way of introducing oral sex into your lovemaking if you haven't tried it before. Before you begin you should, of course, make sure that both of you are scrupulously clean, which is why tongue bathing is best attempted as an erotic and pleasurable follow-up to the delights of a sensual shared bath or shower.

HEAD TO SHOULDERS
Begin your oral exploration of your partner's body at the top, kissing and licking his or her mouth and face, then work your way slowly and sensuously around the ears and down the neck and throat to the shoulders.

Take your time, and make your tongue movements as sensuous as possible

ARMS AND CHEST From the shoulders, kiss and lick your way down the arms to the wrist and back up again. Then move on to the chest, including the breasts, areolae and nipples.

Accompany your oral caresses with varying hard strokes

If encouraged, turn the gentle licks of tongue bathing into more stimulating sucks and nibbles

ABDOMEN AND LEGS From the chest, move down to the abdomen and the insides of the thighs, going close to (but not actually touching) the genitals. Work down to the toes then back up to the abdomen, this time gently kissing and licking the genitals. If your partner enjoys this, you can turn your tongue bathing into an oral sex session.

ANAL STIMULATION

Manual stimulation of the anus, because of its illicit overtones, can be terrifically arousing as long as both partners are happy to practise it, or have it practised on them. Both sexes find it heightens sexual response, both before and during intercourse, and for women it is especially exciting when it is combined with simultaneous clitoral massage. For men, the pleasure of anal stimulation can be greatly increased when it is extended to include massage of the prostate gland (see page 93).

RIMMING AND PENETRATION
Surface rimming involves you gently drawing your fingertip (lubricated with KY jelly) in circles around the outside of your partner's anal passage. This could be followed by internal rimming, in which you slip your lubricated fingertip inside your partner's anal passage and rim on the inside.

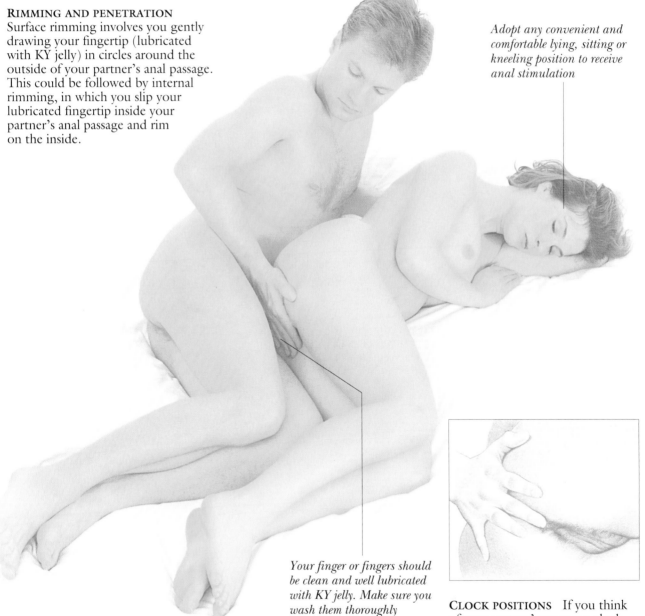

Adopt any convenient and comfortable lying, sitting or kneeling position to receive anal stimulation

Your finger or fingers should be clean and well lubricated with KY jelly. Make sure you wash them thoroughly afterwards

CLOCK POSITIONS If you think of your partner's anus as a clock, with the 12 o'clock position nearest the vagina (or testicles), the most sexually responsive points are usually at 10 o'clock and 2 o'clock.

MUTUAL MASTURBATION DURING LOVEMAKING: 1

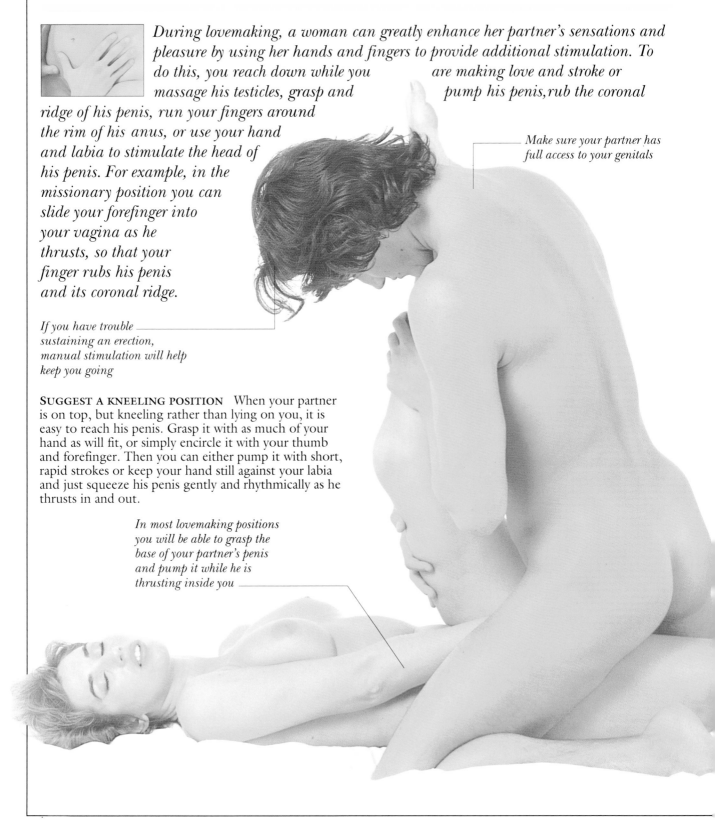

During lovemaking, a woman can greatly enhance her partner's sensations and pleasure by using her hands and fingers to provide additional stimulation. To do this, you reach down while you massage his testicles, grasp and are making love and stroke or pump his penis, rub the coronal ridge of his penis, run your fingers around the rim of his anus, or use your hand and labia to stimulate the head of his penis. For example, in the missionary position you can slide your forefinger into your vagina as he thrusts, so that your finger rubs his penis and its coronal ridge.

Make sure your partner has full access to your genitals

If you have trouble sustaining an erection, manual stimulation will help keep you going

SUGGEST A KNEELING POSITION When your partner is on top, but kneeling rather than lying on you, it is easy to reach his penis. Grasp it with as much of your hand as will fit, or simply encircle it with your thumb and forefinger. Then you can either pump it with short, rapid strokes or keep your hand still against your labia and just squeeze his penis gently and rhythmically as he thrusts in and out.

In most lovemaking positions you will be able to grasp the base of your partner's penis and pump it while he is thrusting inside you

With eyes closed you can encourage fantasies that enhance your reactions

Having your buttocks fondled and stroked is a highly arousing sensation

STROKE THE ANAL REGION When you are on top of your partner in a position such as this one, you will find it easy to lean back in order to stroke the rim of his anus with a fingertip and to stimulate his perineum.

KEEP ONE HAND FREE Before making love in a rear-entry position that involves you kneeling or bending over, get your partner to support you securely so that you will have a free hand with which to masturbate him. The easiest way to give your hand access to his genitals is by reaching back between your legs, and you can reach around behind you to caress his buttocks.

GAIN EASY ACCESS When you are astride your partner and with your back to him, it is very easy to reach the base of his penis to squeeze it as he thrusts, or to masturbate him.

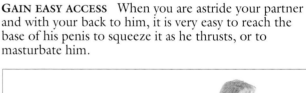

FONDLE HIS TESTICLES Massage his testicles gently from underneath, cupping them loosely in the palm of your hand. This is easy to do when you are making love with you on top, astride him and with your back to him, and he opens his legs.

MUTUAL MASTURBATION DURING LOVEMAKING: 2

One great benefit of the so-called sexual revolution of the 60s and 70s was the realization of the value of masturbation for women. Men have always known that it feels good to fondle yourself, and now women are finding that they are more likely to experience orgasm from masturbation than from intercourse. If a woman knows what type of masturbation works best for her, she is in an excellent position to convey this useful information to her lover. Ask your partner what really turns her on and, while you are making love, make sure you give her maximum pleasure by masturbating her in that way.

Insinuate your body against your partner, maintaining contact at all times

ADOPT A SUITABLE POSITION   Rear-entry lovemaking positions allow you to reach around easily to your partner's genital area. Because you are entering her from the rear, your partner's clitoris will not be getting any stimulation from direct contact with your pubic area as it would if you were making love face-to-face.

The slow exploration of hands around your genitals during intercourse will be unbelievably arousing

Continue to pat and stroke her buttocks, mimicking the movements of your hand on her genitals

Use a fingertip to massage your partner's clitoris during lovemaking; this is a very effective way of exciting her and bringing her to orgasm

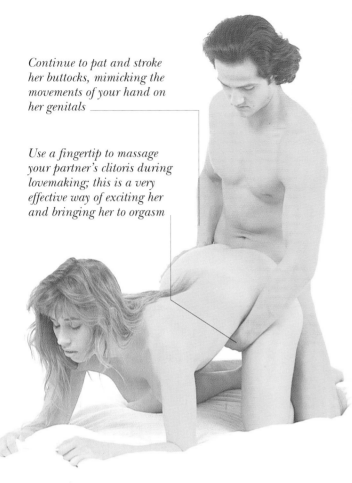

STIMULATE HER CLITORIS   Clitoral massage is especially useful when you are making love in this rear-entry position. Every woman has her own preferences when it comes to clitoral massage, so check with your partner that what you are doing is what she likes best.

DON'T BE AFRAID TO SHOW YOUR INTEREST   If you are able to see what you are doing while you are masturbating your partner, and you can watch her reactions, it adds extra excitement to your lovemaking.

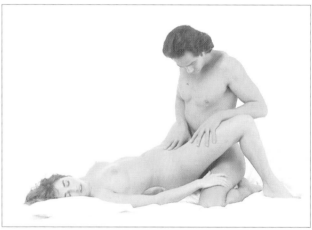

VARY YOUR ACTIONS   Extend your caressing and stimulation of your partner beyond her genital area, for example by gently stroking her belly and running your fingers along the insides of her thighs.

KEEP YOUR HANDS FREE   In any lovemaking position where you lie flat on your back with your partner on top of you, you will have both hands free and so will be able to masturbate her and to stroke and fondle her breasts and nipples.

CHAPTER 10

HOW CAN WE INJECT VARIETY INTO OUR LOVE~ MAKING?

"One of the reasons we settle on a sexual pattern is because we think that we ought to have an orgasm every time we make love, and that there is something wrong if we don't. When we find a routine that works, we tend to stick with it."

A FASCINATING insight into sexual patterning came from the Institute for the Advanced Study of Human Sexuality in San Francisco, in a comparison of two films.

A student couple had been filmed making love. These were real people, being sexual together in their own home and they were not performing anything special for the camera. Once the film had been edited it was shown to them so that they could accredit it as being truly representative of their genuine lovemaking patterns and habits. This they duly did, and the film was used as part of a Human Sexuality Teaching Programme for many years.

Twenty years on, the educators had the bright idea of returning to this couple's home (they had married and stayed together) and filmed them making love again. The fascinating fact to emerge from the second film was that two decades later the couple's lovemaking pattern was identical to the earlier one.

A person can rapidly become set in his or her ways, and so can a couple, and this applies to sex as much as it does to anything else.

CASE STUDY *Ben & Ellie*

Ben and Ellie were representative of many couples. Their lovemaking had got into a rut, because having hit upon a good routine they found it difficult to change and it had become institutionalized. In Ben and Ellie's case, just altering the primary rules was all that was needed.

Name: BEN
Age: 26
Marital status: SINGLE
Occupation: PICTURE RESEARCHER

Ben was a thin, rapid individual. He was tense, but funny and charismatic. He had been with the same steady girlfriend for two years, and the couple spent a great deal of time together, usually at Ben's home.

"I'd like to live with Ellie," he said, "But she refuses to move in with me while I'm still living at home, and I can't yet afford to move out. She does stop with me for weekends, but that is always with my parents somewhere nearby.

"We first met at university, where I had my own room, and I think we had our best sex there. But now we're always in a rush so we go through the same old routine, which is short, sharp and sweet, and over and done with before my parents come up to their bedroom next to mine.

"And it is always the same. First we embrace with me lying on top of her, and then I stroke her clitoris and so on and so forth, the same routine every time. I know there is more to good sex than that, but how do we get out of always doing the same thing? I actually tried doing something different but after a while she deliberately moved my hands back into the old routine."

Name: ELLIE
Age: 24
Marital status: SINGLE
Occupation: SALES REPRESENTATIVE

Ellie looked younger than her age, and she was pale and a little nervous. Her glance habitually darted around the room as if she were afraid of surprise attack.

"It just doesn't work for me if we make love differently," she told me. "I just keep thinking 'When is he going to hurry up and stroke my clitoris so that I can get the real sensation through?' I'm impatient, I know. But it took me long enough to have orgasms at all and I suppose I'm anxious that I'm not going to make it.

"I do feel enormously inhibited by Ben's parents being so close by, and I'm pretty depressed by his criticisms. He says they're not criticisms, but to me it sounds as if he's complaining that I'm boring."

THERAPIST'S ASSESSMENT

The primary rules for good sex are that it should feel safe, be open-ended with regards to time, and be carried out in private. The secondary rules, which we often understand only when we are older, are that sex doesn't have to end in orgasm in order to be good, that orgasm doesn't have to happen through intercourse, and that a sexual encounter can end with orgasm acquired through masturbation and still remain a gorgeous shared experience.

MIND CHANGES
These secondary rules are not excuses to cover those people who aren't very good at lovemaking. They are positive mind changes that enhance and provide valuable variation for randy men and rapacious women. What do I mean by mind changes? As time passes we acquire fixed ideas, which can be hard to alter because they feel like 'givens', facts as solid as rocks which are unshakeable, immovable. One of a human being's most valuable attributes is the possession of a flexible mind. Without it, a person rapidly becomes set in his or her ways. This applies to sex as much as it does to, say, eating habits.

The secondary sexual rule that is perhaps the hardest to understand is the idea that sex doesn't have to end in orgasm. To many, this is a kind of heresy. Yet accepting this idea provides not only extra options but also increases the emotional response we bring to our partners during the sex act. A soon as orgasm as an end is dispensed with, an infinite number of sexual variations are opened up.

ALTERING THE RULES
Since Ben was already paying rent to his father, and Ellie was paying rent for her shared apartment, they realized that it really wouldn't cost them much more to rent a place of their own. So Ben moved out of the parental home and into a cheap but comfortable apartment, which Ellie readily agreed to share with him.

This immediately removed the need for Ben and Ellie to be quick, quiet and discreet in their lovemaking, which in addition no longer had to be restricted to the bedroom. Making love in the kitchen was uncomfortable but different, and aroused the young couple in a way they'd practically forgotten. Ellie deliberately made love (occasionally) in positions and situations where orgasm wasn't guaranteed and Ben (sometimes) declared at the beginning of lovemaking that intercourse was forbidden on this occasion and only masturbation or oral sex was allowed. Sexual boredom evaporated immediately.

My programme for
CHANGING FIXED IDEAS ABOUT SEX

We've been battling with fixed ideas about sex for aeons, probably since the human race first appeared on earth. No doubt the original cave people were convinced that sex had to start with a bump on the head. What fascinates me is, how on earth did primitive man (and woman) know how to do sexual intercourse in the first place? Whatever the reason, there's no doubt we need to do it if we want to continue the race, but what we shouldn't do is allow our lovemaking to become a boring routine, constrained by rigid ideas about what is and is not acceptable.

Intercourse isn't, of course, the only form of enjoyable sexual experience. For example, there are women who can fantasize to orgasm, and both sexes can have wet dreams. There is also the great range of more common sexual activities, such as masturbation, mutual masturbation and oral sex.

Some people even reckon that sexual thoughts or fantasies are sexual experiences — ex-President Jimmy Carter, for example, once confessed to 'committing adultery in the mind'. Carter's notion was that thinking about sex with someone was the same thing, morally, as doing it.

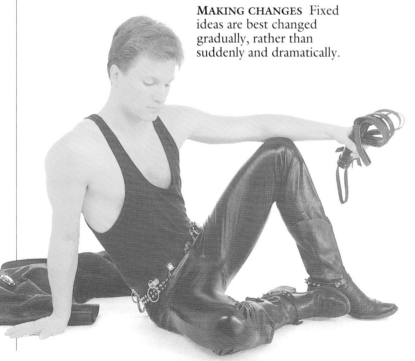

MAKING CHANGES Fixed ideas are best changed gradually, rather than suddenly and dramatically.

Stage | RESIST PURITANICAL PRESSURES

Attitudes to sex change over the years, and since the early 1980s a school of thought has arisen that takes a worthy, but dull, approach to sex. This is typified by objections to fantasy and dressing up, and by disapproval or rejection of lovemaking positions other than the basic face-to-face variety.

For example, although the *Kama Sutra* was fashionable in the 1970s, these days most people's eyes glaze with boredom as they contemplate page after page depicting women apparently hovering in mid-air while a snake-like penis assumes angles of 300 degrees and still manages to penetrate them.

Looked on now as similarly old-fashioned (a hark-back to the swinging, sexual 60s and 70s) is the pastime of dressing up for sex. Instead, in have come new views: for sex to be real, to possess true meaning and emotion, it should be straight; women shouldn't even wear face make-up let alone rouge on their nipples; men ought to relate to women as human beings regardless of their appearance (after all, this is how women relate to men, isn't it?); and fantasies involving anyone other than an actual partner are out because this indicates we aren't capable of a truthful relationship focused on a real person.

PURITANISM IS A DOWNER This new form of puritanism is to be resisted, because it fails to acknowledge that variety in lovemaking will stave off the boredom that can set in and which often can endanger a relationship.

The theories arising from it ignore the fact that altering the angle of entry during intercourse may also alter the emotions that accompany it. They don't take into account that dressing up is an indication of a mind behind the decoration. That when you relate to rouged nipples you are also relating to a woman who is telling you something about her eroticism. That when a woman fantasizes about a movie star while making love she may be trying to keep a relationship alive sexually because she values it for other reasons.

Of course, any activity taken to excess is an intimation that something is unbalanced. But the same is true when, out of many options, only one is ever pursued.

Stage 2 — MAKE GRADUAL CHANGES

Making instant, major changes to our ideas, whether about sex or about anything else, is difficult to do. It is far easier to slip in a few minor variations and gradually build on them. For instance:

• If you always lie on one side of a partner in bed, try the other side for a change
• If you always caress your partner with your right hand, use the left for a change
• If mutual masturbation has involved using the forefinger, use the middle finger instead
• If you usually climax after a certain sequence of events, add to the sequence to make it a little longer each time.

Such changes are simple to make and, apart from adding some pleasant variety to your lovemaking, they help to get you out of fixed routines. They thus pave the way for bigger changes, should these be wanted or needed, and give you and your partner the confidence to be more experimental.

Stage 3 — EXPERIMENT WITH YOUR LOVEMAKING

Use your imagination creatively, and experiment by deliberately changing your lovemaking scenario from time to time. For instance, you and your partner might want to break away from the mistaken idea that lovemaking should only be done at night, and in bed, by making love at other times and in other places. You could also try experimenting with different lovemaking positions, both in bed and elsewhere.

Spontaneous lovemaking p116

NUDITY   Another common fixed idea about lovemaking is that it should be done in the nude, and that the state of nudity should be reached as fast as possible. Substitute the idea of nudity with a different one — that of deliberately leaving your clothes on.

By doing so, you enhance the eroticism brought to the bedroom and therefore the strength of feeling you endow your partner with. Try using your clothes to create ideas for a sex scenario. I'm not suggesting that you have to wear something outrageous, or that you should go out and spend a fortune on a whole new wardrobe. But, in future, buy your clothes with an eye to the erotic effect that they will have on your partner.

DEALING WITH ANXIETIES

Introducing changes into your sexual routine can often lead to anxieties. But you can help your emotions move on by opening up to your partner and discussing your anxieties with him or her. If you have trouble doing this, ask yourself the following questions:

• Do I usually confess my sexual anxieties to my partner? If the answer is no, ask yourself:

• What do I fear about revealing these anxieties?

• Am I anxious about worrying my partner and adding to my own load of worry?

• Do I think my partner will be critical and unsupportive?

• Do I fear my partner will see me as less of a person if I confess to weaknesses?

• Will this make me unattractive and unlovable?

• Do I fear my confessions will unbalance the relationship in some way that is disastrous?

• Are my fears based on the reality of my partner's likely reactions or on my own past experience in my youth?

Thinking through your answers to these questions will show you what is holding you back from discussing your anxieties with your partner. The act of expressing a real fear, of hearing it accepted by your partner and finding that he or she is supportive of you, is enriching — just as releasing anxiety can be cathartic in social aspects of life, so too can it be when it comes to sexual matters.

SPONTANEOUS LOVEMAKING POSITIONS

Quick sex, if it works well for you, can extend your opportunities for making love. The occasional 'quickie', at home, outdoors or even at work, can be terrifically stimulating. Just because sex is sandwiched between a working morning and afternoon, for example, doesn't mean it can't be therapeutic. And 'quickie' positions can be very useful for a man who tends to ejaculate prematurely.

SUPPORT YOURSELF
Use the chair arms to support yourself comfortably and securely and to help you to angle your body most effectively

ADJUST TECHNIQUES Spontaneous lovemaking often involves making the best use of the available locale or furnishings. With a little care, you can make love on a swivel chair quite easily if it has solid feet, especially if its height can be adjusted, but chairs with castors are tricky to use and usually prove more trouble than they are worth.

Lie back with your legs apart and wrapped around your partner as he kneels in front of you

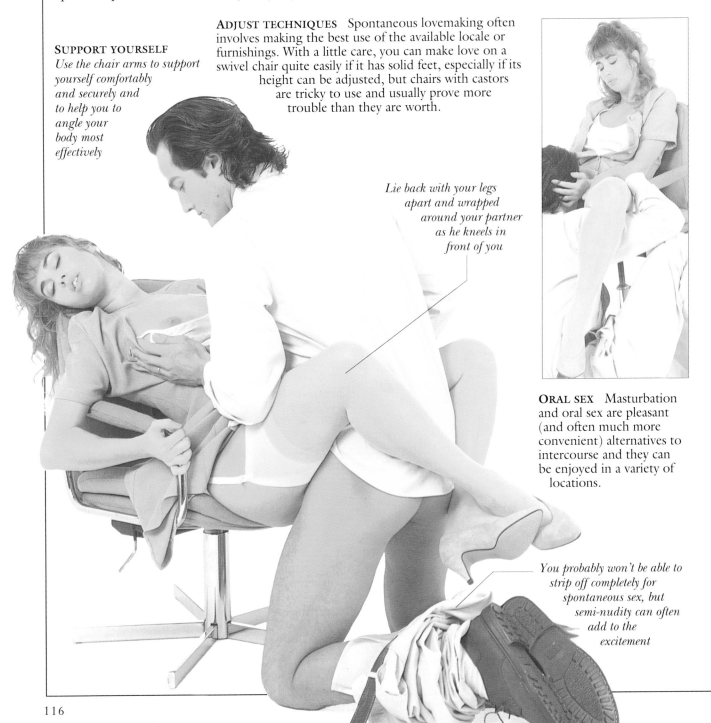

ORAL SEX Masturbation and oral sex are pleasant (and often much more convenient) alternatives to intercourse and they can be enjoyed in a variety of locations.

You probably won't be able to strip off completely for spontaneous sex, but semi-nudity can often add to the excitement

Support yourself on a convenient chair or table if you engage in rear-entry sex

One of you should lean against a wall or other support to help you keep your balance when you are making love standing up

Stockings and suspenders will allow quicker, easier access than tights

CONVENIENT POSITIONS The rear-entry 'doggy-fashion' position (above) is one of the most convenient to use when time is of the essence. It calls for minimal undressing, it is easy to do and it can be very enjoyable for both of you. Having sex in a standing, face-to-face position (right) is often the best option in those situations where you want to make love but you are in a place where there is a lack of suitably private space. It works best if you are both of more or less the same height, and if neither of you is seriously overweight.

You can often achieve deeper penetration if the woman stands on one leg and hooks the other around her partner

MUTUAL MASTURBATION When the time available for lovemaking is limited, use your hands to stimulate your partner during intercourse to maximize enjoyment.

BEYOND THE BEDROOM

Most couples don't think twice about where they make love in the early stages of romance, but rigid patterns tend to set in and, before they know it, lovemaking is restricted to the bedroom. But variety, necessary for the continued vigour of long-term relationships, can be reintroduced easily by changing the setting.

SIT ON A CHAIR Try making love sitting on a wooden chair — in your bedroom, the dining room, the living room, the kitchen or anywhere else in the house. Here, the woman is on the man's lap and faces away from him, but she could also sit astride and face him.

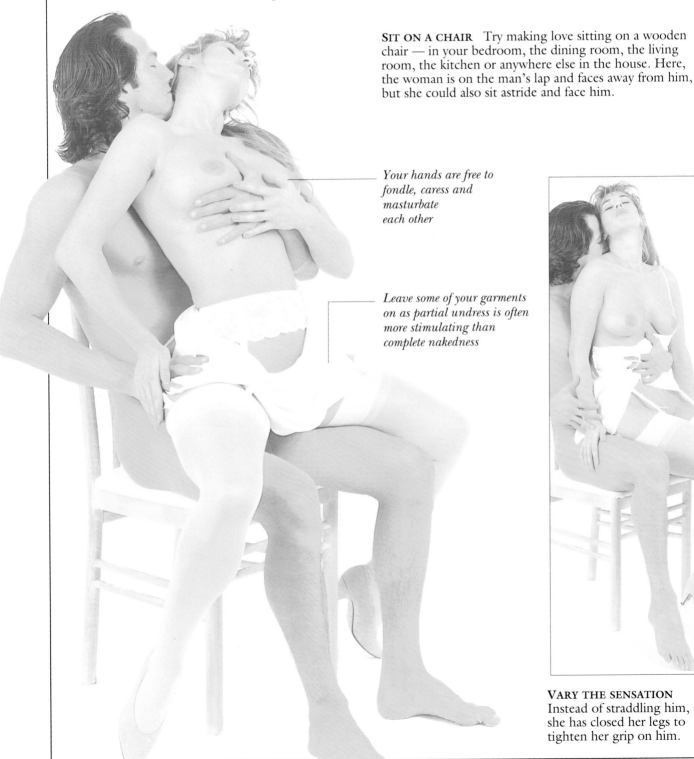

Your hands are free to fondle, caress and masturbate each other

Leave some of your garments on as partial undress is often more stimulating than complete nakedness

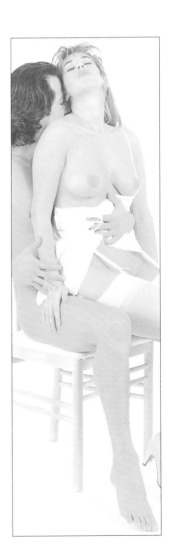

VARY THE SENSATION
Instead of straddling him, she has closed her legs to tighten her grip on him.

DO IT ON THE FLOOR Move the furniture out of the way and make love on the carpet or floor. The hard surface makes a change from the resilience of a bed, and if there is enough room you can experiment with all sorts of different positions.

Be careful not to press your partner against rough-textured surfaces

MAKE LOVE IN AN ARMCHAIR A large, sturdy armchair offers you the opportunity of making love in several positions. For instance, you can both kneel on it, the woman can kneel or bend over with the man standing behind her, or he can sit with her on his lap.

Closing your eyes helps you to savour the sensation, but watching your partner's moves will increase your erotic stimulation

Use the floor's sturdy surface to push off against

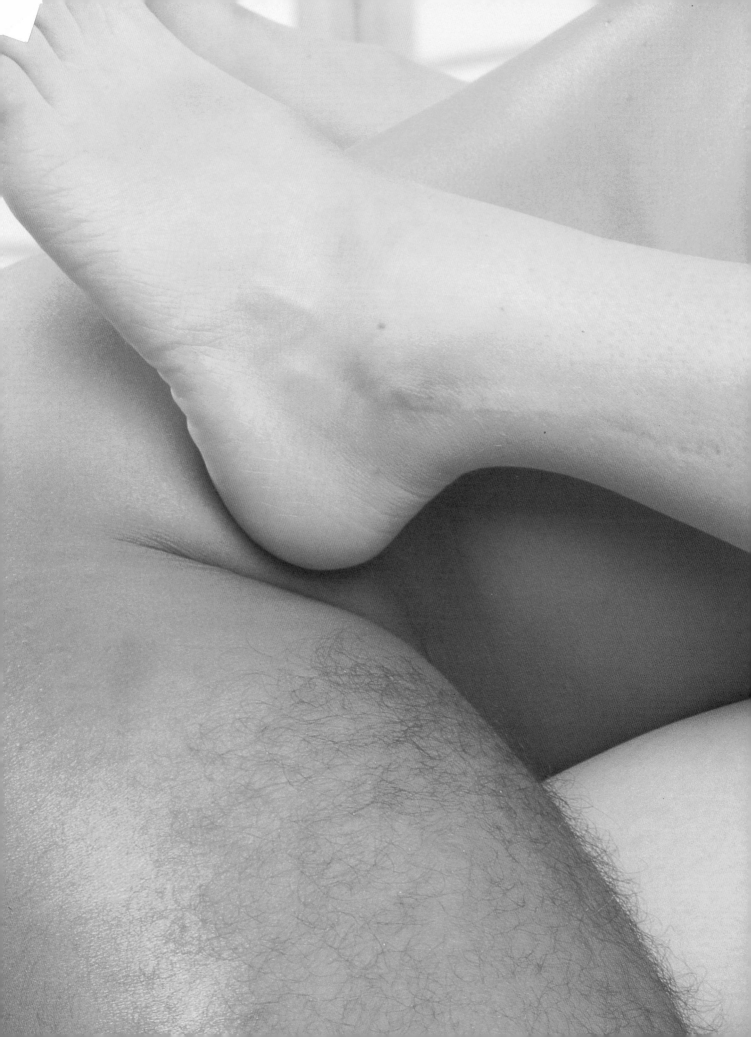

CHAPTER

11

HOW CAN I REVIVE A PARTNER'S WANING INTEREST?

"A decline in spontaneous desire can be compensated for by imaginative stimulation."

ONE OF THE great killers of marriages and other long-term personal relationships is sexual boredom. Age plays a physical part here, and the effects of advancing age on sexual desire and performance are not often anticipated by couples when they are still comparatively young.

Yet couples who are in their late thirties and early forties may, without realizing it, be experiencing subtle health and hormone changes that are progressively reducing their capacity for erogenous sensation. In plain terms, this means that they will need stronger stimulation in order to enjoy sex as much as they formerly did.

The effects of aging cannot, of course, be avoided, but we can come to terms with them and, by adopting suitable attitudes and strategies, prevent them from ever taking the fun and excitement out of our sex lives.

CASE STUDY *Jules & Angie*

Jules was something of a workaholic, spending many extra hours in the office including working at weekends. This, combined with the effects of age, stress and fatigue, had begun to impede Jules' sex drive and put his marriage to Angie in jeopardy.

Name:	JULES
Age:	40
Marital status:	RE-MARRIED
Occupation:	ARCHITECT

In spite of his receding hairline and being slightly overweight, Jules was a good-looking man who exuded energy and dynamism.

"Angie's my second wife," he told me. "We have two youngsters aged five and three, and we live in an idyllic spot with every luxury and comfort you can think of. When I come home from work, I want to be able to switch off from all the stresses of the office and enjoy myself with the family. Part of that enjoyment is my sex life with my wife, and yet I don't often feel sexually interested these days.

"I don't understand it. Angie is as gorgeous-looking as she always was, there's no loss of interest on her part, and everything functions wonderfully once I make the effort and get going. But why is it so difficult for me to get started? I'm worried about the long-term effect this will have on Angie. I couldn't face going through another divorce."

Name:	ANGIE
Age:	36
Marital status:	MARRIED
Occupation:	HOUSEWIFE

Angie was a picture-book blonde beauty, with wide blue eyes, a model's body with long, shapely legs, and a loving and amenable nature. She adored her husband and children and appeared unspoiled by wealth.

"I've been racking my brains to understand what's going wrong between us," she said. "And I wonder if it's a stress problem. Jules is very stressed by work, and in spite of what he says about leaving it behind him, he finds that much harder to do than he admits. I get a lot of stress, too. In spite of having wonderful help, the kids are exhausting at this age, especially since the youngest doesn't sleep, and much of the time I'm wandering around like a zombie.

"I know this means I don't have so much energy to put into our lovemaking but there's not a lot I can do about that. I do make a special point of getting a couple of unbroken nights towards the end of the week, when a child-minder takes over, so that I'm fresh for the weekend. But then Jules doesn't want to know."

THERAPIST'S ASSESSMENT

Angie's description of Jules as being much more stressed than he admitted was an important insight. Stress can actually alter the body's testosterone levels, which are linked to sexual interest and response, so Jules might have been labouring under a physical disadvantage.

PHYSICAL AND SITUATIONAL PRESSURES
But even without the effects of increasing stress levels, older men often need greater physical stimulation. Without it, it naturally would become more difficult for him to enjoy good erotic sensation and he would therefore have less and less incentive to start proceedings in the first place. Angie's extraordinary beauty had been enough stimulation for him six years earlier, but now he needed something more.

Angie, on the other hand was struggling with the fatigue that all mothers of young children will recognize. When you are constantly exhausted it is very hard indeed to turn into a temptress at the end of the day. Angie, however is in a more fortunate situation than most since she can afford a child-minder. Her scheme of having someone look after the kids for two nights of the week, giving her a chance to catch up on her sleep, was a wise one, because it gave her the energy she needed to brighten up her own interest in sex. But, as she had found out, there is never any guarantee that one partner's renewed interest in lovemaking will rekindle the other's.

STIMULATING MIND AND BODY
Jules' options were to try and rethink what was happening to him with regards to work, to seek extra rest himself, and to work out with Angie what some of his most sensuous and erotic desires might be, so that they could bring these into their lovemaking.

As part of the enhancement programme, Angie focused particularly on giving Jules strong penile stimulation by hand, not something she'd ever done previously and yet which turned out to be one of the most exciting and erotic experiences he had ever enjoyed. Having this to look forward to did not mean he felt desire in the spontaneous manner of earlier years, but it did mean he was delighted to set aside regular time each week for a wonderful sensuality session.

My programme for USING SUGGESTION AS A TURN-ON

One of the most skilful arts of lovemaking lies in using the power of suggestion to such effect that a partner is turned on to the point of orgasm before you've even laid a finger on him or her. If, as you proceed to pay attention to their body, you talk them through a scenario, letting your fingers (or indeed, any other part of your body) enact your words, you can create a sense of anticipation so overwhelming your partner goes crazy with excitement.

Stage 1 ESTABLISH YOUR GUIDELINES

The secret of success is to be absolutely in charge of the story and not to let up despite the reaction of your lover. Having said that, it is vital that before you let loose with your imagination you have a very clear idea of what is going to be acceptable to your lover and what isn't. If you don't know what activities are likely to be acceptable, you need to find out well in advance.

GUIDELINES One couple who developed their interest in mild bondage and spanking drew up some clear guidelines between them. If either of them shouted "Stop!", "No!", "I can't bear it any longer!" or any permutation of these, they agreed to take no notice.

If, on the other hand, the partner being dominated spoke an agreed codeword when he or she wanted to stop, that was serious stuff — it meant that all activities should cease immediately. They stuck to the agreement, and it worked.

TRUST It worked, of course, because the couple trusted each other completely. If you are going to give yourself into someone's power and allow them total control of your body, even if it is only for a short time, you need to have developed an exceptionally trusting relationship with that person.

One sex researcher even described such a pairing as the height of emotional trust — a rather different view from that of the grubby image that mild spanking relationships have hitherto enjoyed.

Stage 2 PLAN A SUGGESTIVE SCENARIO

Some people like to plan their scenario in advance. One person actually made reminder lists which included items such as 'leave sharp objects such as scissors and knives in conspicuous positions'. The mere reading of this reminder makes clear the premise of such an arrangement. What came into your mind when you read that? Suspicion? Apprehension? Anxiety? Whatever it was you felt something. Your emotions were aroused, which is the whole point. Such is the power of suggestion.

So, by subtly dressing up the meeting place, you can alter it to send some very distinct messages to the person visiting. It is up to you to choose what those might be.

AROUSAL Another arousing move, once you are in bed together, is to tell your partner what is going to happen and then leave things for a while so that their expectations are aroused by the wait. The same person who made the reminder list once left a partner waiting for half an hour, while he went into a separate room. By the time he returned she was so angry she was fully aroused, sexually as well as emotionally.

GIVING ORDERS One situation that turns some people on is to order them about before every erotic move. For example, in *The Story of O*, O was ordered to stand with her legs slightly apart in front of her master. Just the act of being ordered renders some people a little helpless, a little vulnerable, a little out of control and therefore very erotically aroused.

TAKE IT SLOWLY   If you are a complete newcomer to suggestion and games playing it's a good idea to progress slowly with your ideas and activities. If at some stage you come to a boundary for one or other of you it is vital that this boundary is respected. That doesn't mean to say it shouldn't be examined, even tested, provided the other agrees, but when finally one of you says "This is my limit," that limit must be observed: if it isn't, trust disappears and the relationship is destroyed.

Stage 3 SEXUAL GAMES

The variety of sexual games that you and your partner might want to play is limited only by your combined imaginations and inclinations.

If these are strong enough and you choose suitable imaginary scenarios, you can play an endless variety of sexual games without the need for dressing up or for equipment such as ropes or blindfolds. But the use of such props can make the games more realistic and easier to play, and may also help you to dream up new scenarios.

Love games pp 64, 66,126, 138-143

And don't feel restricted to a particular scenario once you have begun to enact it. If it evolves into something different, let yourselves be carried along by it — you can never tell what exciting paths it may lead you down.

Using a blindfold enables you to play tricks on your partner as part of your sexual games

SEXY GAMES TO PLAY

Here are some suggestions for sexy games you might like to play, or to use as a basis for your own imaginative inventions.

• Agree that you will do whatever activity your partner orders

• Take it in turns (for example on alternate nights) to do anything enjoyable and sexual with each other except for intercourse

• Try a bit of role-playing: pretend that she's a shy, totally inexperienced young virgin and he's a sophisticated seducer

• Pretend that he's an inexperienced youth and she is a seductive older woman

• Give your partner boundaries to their behaviour and punish them if they move beyond them. One punishment might be light caning or spanking. The game is more fun if the boundaries that you choose are impossible to stick to

• Tie your partner to the bed with silken cords and tickle and tease them to climax

• Blindfold your partner and announce that he or she must obey you precisely. Tell them that they are going to be the sexual slave of yourself and another person and that your partner will not know which of you will be having their way with them. There will, in fact, be no other person present, but the key to making this game a success is to convince your partner that there is. In order to do this you will either need to disguise your voice or, better still, not use it. Tread differently, behave differently sexually in your other persona. Penetrative sexual toys such as vibrators, dildos and anal vibrators, anything safe, can come into their own in this game, provided that you use them gently and carefully and that you are sure your partner has no objections to their use

• Another version of the blindfold game is to tie your partner face-down across a bed or even across a comfortable stool. You tell your partner that you have decided to invite some friends around for the evening (friends your partner has never met) and that you will be with them in the next room. One or more of them may be using your partner's body, you say, during the evening. When subsequently you enter the room disguised, if you want to be really convincing in your role as a stranger you can put a scarf or wrap across your mouth, so that when talking through it you sound different

INVENTIVE LOVE GAMES

The use of unusual sexual techniques is often necessary where sexual tension is low and partners feel the need to reinvigorate their desire for each other. Symbolic aggression, in the form of gentle bondage for instance, often finds favour with both men and women, once they overcome the understandable fear of showing that they like to dominate another person or that they enjoy being dominated. Like most other natural drives, sexual excitement is increased by restraint; but this should never get out of hand. If there is any sign that your partner is not enjoying what you are doing, stop at once.

TIE HANDS GENTLY Use scarves, ribbons, pajama cords or stockings to bind your partner's hands. Other areas where compression boosts sexual feeling are the ankles, elbows, soles of feet, thumbs and big toes.

TANTALIZE YOUR PARTNER Once he or she is immobilized, teasingly caress the length of his or her body as you will. Your partner shouldn't know what to expect or when, which will increase their suspense and sensations immeasurably.

HINTING AT RESTRAINT A scarf or tie used to pull your partner gently closer is a loving way of showing him or her that you need some attention.

Encourage your partner's responses by telling him how much you are being turned on

Slide under your partner's arms and insinuate your body against his

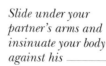

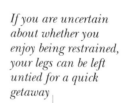

EMPHASIZE YOUR DOMINANCE Manipulate your partner into positions that serve to show how powerless he or she is to resist your attentions.

If you are uncertain about whether you enjoy being restrained, your legs can be left untied for a quick getaway

BE GENTLE AND LOVING
Always treat your partner tenderly. The object is to excite, never to hurt or frighten.

Pretend to struggle against your bonds; this can be very exciting for your partner

TAKE TURNS Pre-arranged signals or simply saying "It's my turn now" must be heeded immediately. Unless it's fun for both, it shouldn't be done.

Use whatever limbs are free to caress your partner in a teasing way

DON'T BE TOO SERIOUS A little light relief lets your partner know that this is fun and you are enjoying his or her attentions. You can only play games of this sort if you are very secure with your partner.

REVIEW THE EXPERIENCE If you've managed to inject further passion into your lovemaking, and both of you have found the technique useful, you should agree how you'll continue in future. If, however, one of you has found it distasteful, it should be dropped from your repertoire.

Express your feelings, so that you both feel comfortable with the experience

GIVING HIM A SENSUAL MASSAGE

Massage can lay the foundations for relaxation, but once the quality of the touch itself is changed, from using a firm hand to fingertip skimming, from working on the whole body to touching tantalizingly around the genitals, the experience shifts from relaxation to arousal (for the basic massage strokes, see pages 60-63).

LEGS AND BACK Begin the session with your partner lying face-down, and sit astride his legs. Use warm massage oil to make your hands and his skin slippery and sensuous, and start by leaning back and drawing your hands along the soles of his feet and over his ankles and calves. Then work up from his thighs to his neck.

Use all the basic massage strokes, first firmly, then with relaxed pressure and finally with light fingertip pressure

LOWER BACK Using gentle, erotic pressure, work your hands slowly up from his thighs and buttocks to his lower back.

UPPER BACK Pay special attention to the muscles between his shoulder blades and at the base of his neck.

If your bed is too soft, put a duvet or folded blankets on the floor and give your massage there

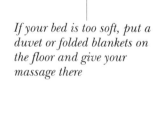

BODY CONTACT When you have finished massaging his back and shoulders, lean forward on to him and slowly and sensuously slide your body from side to side against his. Tighten your thighs against his, and rub your breasts softly across his back.

FRONTAL MASSAGE Ask your partner to roll over onto his back and then, again using plenty of warm oil, massage his abdomen and chest. Lightly massage his breasts and nipples, but avoid touching his genital area.

HEIGHTEN HIS AROUSAL Turn your partner on by first running your fingers lightly around his breasts. Then circle his nipples with featherlight strokes of your fingers, and gently caress their tips. If your hair is long enough, let it trail seductively across his naked body.

Intensify his pleasure by gently gliding your hands up the sides of his chest and along his soft underarm skin

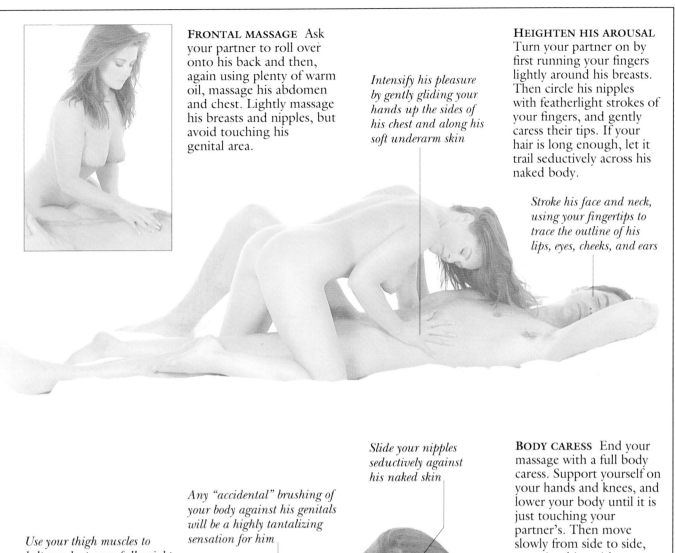

Stroke his face and neck, using your fingertips to trace the outline of his lips, eyes, cheeks, and ears

Slide your nipples seductively against his naked skin

BODY CARESS End your massage with a full body caress. Support yourself on your hands and knees, and lower your body until it is just touching your partner's. Then move slowly from side to side, caressing him with your breasts and belly. Finish off by sliding your body up and down his, then finally sweeping your hands up over his belly and chest to his arms.

Any "accidental" brushing of your body against his genitals will be a highly tantalizing sensation for him

Use your thigh muscles to help you keep your full weight off your partner as you slide against him

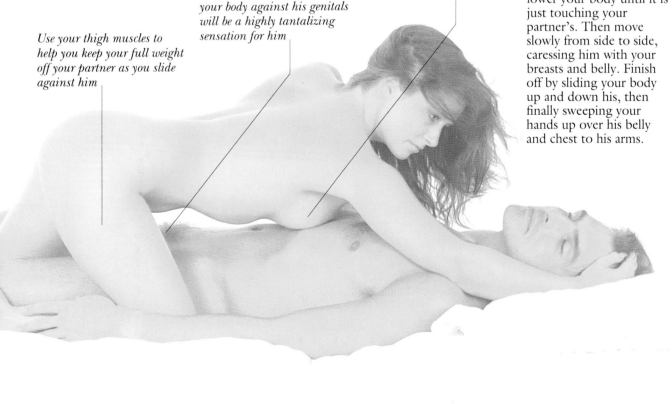

GIVING HER A SENSUAL MASSAGE

Giving your partner a loving, sensual massage will reinforce the bonds of love between you, and it will be a highly erotic experience for both of you. Make yourselves comfortable in a warm, draught-free room, and if your bed is too soft put a mattress, duvet or folded blankets on the floor and give her your massage there (for details of the basic massage strokes, see pages 60-63).

START AT THE BUTTOCKS
The female buttocks are rich in nerve endings and so they are highly erogenous. Using warm massage oil to make your hands and her skin slippery and sensuous, lightly run the flats of your hands across each of her buttocks.

BACK MASSAGE Put your hands on each side of her hips, thumbs pointing towards her spine, and gently glide them up the sides of her body towards her shoulders. Do this several times, then repeat with your hands flat on her back.

Use all the basic massage strokes, first firmly then increasingly lightly until your fingertips are just brushing her skin

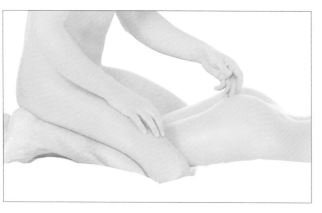

INNER THIGHS Using well-oiled fingers, stroke firmly up the inside of each thigh in turn, from just above the knee up to the buttocks and back. Use only the lightest of finger pressure on the return strokes.

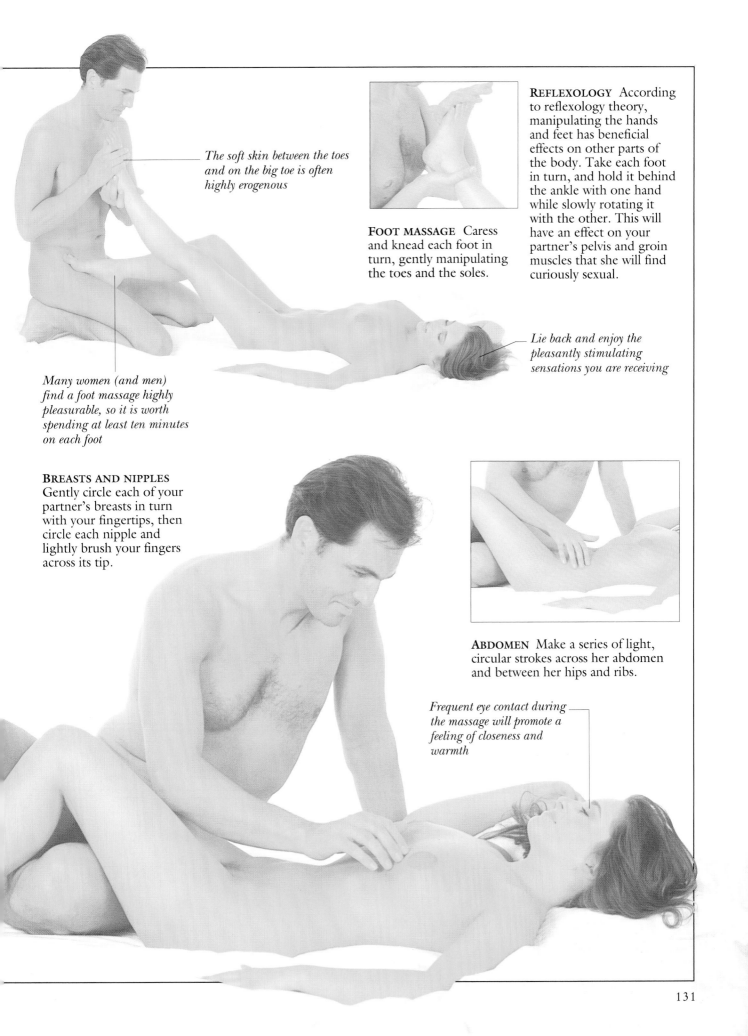

The soft skin between the toes and on the big toe is often highly erogenous

FOOT MASSAGE Caress and knead each foot in turn, gently manipulating the toes and the soles.

REFLEXOLOGY According to reflexology theory, manipulating the hands and feet has beneficial effects on other parts of the body. Take each foot in turn, and hold it behind the ankle with one hand while slowly rotating it with the other. This will have an effect on your partner's pelvis and groin muscles that she will find curiously sexual.

Lie back and enjoy the pleasantly stimulating sensations you are receiving

Many women (and men) find a foot massage highly pleasurable, so it is worth spending at least ten minutes on each foot

BREASTS AND NIPPLES Gently circle each of your partner's breasts in turn with your fingertips, then circle each nipple and lightly brush your fingers across its tip.

ABDOMEN Make a series of light, circular strokes across her abdomen and between her hips and ribs.

Frequent eye contact during the massage will promote a feeling of closeness and warmth

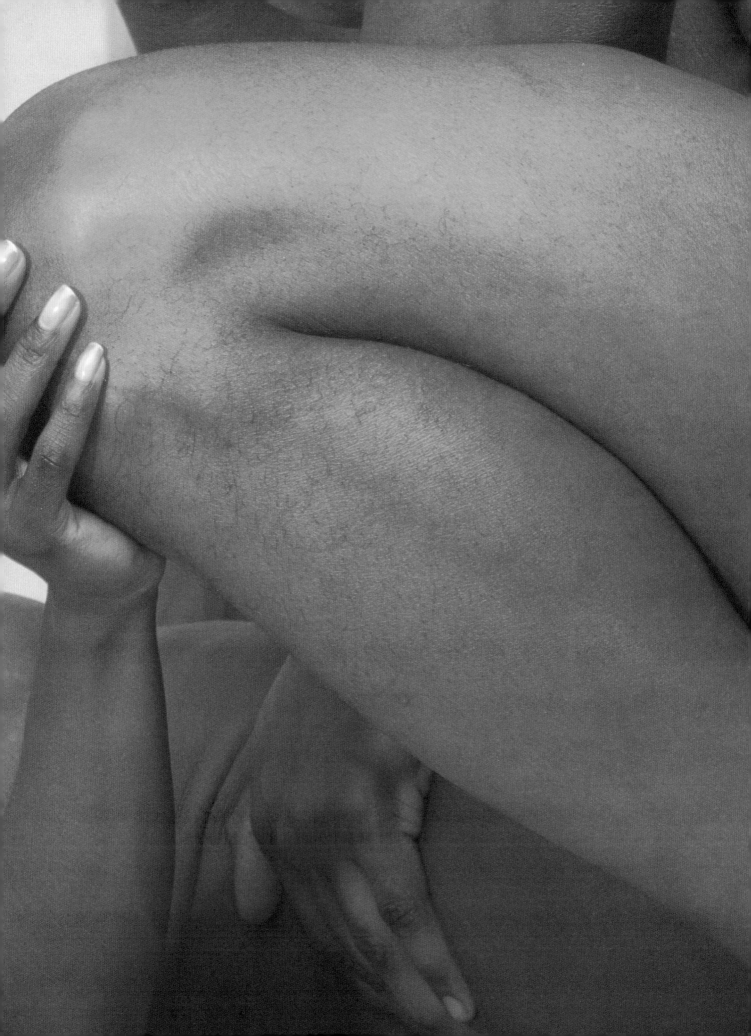

CHAPTER
12

HOW CAN WE EXPLORE OUR DEEPEST FANTASIES?

"Not everyone has sexual fantasies, but many of those who don't fantasize are capable of learning how they can do so."

SEXUAL FANTASY IS regarded by some as a marriage rescuer and an enhancer of eroticism, by others as an escape from reality and politically undesirable. The latter attitude ignores the fact that judicious use of fantasy can be of great value. It can, for example, help some women to experience a climax when they have never been able to do so before.

The use of fantasy allows couples to explore their imaginations and transform their lovemaking into a sexual adventure fully involving their minds and emotions as well as their bodies.

There is thought to be a link between an individual's sex drive and the likelihood of him or her having sexual fantasies, with people who have a high sex drive being more likely to use fantasy than those with lower sex drives.

In addition, those whose upbringing has conditioned them against sexual feeling, and who thus through guilt have learned to suppress their sex drives, will be less likely to have sexual fantasies.

However, the good news is that we can all learn how to overcome such inhibitions and enjoy the erotic potential of our imaginations.

CASE STUDY *Joyce & Neil*

Both Joyce and her partner, Neil, understood the usefulness of sexual fantasy in a relationship and both of them wanted to introduce it into their sexual activities. But their problem was that neither of them knew how to mention this secret desire to the other.

Name:	JOYCE
Age:	27
Marital status:	DIVORCED
Occupation:	POOL ATTENDANT

Joyce was a pretty but indecisive woman who worked part-time at her local swimming pool. She had a two-year-old son, and was trying to decide on a suitable retraining programme to improve her career prospects.

"I was married for eight years to a man who simply couldn't turn me on," she said. "His particular brand of sexuality just didn't tune into my erotic wavelength and the marriage eventually fell apart. After that, I had brief, unsatisfactory relationships with two other men and then ended up with Neil.

"Neil is imaginative, very good in bed, gives me wonderful oral sex and gets me farther in the direction of climaxes than anyone else has ever managed, but I have never had a climax with him. I know I can have them because I can get them through masturbation and fantasy. I feel sure sex could really work with Neil, I'm so far along the pathway with him now, but somehow or other I need him to bring fantasy into it. I really don't have a clue where to start. Do I just ask him? How would he know what I mean? Is there any way in reality in which he can somehow enter my fantasies, or am I just kidding myself?"

Name:	NEIL
Age:	30
Marital status:	SINGLE
Occupation:	ILLUSTRATOR

Neil was a short, dark illustrator who painted lyrical pictures of knights and dragons, and women warriors fighting orcs and trolls. His work was much in demand for science fiction book covers and calendars.

"I think Joyce is one of the sexiest women I've ever encountered," he said. "Yet she is only just beginning to understand that. She has yet to be awakened sexually. What she really needs is some kind of romantic yet directly erotic scenario, and what I'd really like to do is to pretend she has been tied down by a cruel guardian with ropes and left there vulnerable to me. I think this could be wonderful for both of us but I'm terrified of blowing it. I don't want to take the risk of overstepping the mark. What can I do?"

THERAPIST'S ASSESSMENT

When Joyce and Neil discussed their problems with me individually, it soon became clear that what they both wanted was to enhance their sexual activities by the use of fantasy, and that the only thing that stopped them from doing so was the fact that neither knew how to raise the matter with the other. But once they were able to discuss it freely they were soon confiding and acting out sexual fantasies, and Joyce was climaxing regularly and easily.

Difficulties of communication can sometimes put up the greatest barrier of all to a special sexual activity which, ironically, both partners may desire. Asking for something out of the ordinary is not easy; to do it successfully you need to take risks, yet give reassurance at the same time.

UNSPOKEN SIGNALS

You also need to read a partner's unspoken signals very carefully. One reason these can be misinterpreted is because your own desire for a particular activity is so great that you project it on to a partner when it is not necessarily there. The only way to find out just whose mind a certain sexual desire or activity lodges in is by talking. Ask questions at a neutral time, not when you are poised over your partner complete with thigh boots and whip. Choose a relaxed time for asking these intimate questions, for example when you are lazing on the grass on a hot summer's afternoon, or during a long car journey.

ASKING QUESTIONS

When asking questions, avoid doing so in an accusatory fashion. Don't say, "You look as if you might get behind a bit of mild spanking in bed." Instead, use a more indirect approach, such as, "I get the feeling you might quite like it if I spanked you very lightly when we make love next time. What do you think?" And if you are very uncertain indeed about how your partner might receive even such a tentative question, you could precede that by saying, "There's something sexual I really want to talk about, but I'm finding it very hard. I'm afraid you might get the wrong idea about me."

Most partners on hearing this are going to want to know what it is that is so difficult, and will offer reassurance. You can then follow up the reassurance by saying, "This is just a question and in no way alters anything we already love doing together in bed. But...." There is no avoiding the fact that you are taking risks in opening up the subject but, on the other hand, if you never do this, you will never get to move on in your erotic life at all.

My programme for
USING SEXUAL FANTASY

Sexual fantasy is one of those unquantified facets of everyday erotic life that are virtually unmeasured so far by psychological testing. But we do know that even though not everyone has sexual fantasies, and even though there are some people who never have one at all, many of the people who don't have them find that they can learn to. This programme shows you how to help your own fantasies to develop by using mental and physical stimulation, and how to use fantasy to enhance your lovemaking.

Dr Glenn Wilson, one of the few psychologists who have been brave enough to study sexual fantasy, says that it is directly related to sex urge or libido. The higher the sex urge a person possesses, the higher their likelihood of having sexual fantasies. This conclusion may tie in with findings of Dr John Bancroft at Edinburgh University who relates higher testosterone levels in women to the greater likelihood of their ability to fantasize. Higher levels of testosterone are also thought to be responsible for greater sexual libido.

UPBRINGING AND CONDITIONING However, upbringing plays a large part in how an individual uses his or her sexual libido. If a person has been conditioned from a very early age against sexual feeling (as many of us have been) their sex urge may be inhibited by guilt feelings. And the guilt stifles fantasy when it tries to make an appearance. But we can learn how to overcome these inhibitions and enjoy the erotic display for our imagination only.

Stage 1   MENTAL STIMULATION

Plan to give yourself at least an hour and a half of undisturbed time for the first two stages of this programme. After a warm, relaxing bath, lie on your bed in a bedroom that is warm enough to allow you to feel completely comfortable while lying there nude.

EROTICA If you find it hard to make up your own sexual fantasy you may like to read some of the collections of erotica available. For example, *My Secret Garden* by Nancy Friday appeals to women, and is available in paperback, while magazines such as *Penthouse* and *Playboy* appeal to men and some of the better

sex magazines contain very arousing material for both sexes. You may also enjoy reading sexual scenes from certain favourite novels.

Or you may like to consider the illustrated fantasies on the pages following these. One is written to please men, another is specially aimed at arousing women and the third one works well for both sexes.

Stage 2   PHYSICAL STIMULATION

As you read your erotic book or sexy magazine, become aware of any feelings of physical arousal in your body. If these are inspired by a particular part of what you are reading, focus your thoughts on it. And while doing so, try fondling and caressing your genitals, paying very special attention to your clitoris or penis. Try keeping the sexiest aspects of the fantasy in your mind as you become aroused.

Self-stimulation p226

CUT-OFF POINT Some women find they can get turned on easily this way, but then they reach a stage that many of them describe as the 'cut-off point'. If this cut-off point is a problem for you, the way through it is to focus very deliberately on the most arousing part of the fantasy. Every time your mind wanders off, insist that it returns. Many women find that this is a very effective way to overcome any final inhibition to climax. And many men find that, by using the same methods, they can enjoy an orgasm of greatly enhanced sensation.

Other ways of using sexual fantasy to overcome those final inhibitions are by having your partner whisper the fantasies to you as you near climax, or by watching an erotic video from your bed.

Stage   USE FANTASY IN YOUR LOVEMAKING

Thousands of people secretly use fantasy to enable them to climax during lovemaking. And most of them don't own up to this because of fears of spoiling the sexual relationship or of spoiling the fantasy by exposing it to the true light of day. Very few people have the courage not only to confide their fantasies to their partners but also to suggest trying to act them out together.

Playing innocent p142

LOSING FANTASIES   It is important to note that if you lose a sexual fantasy because you reveal it, this doesn't mean you will never be turned on again. Most people are capable of replacing an old fantasy with a new one, of developing existing fantasies until they are totally changed, and of moving on easily from one fantasy to another.

ACTING OUT FANTASIES   Listen to how one couple, Mimi and Roger, negotiated the move from imagination to real life.

"It was apparent, quite early on in our relationship, that we shared an interest in sexy underwear. I loved wearing it, he adored seeing me in it and taking it off me. As I bought the stuff, trying it on in changing room cubicles, I would long for Roger to be there. When I mentioned the idea to Roger, he instantly went off into a fantasy. I could see it happening, mainly because I'd already had the same fantasy. What we both actually wanted was to act out our changing-room fantasy — the situation where I would let my legs, in filmy stockings and suspender belt, linger between the drapes where he could see them, where I would draw the curtain half-way back so that he could see me in the gauzy pieces of lace that hid virtually nothing. And the problem was that we needed to do this for real. If we had pretended to do it, at home, it just wouldn't have worked.

"After we had fleetingly alluded to the idea a couple of times, I made a date with him. 'Meet me at the department store at 11.00 on Wednesday,' I said, naming a store which I knew tended to be relatively empty at mid-week, particularly at that time of day.

"There was a range of Edwardian underclothes on sale on that occasion. The place was empty and the only saleswoman there wasn't remotely interested in our movements. I started off by demonstrating the clothes in front of him for his approval and ended up finding it impossible to undo one of them and needing his assistance in the cubicle. We made love very rapidly standing up, incredibly aroused by the exhibitionism of the situation. No-one noticed us, luckily, and that still remains one of the most exciting episodes in my life. Afterwards we re-enacted it at home and that, too, was wonderful.

"Having risked doing something we'd only previously thought about, and having got so much out of it, we dared then express other fantasies. On one occasion I made him up like a girl and made love to him quite aggressively. On another, he tied me to the bed and stimulated me for hours before letting me climax. We don't do this all the time, of course, only very occasionally as a special treat, but apart from feeling sensational it draws us very close together emotionally."

EROTIC INSPIRATION
If you find it hard to make up your own sexual fantasy, you may find inspiration in erotic literature or sexy magazines.

Some of the better erotic books and magazines contain material that is very arousing for both sexes

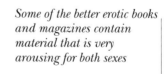

ENACTING HIS FANTASY

Sexual horizons are enlarged most easily by using fantasy to accompany your lovemaking or masturbation. Without having to resort to new partners, you can experience, if only in your mind, an entire range of arousing activities. Punishment and bondage are among the more common types of male fantasy, as evidenced by the number of advertisements that appear offering 'discipline' or 'correction' services to male clients. Provided that both partners involved in such activities are willing participants, punishment and bondage games can be great fun and highly erotic.

Black leather or PVC clothing, perhaps combined with lace or other see-through materials, helps create the right atmosphere

SHOWING HIM WHO'S BOSS Dressed in thigh-length boots and armed with a riding crop or whip, make it plain to him that he has misbehaved, and so now he is going to be punished. You are in charge, and he will have to do whatever you tell him to.

A feeling of helpless vulnerability will be heightened by your nakedness

THE PUNISHMENT BEGINS Order him to sit; press the hard leather riding crop firmly against his naked skin to give him a hint of what is to follow.

BLINDFOLDING Increase your power over him, and makes him feel even more vulnerable, by making him kneel and covering his eyes with a blindfold so that he can't see what you are going to do to him next.

Use alternate backhand and forehand strokes to strike each of his buttocks in turn with the riding crop

NO SERIOUS PAIN
Although your strokes may sting, make sure they aren't seriously painful

BINDING HIS HANDS By pushing him forward so that his forehead is touching the floor, force him into a totally submissive posture. Then pull his hands behind his back and binds his wrists loosely but securely — he is now naked, blindfolded and bound, and completely in your power.

Tie the cord around his wrists fairly loosely to avoid discomfort

GIVING HIM A BEATING Unable to defend himself, he can only plead for mercy as you beat his naked buttocks with your riding crop, first on one side and then on the other. Eventually, though, you relent and stop hitting him, but only on condition that he makes wild, passionate love to you.

Despite the pain and humiliation, the experience will be highly arousing

ENACTING HER FANTASY

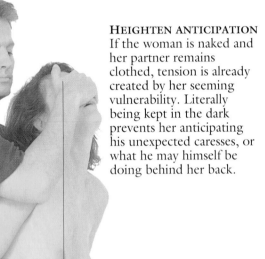

As a way of introducing variety into your sex life without undue effort or threat to an existing relationship, unexpected sexual behaviour can be a real turn-on. Women often use the fantasy of a secret lover, occasionally coupled with a feeling of helplessness, to induce increased ardour. A male partner often finds this type of fantasy, acted out, helps to liberate unknown desires within himself as well.

HEIGHTEN ANTICIPATION
If the woman is naked and her partner remains clothed, tension is already created by her seeming vulnerability. Literally being kept in the dark prevents her anticipating his unexpected caresses, or what he may himself be doing behind her back.

Gently cover her eyes and be as soft in your movements as possible so as to induce feelings of eroticism, not fear

Rough textures against smooth skin will encourage a variety of feelings, both real and projected

BE SUGGESTIVE Speak in a low voice and tell her what you are going to do with her, and what she will have to do for you. Try to keep humour and levity at bay.

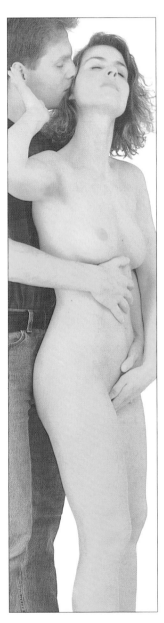

ENCOURAGE HER When she begins to respond to your suggestions, ease up by freeing her eyes and begin to let your lips and hands caress her body.

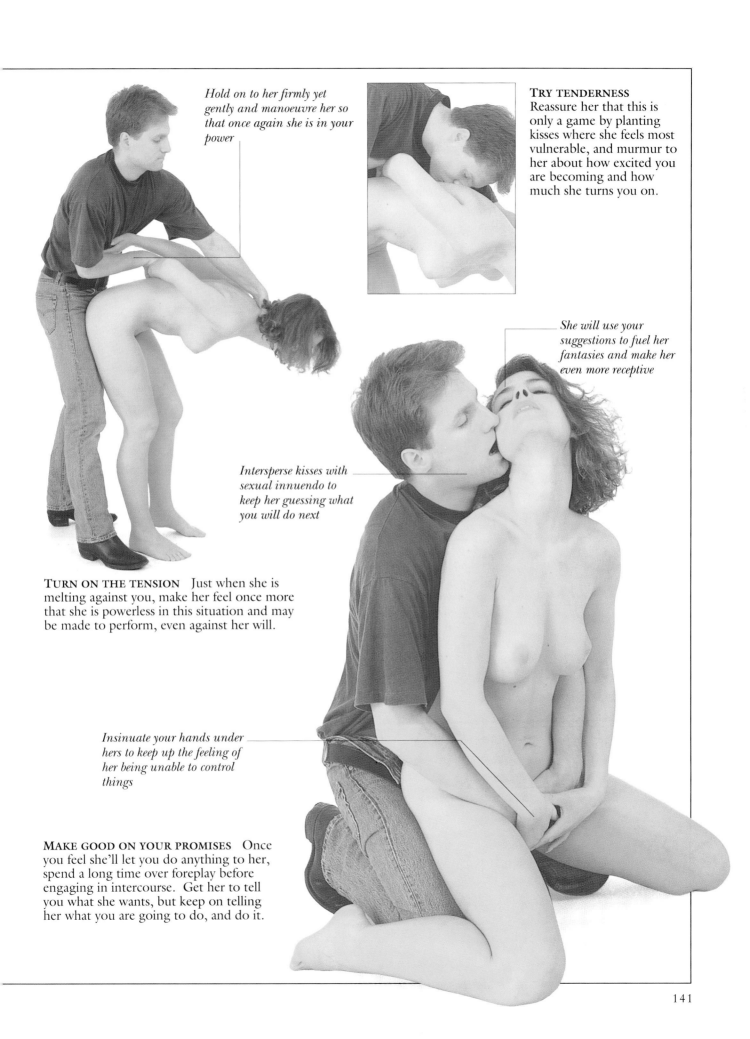

Hold on to her firmly yet gently and manoeuvre her so that once again she is in your power

TRY TENDERNESS
Reassure her that this is only a game by planting kisses where she feels most vulnerable, and murmur to her about how excited you are becoming and how much she turns you on.

She will use your suggestions to fuel her fantasies and make her even more receptive

Intersperse kisses with sexual innuendo to keep her guessing what you will do next

TURN ON THE TENSION   Just when she is melting against you, make her feel once more that she is powerless in this situation and may be made to perform, even against her will.

Insinuate your hands under hers to keep up the feeling of her being unable to control things

MAKE GOOD ON YOUR PROMISES   Once you feel she'll let you do anything to her, spend a long time over foreplay before engaging in intercourse. Get her to tell you what she wants, but keep on telling her what you are going to do, and do it.

PLAYING THE INNOCENT

Both a mastery of sexual techniques and a lack of experience are powerful stimulants of sexual desire for both sexes. Women often fantasize about a sexually adroit partner or about initiating a younger man into sex, while men occasionally like an aggressive partner who has them at their mercy but usually prefer to see themselves as the more experienced partner in any relationship. Rediscovering the excitement of 'first time' sex is an easy way to put an edge on sexual feelings.

When possible, slightly resist your partner's advances and appear reluctant throughout

Wear white to emphasize your 'virginity' but make it exceedingly tactile

LET YOUR PARTNER TAKE THE LEAD Pretend this is your first sexual experience. Simple gestures of affection are permitted but don't be too overt in your receptivity.

TAKE THINGS SLOWLY Gestures should be long, lingering and langorous — the slower the movement, the more erotic and arousing it will feel. Your body needs to be treated as though it were undiscovered territory.

USE A VARIETY OF CARESSES Use your mouth and hands up and down your partner's body, listening to the responses that tell you she is enjoying what you do.

Remove her garments for her as though she were a child

SLIP THINGS OFF As you remove each garment, ease it off in a non-forceful way yet one that is charged with sensuality.

REMOVE HER GARMENTS ONE AT A TIME Don't be in too much of a hurry to strip your partner naked. Intersperse removing her garments with gentle caresses as each new part is revealed.

GIVE HER REASSURANCE As you make love to your partner, tell her how good you will make her feel and how she is going to enjoy the experience. Never mind that you've made love to her a hundred times before; this is the first time all over again.

Adopt an on-top position so that she is cradled underneath

Manipulate your partner's body to suit you

Press your legs up against her so that she feels enclosed by you

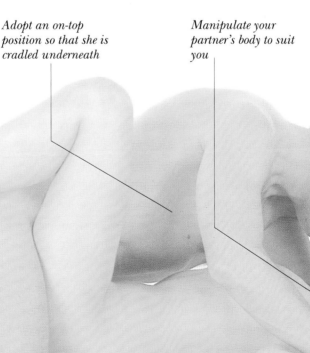

CHAPTER 19

HOW CAN I KEEP SEX SAFE WITH A NEW PARTNER?

"AIDS has forced us to change our sexual habits. Promiscuity threatens not only ourselves but, through us, it threatens others."

BECAUSE OF the spread of sexually-transmitted diseases, especially of herpes and AIDS, unless you are certain that you and your partner are virgins you cannot afford to take risks with unprotected intercourse. If you want to avoid the risk of infection with HIV (the virus that causes AIDS) you might find that you have to make distinct changes to your dating habits. Instead of assuming that intercourse is going to be available immediately, assume that it isn't. Focus on what used to be called, in the old days, 'heavy petting'. It may not be the same as intercourse, but mutual masturbation, and using fingers instead of the penis, can lead to some remarkably satisfactory experiences.

If you or your partner are or have been intravenous drug users, and you shared needles with other users, you cannot be sure that unprotected sex will ever be safe.

It is, of course, possible to have tests, including AIDS tests, which give you a pretty good idea of your sexual health, but even these might not indicate the presence of HIV during the early stages of the infection.

To reduce the risk of infection, using a condom or making love by using methods other than intercourse may prove necessary and sensible. How to handle that and how to make it desirable is, of course, another matter altogether.

CASE STUDY *Andrew*

Andrew had a lot of sexual experience and usually preferred to make love to several different women rather than stick with a single partner. But one of his former lovers had tested HIV positive, and although tests showed that he was free of the infection the episode had made him scared to have sex.

Name:	ANDREW
Age:	36
Marital status:	SINGLE
Occupation:	ENGINEER

"There's nothing like thinking you may actually have caught HIV to change your outlook on life," said Andrew. "Up until then, I had been blatantly promiscuous and really I just didn't give a damn about any consequences of my sexual behaviour. To be truthful, I didn't think HIV could happen to me — until I was contacted by a hospital tracing department who informed me that a girl I'd had a brief affair with some months previously was HIV positive. They advised me to go for testing, and I did so immediately. The days between the call and getting the result of the test were the worst in my life. I was sure that I'd caught it. I've had my share of sexual infections and I was convinced I'd be HIV positive. I wasn't. I waited three months and then had a second test to make absolutely sure. Thank God, I was alright.

"But I haven't dared to make love to anyone since then. I'm scared. There is no way I'll let myself in for that again, and I might not be so lucky next time. But now, I don't know where to start. Do I avoid sex altogether? I certainly don't want to, but if I've got to use condoms I'm going to feel terrible. For one thing, I've always hated the feel of the things. And for another thing, I can't stand their smell.

"I can certainly understand why people prefer a permanent partner nowadays. But my problem is, the better I get to know and like a girl, the less I fancy her. I wish this wasn't the case but it is. What am I going to do?

"My mother would love to see me married, and to tell the truth, sometimes I think that I would like that too. And I'd like to become a dad. So I've got other reasons for wanting to settle down, and sharing a house seems a small price to pay for staying alive and well.

"But I've lived on my own for years now and I suppose I've got accustomed to it. I value my privacy, but I also value my health. I know it won't be easy, but how can I ensure that sex stays safe?"

THERAPIST'S ASSESSMENT

I advised Andrew to become self-revealing, to get comfortable with condom usage, and to make love without intercourse more than formerly. Since these suggestions, by their nature, meant that he was likely to become more intimate with a partner than in the past, he was also likely to form a longer-term relationship.

INTIMACY AND SAFE SEX

If the heat of your passion overcomes you and you want to have intercourse, this is the signal to talk about sexual health. Waving your HIV test certificate would be a way of doing it but not exactly a sensitive one, especially if your partner felt insulted at being asked about his or her sexual health. Leading the conversation around to such questions would be better, and the best way to do this is to begin by talking about your own sexual history rather than asking for details of your partner's. Self-revelation is always the best way to introduce a tricky discussion. I told Andrew that if he could tell his next new partner about his recent unpleasant experience, and use it as an explanation and apology for asking about her, she would most likely understand and sympathize.

SAFER OPTIONS

Lovemaking without intercourse, or intercourse with a condom, really have to be your options. For inspiration on lovemaking without intercourse see page 96, and for details on how to use a condom see page 152. Many people have developed an aversion to the smell of condoms, but it is important to understand that this is a learned response and can be unlearned. You might even find, as many people do, that the rubbery smell of condoms actually becomes erotic because it is associated with a time of great pleasure.

Sometimes the emotional discomfort of getting out the condom and putting it on is the difficulty. This in itself may mirror the lack of trust or of knowledge between the people involved, particularly at the beginning of a relationship. Putting in some work on talking through your views and feelings would go a long way to making the condom moment easier and acceptable.

Some, usually slightly older, men find that wearing a condom numbs them so that it is hard for them to feel really stimulated, sometimes to such an extent that it is very difficult for them to climax. There are no real answers to this one, except to experiment with different types of condom in a search for the one that allows most sensitivity.

My programme for SAFE SEX

'Safe sex' is the term commonly used to describe forms of sexual activity that are unlikely to expose the participants to HIV infection and thus to AIDS. Safe sex is generally regarded as any form of sexual activity where there is no exchange of bodily fluids between the partners involved — an exchange of bodily fluids being the most common way in which HIV infection is passed from one person to another. But as well as offering you a high level of protection against HIV infection, safe sex techniques can help to prevent you catching (or passing on) most other sexually-transmitted diseases, including gonorrhoea, syphilis, chlamydia and genital herpes.

Stage I UNDERSTANDING HIV AND AIDS

Once it gets into the bloodstream, HIV — the human immunodeficiency virus — destroys the body's ability to fight disease. The virus invades, and then multiplies in, the white blood cells that play a vital part in the body's immune system, its defence against infection and disease.

AIDS Eventually, the damage to the body's white blood cells reaches a level at which the immune system can no longer function properly. This condition is called AIDS (acquired immune deficiency syndrome) and it makes the body vulnerable to 'opportunistic' diseases, including certain pneumonias and cancers, that are often fatal. The time be-

tween initial infection with HIV and the development of AIDS can be up to eight years, and so people who have been infected without knowing it can, through unprotected sex, unwittingly pass it on to other people.

THE SPREAD OF INFECTION The first thing to bear in mind about HIV infection and AIDS is that the problem is not confined to the homosexual community. It is true that in Europe, North America and Australasia the gay population has been hardest hit by the infection. But there, as elsewhere in the world, it is becoming increasingly prevalent among heterosexuals. We are all potentially at risk.

HIV TRANSMISSION The most common means by which the human immunodeficiency virus spreads from one person to another is through sexual contact involving the exchange

Caress your partner's genitals; it's both safe and pleasurable

SAFE SEX IS ALSO EXCITING Mutual masturbation, coupled with the sharing of your sexual fantasies, is only one of the many 'permitted' activities.

of body fluids — that is, the passing of semen, vaginal secretions or blood from one person to his or her sexual partner. An infected (HIV-positive) man can transmit the virus to his sexual partners — of either sex — because his semen will contain the virus in very large numbers. And a woman who has become infected with HIV can pass the virus on to her subsequent sexual partners because it will be present in her vaginal secretions.

In addition, because the virus is found in the blood of infected people as well as in their semen or vaginal fluid, infected drug addicts can spread the virus relatively easily by sharing hypodermic needles with uninfected friends. There have also been instances of haemophiliacs being infected by transfusions of contaminated blood or blood products, and an HIV-positive mother can pass the infection on to her baby (although many infected mothers give birth to uninfected babies).

ONE MAY BE ENOUGH   The ease with which the infection can pass from one person to another, during unprotected intercourse, is clearly illustrated by the numerous cases in which only a single sexual contact with an infected person, without using any form of protection, has been enough for someone to become infected with HIV.

For example, there has been many a well-documented case in which a woman has contracted HIV through a single sexual contact with a man who, unknown to her, was a drug addict who had become infected with the virus by sharing his drug-taking equipment with other users.

In a number of other cases, married women have been infected with HIV by their husbands, who caught the virus through having heterosexual or homosexual affairs or as a result of a single, unprotected sexual contact with an infected prostitute.

SOURCES OF HIV INFECTION

HIGHEST RISK

- Vaginal sexual intercourse without a condom

- Anal intercourse with or without a suitable condom

- Fellatio, especially to climax

- Any sexual activity that draws blood, whether accidentally or deliberately

- Sharing penetrative sex aids, such as vibrators

- Inserting fingers or hands into the anus

ACTIVITIES INVOLVING SOME DEGREE OF RISK:

- Vaginal sexual intercourse with a condom

- Lovebites or scratching that breaks the skin

- Anal licking or kissing

- Sexual activities involving urination

- Mouth-to-mouth kissing if either partner has bleeding gums or cold sores

- Cunnilingus using a latex barrier

- Fellatio using a condom

RISK-FREE

- Dry kissing

- Wet kissing as long as neither partner has bleeding gums or cold sores

- Stimulating a partner's genitals with your hands, or having your genitals stimulated by a partner's hands

- Self-masturbation

- The bites of bloodsucking insects

- Toilet seats

- Swimming pools

- Other people's bed linen or towels

- Swallowing another person's saliva (assuming there are no cuts or sores in your mouth)

- Sneezes

- Cheek-to-cheek kissing

- Shaking hands, embracing or cuddling

- Sharing a glass or cutlery

- Being a blood donor (in developed countries where the needles used are sterilized)

Sensual condom p152

CONDOMS By creating a physical barrier that prevents the exchange of bodily fluids during intercourse, condoms provide a simple way of having 'safe sex'. Spermicidal jellies and creams help, too, because they appear to make the virus less active. So simply by ensuring that we use condoms and spermicides we can greatly reduce the danger of infection with HIV, and also the risk of catching other sexually-transmitted diseases.

Stage 2 ASKING FOR SAFE SEX

Put bluntly, the safest ways to avoid AIDS are by choosing to be celibate (unlikely for readers of this book), by careful use of condoms and spermicides, and by engaging in and enjoying the many types of sexual activity that are alternatives to intercourse.

When you are with a partner you know well, suggesting that you use condoms or indulge in non-coital sexual activities is usually not too difficult, but raising the subject with someone new can often be embarrassing and awkward.

ATTITUDES This potential awkwardness is often made worse by the different attitudes people have towards HIV, AIDS and safe sex. For example, many people erroneously believe that AIDS is not a heterosexual problem and refuse to take precautions, while there are many others who understand there are dangers from HIV but feel they are slight, and anyway find it impossible to ask a partner to use a condom or to consider whether or not he or she might have encountered the virus.

On the other hand, some people are fearful of getting HIV and use precautions conscientiously, although a few take this too far and become phobic about HIV and AIDS and, even in circumstances where they know they cannot possibly have caught the virus, cannot relax until they have had a blood test that shows them to be HIV-negative.

HOW TO ASK Some people find it very hard to talk about any aspect of sexuality let alone to ask whether or not a potential sex partner is HIV-free. Indeed, even the most suave amongst us find this difficult. Unfortunately, for anyone entering a new relationship the tricky and embarrassing HIV/AIDS discussion has to be tackled.

In our section on how to use assertion techniques (pages 72-73) we outline how to approach challenges by working our way up to them in small ways. A similar approach is relevant here. When developing a relationship with someone new, try getting comfortable first with small aspects of sexuality. Tackle them slowly, with the easiest discussion first. Remember that self-disclosure (see page 79) is a good way of approaching something difficult.

CONTACT WITH FLUIDS
During masturbation, avoid contact with your partner's semen or vaginal fluids if you have any cuts or open sores on your fingers or hands

PRACTISE NON-PENETRATIVE SEX
Caressing and masturbating a partner are enjoyable alternatives to sexual intercourse.

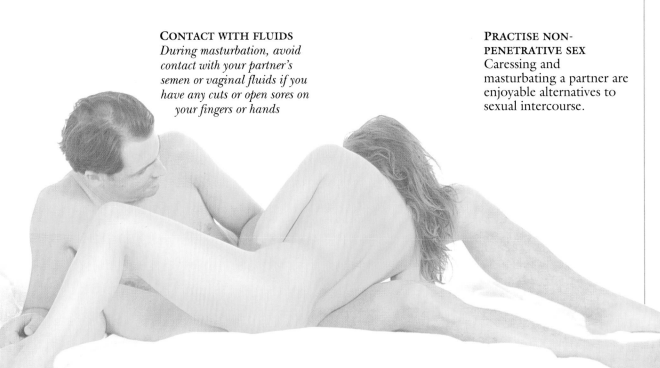

Try phrases such as: "I feel very nervous about asking this question, but it's something that's very important to me." "What's your feeling about safe sex?" "I know some people think women [or young people] shouldn't carry condoms but I think it's very important. I carry them. Do you?" "I've often wondered about the value of taking an AIDS test. I can see it could be very important. But I've never done it so far. Have you?" "I know some people think me a bit over-careful, but I really only feel safe with sex when using condoms. How about you?"

SAYING NO It may be that the end result of your delicate and carefully-negotiated discussion is that your partner refuses to use condoms or other safe sex practices. Here's how you might say no to unprotected sex: "I like you immensely and I'd love to go to bed with you, but I feel so strongly about safe sex practices that, in the circumstances, I'm going to have to call it a day. But why don't we try and stay really good friends."

ALTERNATIVES TO INTERCOURSE If condoms are not available, or if one or both of you is unwilling to use them, you should avoid having sexual intercourse. But that, of course, doesn't mean you have to abstain from sexual pleasure — there are several very enjoyable sexual activities for you to try that do not involve intercourse.

Mutual masturbation p96

FANTASY AND MASTURBATION For example, you and your partner could take it in turns to describe your sexual fantasies to each other while you both self-masturbate, or while you masturbate each other. You could both use vibrators, or use vibrators on each other, provided you didn't share them. Or you could simply rub your bodies up against each other, perhaps simulating the movements of intercourse.

ORAL SEX Because there is a reasonably high risk of infection, oral sex should be avoided unless you take careful precautions to prevent contact with semen or vaginal fluid. For fellatio, this means using a condom, and for cunnilingus a latex barrier (these are available from chemists).

Massaging each other's whole body, including the genitals, is another option, but, as is the case with oral sex, contact with bodily fluids such as semen and vaginal secretions should be avoided, especially if you have any skin cuts into which the fluids could penetrate.

HIV/AIDS QUESTIONS

Q. Isn't it only homosexuals who get AIDS?

A. No, not at all. This notion arose in Western countries because the first cases of AIDS to be diagnosed, in the early 1980s, were among homosexual males in the United States. Since then, the majority of cases in the West have involved gay men, but elsewhere (for instance in Africa) the majority of people affected are heterosexual. And because, in general, the gay community has adopted a responsible attitude towards safe sex, the rate of increase in the number of AIDS cases in the West is now higher among heterosexuals than among homosexuals.

Q. If my partner and I are both virgins and neither of us haemophiliac or drug users, we don't need to use condoms, do we?

A. There are other possible, but extremely rare, ways to catch HIV, such as through infected and improperly-sterilized dental or surgical equipment, or if blood from an infected person gets into an open cut or scratch on your skin, for example during a fight or when playing a sport that involves hard physical contact.

But these are, as I mentioned, incredibly rare and there is likely to be hardly any risk for you in intercourse without condoms. That is, as long as you are certain you are both monogamous. The problem arises, of course, when you think a partner is sexually faithful when, in fact, he or she has been deceiving you. There has been more than one tragic case of a woman who has only ever slept with one man in her entire life, i.e. her husband, but who nevertheless discovers one day that she has AIDS.

Q. Can lesbians get HIV?

A. It is possible that women can transmit the virus to other women but it is extremely rare. There have been, so far, only a tiny number of cases reported.

Q. I have heard that HIV is a very fragile organism and is actually hard to get. Is this true?

A. Yes. It cannot live outside the body very long, which is why it can't be transmitted by shaking hands or caught from lavatory seats.

Q. Is it true that women get HIV easier than men?

A. It is not known yet whether this is a hard-and-fast rule but, in general, since there are far more men infected it means that women are now at greater risk. A woman is more likely to meet an infected man than vice versa.

THE SENSUAL CONDOM

The condom is not only an effective form of contraceptive, it also acts as a barrier to infection with sexually transmitted diseases such as syphilis, gonorrhoea, chlamydia and HIV — putting on a condom correctly can thus sometimes mean the difference between safety and sickness. Some couples, however, are reluctant to use condoms because they think that interrupting their lovemaking to fit one is unromantic and unerotic. But by following a few simple rules, a woman can turn the mundane act of slipping a condom on to her partner's penis into a truly erotic experience.

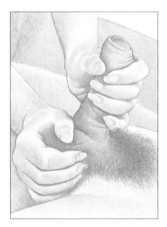

CHOOSING CONDOMS
As a general rule, avoid unknown brands and always check the expiry date on the package. Avoid the strangely-shaped condoms with knobbly edges and clitoral 'ticklers' — although they heighten the sensation they are, alas, generally unsafe because they do not fit the penis tightly enough and so may slip off or allow semen to leak into the vagina during intercourse

START WITH A GENITAL MASSAGE To make the donning of the condom as erotic an experience as possible, begin by treating your lover to a brief but sensuous genital massage.

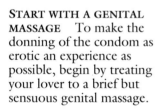

Make putting on a condom part of foreplay; don't wait until your excitement gets the better of you

When slipping a condom on to your lover's penis, use slow, sensuous movements to make the occasion as erotic as possible

MASTURBATE HIM
Change your hand action from genital massage to gentle masturbation of him as a preliminary to fitting the condom on to his penis.

SQUEEZE OUT THE AIR
Gently press the tip of the condom between thumb and forefinger to ensure it contains no air — an air bubble could cause it to split during intercourse.

THEN FIT THE CONDOM
Put it on the tip of his penis with one hand and roll it down to the base with the other. If he is uncircumcised, first push back his foreskin.

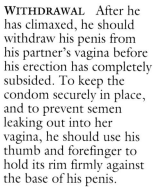

WITHDRAWAL After he has climaxed, he should withdraw his penis from his partner's vagina before his erection has completely subsided. To keep the condom securely in place, and to prevent semen leaking out into her vagina, he should use his thumb and forefinger to hold its rim firmly against the base of his penis.

USING CONDOMS Condoms should be used to make oral sex safe (above) as well as to provide protection during intercourse (below). For oral sex, use flavoured condoms to make the act of giving fellatio through a condom more enjoyable for her.

You may find that using a condom helps you to maintain your erection longer and delays ejaculation

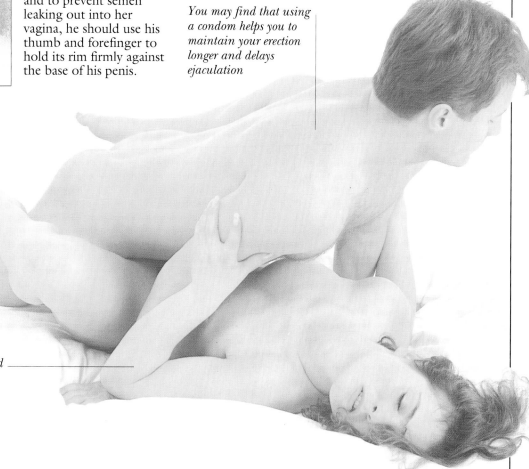

Your vaginal sensitivity and the physical sensations that you feel during intercourse are unaltered by the use of a condom

CHAPTER 14

HOW CAN WE HAVE GOOD SEX WHILE I'M PREGNANT?

"When a woman is pregnant, she and her partner may need to change their ideas about what constitutes a display of love."

YOUNG COUPLES who associate intimacy with lovemaking often find pregnancy unpleasantly divisive. The baby literally gets in the way, and a pregnant woman's change of shape and size, and her fatigue, convert what should be a warm renewal of loving feelings into something done out of a sense of duty or into emotional withdrawal. Small wonder, then, that lovemaking during a pregnancy can sometimes become a cause for anxiety.

Intercourse is usually no problem during the earliest months of a pregnancy, but from about the third month or so a couple may have to start using different lovemaking positions because of the physical changes taking place in her body.

But when intercourse becomes impractical or unwise, for instance in the final month of pregnancy, there are many other ways of showing tenderness through touch and mutual masturbation which make a marvellous alternative sex life.

CASE STUDY *Jane & Nick*

When Jane became pregnant, her sexual needs changed and she found masturbation more pleasurable and satisfying than intercourse. But she didn't explain her changed needs to her partner, Nick, who began to feel unloved and rejected when Jane ceased to enjoy intercourse.

Name:	JANE
Age:	26
Marital status:	MARRIED
Occupation:	HOUSEWIFE

Jane was a short, plump, round-faced woman who looked much younger than her age. She had already given up her job as a telephonist, was in her sixth month of pregnancy and had prepared an immaculate house ready for the arrival of her child.

"I've wanted this baby more than I've ever wanted anything," she said. "I feel just the same towards Nick as I have always done, but he isn't happy. He's not happy with our sex life, and that is really clouding what could be idyllic. I've told him so many times how much I care for him and yet he seems desperate with anxiety. All he wants to do is have sex, far more than he did before the pregnancy, and I can see it's because he's not feeling right in himself. But it simply isn't taking into account that my body is going through changes beyond my control, and because of that I don't have much urge for sex. Affection yes, sex not so much."

Name:	NICK
Age:	26
Marital status:	MARRIED
Occupation:	TEACHER

Nick, edgy and slightly built, came from a single-parent family. His father left when he was six, and Nick experienced problems with low confidence and depression during his teens. He relied on Jane a great deal emotionally and it didn't take much to unsettle him.

"Jane has changed since she's become pregnant," he complained. "She doesn't seem as caring and loving as she used to and I'm getting increasingly unhappy. To begin with she was permanently exhausted. Then, just as things seemed to be improving, she lost interest in sex. I feel as though my life is falling apart. Jane has been the centre of it and if she doesn't love me any more, I'm lost. I really love her and I want to show her that in the closest way I can."

THERAPIST'S ASSESSMENT

The advent of a baby can, unfortunately, bring out the infantile aspects of ourselves. This is what had happened to Nick. The baby already seemed like a rival and so the 'infant Nick' was out in full force, clamouring for mother's attention. And when someone has experienced a difficult and unstable childhood, as Nick had (for a short time he had lived in a children's home), they are especially likely to react in this way. So Nick's infantilism was clashing with Jane's desire for perfection, which in itself was an unrealistic expectation.

DISPLAYS OF LOVE

In addition, Nick subscribed to the belief, as do many others, that sexual intercourse equals love. When he couldn't have this with Jane he felt unloved. It may be, because of tough beginnings, that many men are unable to display or seek love (because this seems an unmanly thing to do) except through bed, this being the only acceptable closeness.

So, on the emotional side alone, deprived men like Nick need their partners to understand their behaviour. They also look for a high level of reassurance and tolerance from that same partner. It is important that they change their ideas about what constitutes a display of love and learn that there are substitutes which demonstrate the same thing. Nick's need for a lot of sex related directly to his anxieties. He felt less sexy when he was calmer.

REASSURANCE

I encouraged Jane to show him patience, understanding and a different type of affection, much as she might do with an unhappy child. I suggested that she maintain a kind of holding role with Nick over the next few months in order to reassure him and help him through his real panic and fear, so that he could discover for himself she wasn't about to leave him and she wasn't going to stop loving him.

SEX DURING PREGNANCY

But there were also ways of improving the couple's sex life to make it more pleasurable for Jane and therefore more welcoming for Nick. It was agreed that Jane should be given some choice about when and if they should make love, and that special attention should be paid to mutual masturbation and oral sex for her so that she was able to have climaxes again.

My programme for
A SEXY PREGNANCY

For some women, pregnancy is a time of heightened sexuality, but even those who don't experience such a physical reaction to the changes in their bodies may nevertheless learn to use those changes sensuously. Providing there are no medical reasons for avoiding it, intercourse during pregnancy is quite permissible and can be as enjoyable and exciting as at any other time, but it helps if both partners understand the physiological and hormonal changes that occur in a woman's body when she is pregnant, and the safety aspects of sex during pregnancy.

Stage — UNDERSTAND THE PHYSIOLOGICAL CHANGES OCCURRING

Alongside the development of a baby go physiological alterations in the body of its mother. The earliest of these affect the breasts: in the first three months of pregnancy their size increases by 25 per cent as a result of tissue and glandular alteration, and the nipples also enlarge. Some women find this painful, and their breasts feel sore and react adversely to rough handling, but the tenderness grows less as the baby advances.

By the time junior arrives, the breasts will have increased by almost one-third of their pre-pregnancy size. They are therefore in a permanent state of arousal and, if caressed and stimulated sensitively, may experience far more turn-on than previously.

SEXUAL TENSION The genitals, too, experience highly increased levels of sexual tension from the fourth month onwards. Sex researchers Masters and Johnson deduced from their studies that the task involved in the body's support of the baby's weight creates unusually high levels of sexual tension. This explains why, as the birth nears, many women become increasingly restless and find it hard to sleep. For a pregnant woman, sexual release in these circumstances can be the difference between sleep and exhaustion.

The high levels of sexual tension also mean that many women who normally find it hard to experience orgasm are able to do so with ease during pregnancy, and some women have multiple orgasms for the first time when they are pregnant.

The genitals actually increase in size due to fluid retention within the body tissues, and there is increased vaginal secretion. Pregnant women are, therefore, literally in a constant state of sexual arousal, and whereas non-pregnant women's bodies return to a normal, relaxed state after climax, and their genitals return to their normal size, those of pregnant women do not.

VAGINAL CONTRACTIONS Despite orgasm, the genitals remain somewhat swollen, and the more advanced the pregnancy becomes, the more enlarged they get. Eventually the vagina is constantly swollen and it can't contract very dramatically, which means that towards the end of the pregnancy climaxes may not feel very intense. At this stage, the contractions during a climax are often felt more markedly in the uterus instead.

Stage — UNDERSTAND THE HORMONAL CHANGES

There are massive hormonal changes during pregnancy, with extra quantities of the female sex hormones oestriol (the predominant oestrogen of pregnancy) and progesterone being produced. Oestrogens are commonly associated with a sense of wellbeing, while recent studies have shown progesterone to be associated with discomfort and typically 'premenstrual' symptoms.

SEX DRIVE The levels of free-ranging testosterone in the body fall slightly in pregnancy. One sexological theory has it that free-ranging testosterone is responsible for the sex drive. If this is true, it would mean that pregnant women are likely to experience decreased sexual interest and response, and although Masters and Johnson's studies didn't find this, there are numbers of other studies which demonstrate a gradual decline in sexual interest as the pregnancy advances.

The truth is probably that we experience such varying combinations of hormone balance, which affect our mood, and such an overlay of emotional experience, which also influences mood, that it is impossible to predict how sexy any pregnancy will be.

Stage UNDERSTAND SEXUAL SAFETY IN PREGNANCY

Sex is perfectly safe during pregnancy unless otherwise advised by the doctor, and there is no reason why intercourse shouldn't be continued up until a month before the expected birth date. There are now doubts about its safety during the last month, as some doctors fear that there may be a link between late intercourse and babies born with certain respiratory diseases. But there is no reason why masturbation need be discontinued, and orgasm itself may prepare the uterus for the more massive contractions to come during labour.

BLEEDING DURING INTERCOURSE However, if there is bleeding during intercourse the doctor should be notified immediately.

He or she will probably advise that intercourse should cease for a short time until the pregnancy settles down. In addition, women with a history of miscarriage are often advised by their doctor to refrain from intercourse in the first few months of pregnancy.

Stage SEXUAL POSITIONS DURING PREGNANCY

Early on during a pregnancy, before the woman's breasts and belly have begun to swell appreciably, she can have sex comfortably and safely in any position that she and her partner choose.

But as the pregnancy advances, and her breasts become tender and her belly swells, using lovemaking positions with him on top

Woman-on-top p162

becomes increasingly awkward and uncomfortable. When this stage is reached (it usually occurs from about the fourth month onwards, but for some women it may be relatively early in the pregnancy), it is better for the couple to use one of the woman-on-top or rear entry positions for their lovemaking.

Among the woman-on-top positions, some of the most satisfactory for use during pregnancy are those where she lies on top of him, with her legs either between his or outside them, and those where she kneels astride him. The rear entry positions have the advantage that her swollen belly doesn't get in the way.

DO'S AND DON'TS IN PREGNANCY

DO'S

• He should be tender, romantic, patient and understanding

• If she wants to breastfeed the baby when it has been born, he should help prepare her nipples during pregnancy by lovemaking involving oral stimulation of her breasts

• When making love, he should use different kinds of stroking, and try using a firm, fatherly hand over her belly if the baby kicks

• He should keep his weight off her bump and breasts when he makes love to her

• If she doesn't feel sexy when her partner wants to make love, she should try to invent some pleasant sexual variations as alternatives to intercourse

• Take your time when lovemaking during pregnancy, and don't be afraid to experiment

• Use lots of pillows for greater comfort and to get the right angles around the curves of her body

DON'TS

• He should not expect her to be able to concentrate on lovemaking if the baby is moving about energetically

• She should not think that she is frigid if she doesn't have an orgasm every time

• Do not expect, or try for, simultaneous orgasm

• Never stick anything up inside her vagina except the penis or fingers

MAN-ON-TOP POSITIONS

Many couples find that lovemaking where the man is on top is powerfully erotic. This may be because the woman's feelings are at their most open and vulnerable — she is caring and trusting enough to allow herself to be thus dominated — and the man may see the position as a pinnacle of his sexual power.

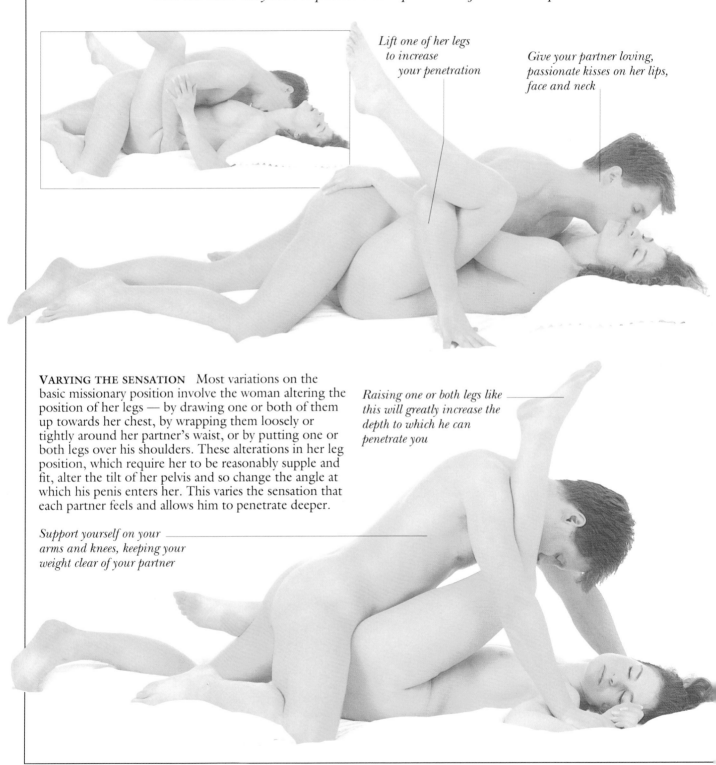

Lift one of her legs to increase your penetration

Give your partner loving, passionate kisses on her lips, face and neck

VARYING THE SENSATION Most variations on the basic missionary position involve the woman altering the position of her legs — by drawing one or both of them up towards her chest, by wrapping them loosely or tightly around her partner's waist, or by putting one or both legs over his shoulders. These alterations in her leg position, which require her to be reasonably supple and fit, alter the tilt of her pelvis and so change the angle at which his penis enters her. This varies the sensation that each partner feels and allows him to penetrate deeper.

Raising one or both legs like this will greatly increase the depth to which he can penetrate you

Support yourself on your arms and knees, keeping your weight clear of your partner

DEEP PENETRATION

A man-on-top position that enables really deep penetration is that in which the woman lies on her back and brings her knees right up towards her chin, so that when her partner enters her, her feet are at each side of his head. When a couple is using this position, which is advisable only if the woman is really supple and fit and not prone to back problems, he should be careful not to hurt her and a little cautious in his thrusting because of the deep penetration possible.

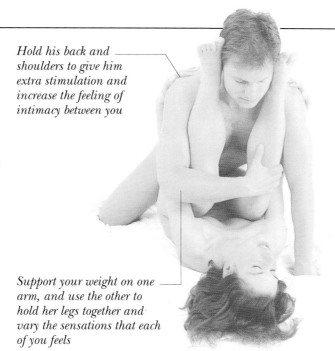

Hold his back and shoulders to give him extra stimulation and increase the feeling of intimacy between you

Support your weight on one arm, and use the other to hold her legs together and vary the sensations that each of you feels

KISSING Although opportunities are limited in this position, your partner will be able to kiss your ankles and feet.

MISSIONARY POSITION When it works well, sex operates on a variety of levels. One of these is the physical sensation of close bodily contact, especially contact between stimulated genitals. Another is the way in which partners can show their love and affection for each other while making love. One great advantage of the missionary position is that it combines close bodily contact with the opportunity to show affection.

SHOWING AFFECTION Face-to-face positions like this, whether man-on-top or woman-on-top, allow the partners to be affectionate with each other. However, the opportunities for mutual masturbation and other forms of manual stimulation are somewhat limited.

Raise your legs, spreading them wider apart, to allow him to penetrate you more deeply

Raise yourself on your arms so you can look down to watch yourself thrusting in and out of your lover

USING PILLOWS Putting a pillow beneath her buttocks, so as to tilt her pelvis upwards, will allow deeper penetration.

WOMAN-ON-TOP POSITIONS

The tenor and tempo of sexual intercourse gathers new shape when the woman takes charge. Not only can she better ensure that she is stimulated in all the important areas but also that lovemaking takes on new excitement for her partner as well. One way in which a woman can tease her man into helpless desire is to give much promise of intercourse but then withhold it at the very last moment, drawing away from him even as she allows the head of his penis to slip inside her, and most women find that this is easiest done when in a woman-on-top position. This position also gives the woman a better opportunity to direct the angle of intercourse, so that where the missionary position manages to miss out her clitoris, woman-on-top hits the mark precisely.

VARYING YOUR POSITION
When you are on top of your partner in this semi-kneeling fashion it is easy to vary your position, for instance by leaning forward so that your body is pressed against your lover's, or by sitting half-upright or fully upright.

When you are on top of him, give him extra stimulation by brushing your nipples lightly across his naked chest

Use your bent legs to push his thighs closer together to vary the sensation

If your man tends to come too soon, you can slow down the movement when he is reaching the brink and so prolong your lovemaking

Take advantage of your extra freedom of movement to vary your pelvic thrusts and maximize your own pleasure

LYING ON TOP This is a very comfortable and loving position for both you and your partner. You can lie with both your legs outside your partner's, or vary the sensation by lying with one or both of your legs inside his. This position will excite him by making him feel that you are seducing him.

By holding on to your waist or buttocks he can vary the depth of his penetration

THE FROG POSITION In the so-called frog position, you lie with your legs directly on top of your partner's and the soles of your feet on top of his feet. This position is not especially romantic but it is very sensual and, like all woman-on-top positions, it has the great advantage of removing performance pressures from the male, allowing him to find more fun in lovemaking.

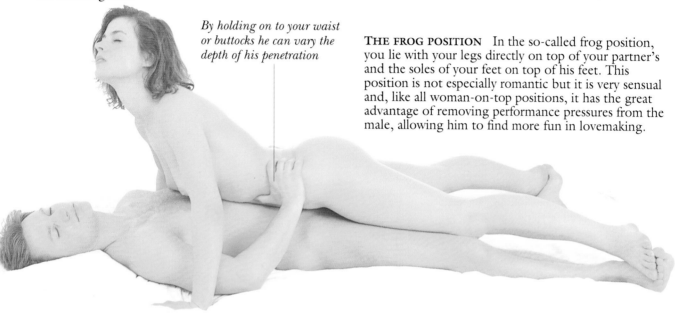

You will need to support yourself on your arms so that he can maintain proper penetration

In this position your partner can easily reach your breasts and clitoris to stimulate them by hand

REAR ENTRY To get into this position, begin with your partner lying on his back. Then sit astride him facing his feet, guide his erect penis into you, and lean back and support yourself on your arms. Alternatively, once he is inside you, you can remain sitting upright while he lies back or he can sit up so that you are sitting in his lap facing away from him.

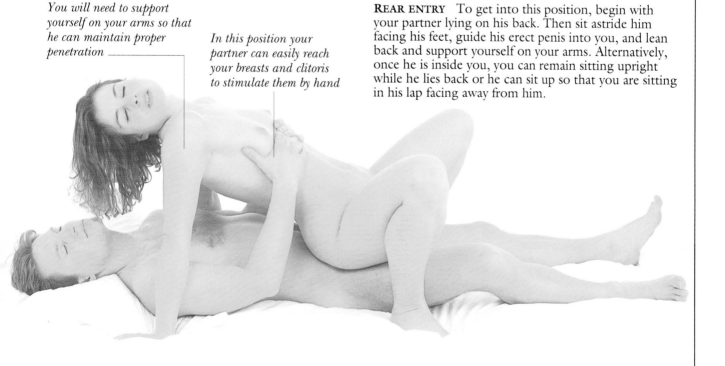

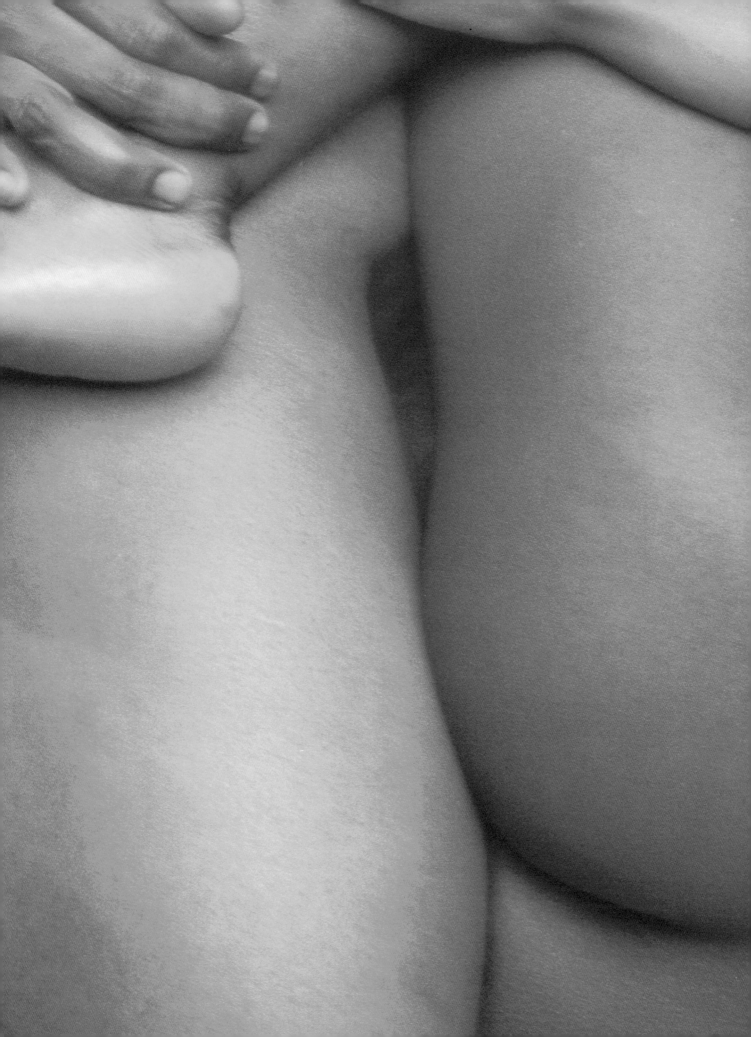

CHAPTER 15

HOW CAN I ACHIEVE A DEEPER ORGASM?

"A feeling of warmth, security and closeness is one of the essential elements in setting the scene for sexual bliss."

IT IS POSSIBLE that to experience bliss, whether sexual or any other kind, we shouldn't look for it too often. If it became commonplace it would lose its special value, because it would then be expected and almost predictable, with a consequent lessening of the wonderful excitement that it brings when it takes us unawares.

Outstanding lovemaking undoubtedly depends on a combination of factors, including surprise. One thing that can't be planned is surprise, but many of the other factors that combine to make lovemaking outstanding can be deliberately invoked.

Among these are feelings of relaxation and security, which are, in most cases, easy to generate. Among the main ingredients of sexual relaxation are physical and emotional relaxation; a sense of being entirely in harmony with each other; a feeling of physical warmth and comfort; mutual caressing; and being able to take your time over your lovemaking.

CASE STUDY *Hayley & Richard*

Hayley and Richard had both, individually, sometimes experienced unusually deep and strong feelings during orgasm. This only ever seemed to happen by accident, and what they both wanted to know was, how they could make such intense and satisfying feelings happen more often?

Name:	HAYLEY
Age:	33
Marital status:	SINGLE
Occupation:	COPYWRITER

Hayley was in her second long-term relationship. She was agile and gypsy-like, with short, curly black hair and punkish but extremely expensive clothes.

"Richard and I have been together for three years," she told me. "And we are pretty committed to each other. We have a very similar outlook on life and, although it sounds corny, this is partly a spiritual one. By that I mean we have a similar sense of morality and feel strongly we want something spiritual out of our life together.

"Which brings me to sex. The best sex for me has been when I have been deeply relaxed and at the same time very focused on the sexual sensation while it is building up. I feel very far away indeed in my head when I finally come to orgasm, and the climax seems to come from somewhere incredibly deep down inside of me.

"This is a wonderful experience but it doesn't happen very often, and only ever by accident. Is there any way of encouraging it?"

Name:	RICHARD
Age:	30
Marital status:	SINGLE
Occupation:	INSTRUMENT MAKER

Richard was a former naval officer who had set up his own business as a maker of naval brass instruments such as sextants. He was comfortable with new acquaintances and felt at home with both 18-year-olds and 80-year-olds.

"I felt when I met Hayley that she had no pretensions. She was completely open to me, in spite of a sharp difference between her earning power and status and mine. She is very senior in her company and very successful. But there's no sense of competition or one-upmanship from her.

"I know what she means about wanting this deeper feeling during orgasm. It's happened to me too. I personally doubt you can achieve it deliberately. With me, it's always happened as a result of a long, peaceful buildup. Maybe we'll talk in bed, for a long time sometimes, while caressing each other, and one thing leads to another. That's great. But it's accidental."

THERAPIST'S ASSESSMENT

In my discussions with Hayley and Richard, I stressed that there were no specific answers to their question. When lovemaking works unusually well, the unexpectedness of this adds poignancy and deeper feeling to climaxes. We may not be able to plan this surprise, but we do know that we can create some of the other ingredients for deeply relaxed lovemaking.

Feelings can be aroused by a variety of techniques. For example, anticipation, mild anxiety, anger and passion can all be deliberately induced. So in order to create extreme sexual relaxation, it is worth identifying its ingredients. These will, of course, differ from one couple to another, but those that Hayley and Richard identified, when they sat down and made a list of their emotions and activities, are fairly typical. They listed:
• open-ended time
• warmth
• the comfort of their double bed
• restful lighting
• mutual caresses during conversation
• awareness of each other's mental state (it is hard to be erotic if you are worried or angry about something)
• an ability to pick up on sexual areas where one partner is asking for encouragement.

KEY POINTS
The most important points, though, were the last two. Among the feelings generated by these ingredients were a sense of nakedness (meaning openness or being entirely exposed to each other) and extreme trust in order to be able to do this; a kind of telepathic sharing of the same feeling (each could look the other in the eye and know that they, too, were flooded with a sense of beauty); and a sense, as climax approached, of letting themselves flow off the edge of everyday consciousness into a tumult completely beyond control.

TAKING TIME
Hayley and Richard agreed that the key to this experience was time — the ability to give themselves enough time in which to relax and experience all their 'requirements'. They resolved to put aside certain weekend mornings or afternoons when they would deliberately cut themselves off from interruptions, for instance by unplugging the phone and disconnecting the doorbell. Then they would just spend time together and see what happened.

My programme for
INCREASING SEXUAL
FEELINGS

The depth and breadth of sexual feelings between yourself and your partner can be magnified by taking turns at giving each other sensual pleasure without expecting anything in return. This unselfish giving of sensual pleasure involves the use of touch and massage, and a gentle, loving form of sexual intercourse that is intended primarily for the benefit of one partner alone.

Stage GIVING PLEASURE

Such is the great emphasis placed on reaching orgasm these days, it is easy to forget that many wonderful and satisfying experiences can be reached through sexual activity not aimed at resolution. Watching your lover unfurl, relax and bask in the sensuality of your unselfish, non-demanding touch is excep-

tionally rewarding: as the giver of pleasure you gain feelings of love, tenderness, caring, nurturing and eroticism.

UNSELFISH TOUCH In your role as the unselfish giver of pleasure, you begin by kissing and caressing your partner's naked body, using the strokes and movements that he or she most enjoys. Everything you do should be geared solely to the pleasure of your partner, who should do nothing but lie back and drift off into sensual bliss.

MASSAGE You should continue kissing and caressing your partner lovingly for about fifteen minutes, and then change roles: you become the receiver of pleasure and your partner the giver. After that, you can move on to give your partner a 'Three-Handed Massage'. This begins as a body massage session — either a basic one (see pages 60-63) or a more erotic sensual type — but it then progresses to become a highly sensuous combination of massage and intercourse.

GIVING AND RECEIVING
This programme will show you the truth of the old saying that it is better to give than to receive.

Stage RECEIVING PLEASURE

The receiver of pleasure absorbs the giver's loving, caring feelings through the skill and texture of his or her touch and relaxes totally, knowing no performance is expected of him or her. Such a deliberate pleasure-giving exercise puts ideas into the receiver's head and provides a blueprint for a treat that they could, in turn, let fall upon the giver.

ECSTASY What exactly does the receiving partner gain from this loving but undemanding sex? Principally, he or she will experience feelings of love and serenity accompanied by greatly heightened sensuality. With the deep sense of inner peace that this receiving of pleasure creates, fine nuances of love and sensation are capable of expanding into great waves of emotion.

For example, the pleasant but unspectacular sensation of receiving a simple caress can enlarge to become an engulfing, prickling feeling of sensuality. In this way, sexual love from a partner can be experienced as an ecstatic rapture of the mind rather than as a localized physical reflex of the genitals.

PASSIVITY In order to be able to give this experience, your partner has to be capable of receiving it. Some people find it peculiarly difficult to lie back and wholeheartedly enjoy pleasure that is aimed at them alone. Some men feel so strongly that theirs is a 'doing' role they find it impossible to be passive. And some women are so used to being the carers and donors of pleasure that they cannot relax into acceptance.

One way of finding out where you stand on the idea of being passive is to give a massage and then ask yourself, "Is it easier to touch for my pleasure or for the pleasure of another?" On a second occasion, switch roles, then ask yourself, "Is it easier to give or receive?" Honest answers to these questions will tell you whether or not you are good at being passive and receiving pleasure.

SELFISHNESS If acceptance of pleasure turns out to be a problem, it may be that you need to learn more about the value of selfishness. Contrary to popular belief, selfishness, in the sense of accepting that it is all right to be pleasured, is healthy. Orgasm is, after all, a supremely selfish experience that no-one else can have for you but you.

Stage GIVING AN EROTIC MASSAGE

Sex exam p82

A sensual, erotic massage is a very good way to give pleasure, and the better you get to know your partner's body (for instance by doing the Sexological Exam) the more erotic you can make the massage. To give such a massage, begin with the usual basic strokes such as circling, swimming and kneading with your thumbs and fingertips.

PRESSURE VARIATIONS Carry out each stroke three times. Use firm pressure to begin with, and then repeat each stroke twice, using first relaxed pressure and then the lightest of fingertip pressure. While you are massaging with firm pressure, work your hands and fingers into your partner's muscles to loosen

---

TAKING TIME OFF FROM EVERYDAY LIFE

Learning to relax into selfishness often means taking time off from everyday life in order to concentrate on yourself alone. This can be practised by:

• Having a frank discussion with your partner about respecting the hour you are going to take for yourself

• Discussing the need for privacy with anyone else in the house

• Putting a lock or bolt on the door of your room

• Hanging up a 'Do Not Disturb' sign

• Re-scheduling your daily activities to free an hour that you can set aside for yourself

• Making a place in your home that is warm, welcoming and sensuous

• Practising the self-pleasuring techniques regularly (see pages 226-233), including setting aside an hour at least once a week when you do whatever you honestly feel like doing

It can be surprisingly difficult to carve this free time from your normal routine, but before long you will begin to feel that there ought to be more of it. The onset of that feeling will mark the beginning of a healthy acceptance of the fact that you are entitled to enjoyment. Relaxing into selfishness is a path to sensuality focused on you alone.

them up and relieve any tension in them. This will help him or her to relax, both physically and mentally, and thus become more receptive to the increasingly sensuous pleasure of the rest of the massage.

FACE-DOWN MASSAGE Massage the whole body in this fashion, first with your partner lying face-down. Start at the neck and shoulders, and then massage each arm in turn, right the way down to the fingertips.

Next, work your way down your partner's back, over the buttocks and down each leg in turn as far as the ankle. Don't massage the feet at this stage, because that is easier done when your partner is lying face-up.

FACE-UP MASSAGE Turn your partner over on to his or her back, and as before begin your massage at the neck and shoulders, working first down the arms and then down the chest and abdomen. As you move nearer to the genitals, occasionally and 'accidentally' brush them with the back of your hand, or with any other part of your body that is conveniently close. Then, just as your partner is expecting you to massage the genital area itself, veer away; he or she will probably find this provocative behaviour outrageously tantalizing.

THIGHS AND FEET Once you reach the legs, work your way down each in turn and pay special attention to the insides of the thighs, which are highly erogenous. When you get to the feet, in addition to giving each one its individual massage, combine foot massage using one hand with inside thigh massage using the other.

Another pleasant way in which to manipulate your partner's feet is to support each one in turn behind the ankle with one hand, while slowly rotating the foot with the other. The effects are felt all the way up the leg to the pelvis and the groin muscles, and the overall sensation that is produced is curiously sexual.

USE YOUR NAILS If you want to take your sensual massage one stage further, try lovingly caressing your partner all over with your fingernails. Before you begin, make sure that your nails are not broken or rough-edged. Use only your nails on your partner's skin, and move them in a variety of ways so as to maximize their sensual effect. Start off by moving them in circles, then change to up-and-down and side-to-side movements, varying the lengths of the strokes you make from very short to relatively long.

EROTIC HELPLESSNESS During all the stages of your sensual massage, do not let your partner move any part of his or her body. If, for instance, an arm needs to be moved so that you can massage it easier, you should move it yourself — part of the eroticism of a good massage (for the person being massaged) lies in the feeling of helplessness it can create.

Stage ## THE THREE-HANDED MASSAGE

A more advanced way to give sensual pleasure is by intercourse for the benefit of your partner alone. One very special version of this has been termed the Three-Handed Massage by US massage master Ray Stubbs. Ray, if not exactly inventing the following idea, certainly put a lot of time and effort into sensitively developing it.

His suggestion to seekers of deep orgasmic feeling is that they should combine the relaxed sensuality of massage with the gentle touch of intercourse. One session may focus on one partner, a second session on the other. The massagee should not try and reciprocate simultaneously because his or her efforts will detract from the inner calm he or she might

Three-Handed Massage p172

otherwise achieve. It is this same inner calm that allows for a deep sensual experience. Here is how a man can give his partner a Three-Handed Massage — the version of the massage that a woman can give her partner is basically similar, and like this one it also begins with a basic massage and ends with penetration.

SETTING UP THE MASSAGE Set the massage up as you would for a basic one. Give your partner fifteen minutes or so of manual body massage before including her genitals. Don't hurry. Take your strokes slowly and don't aim at orgasm — for either of you. After this manual massage, move on to give her the three-handed version, which begins with a straightforward back massage.

BACK MASSAGE With your lover lying on her front, give her a relaxing back massage. Use plenty of warm massage oil to do so. During this attention, after stroking and caressing her, gently bring your legs across her thighs so that you are sitting on her. In order to have exceptionally smooth and slippery mobility during the massage, lavishly oil your own abdomen, genitals and thighs.

Without interrupting your sensual massage of her body, let your well-oiled lower half glide backwards and forwards over her thighs and buttocks so that your genitals are in contact with her skin and, in effect, also massaging her. Do this in a flowing and sensitive fashion to make it as sensuous as possible, like some kind of exquisite dance.

PENETRATION As you continue with this, let your penis find its slippery way between her slightly parted legs and make its own contact with her vagina. Allow yourself to penetrate her exceptionally slowly — the slower you are, the more tantalizing your touch will be. Let your hands and penis slowly massage her simultaneously so that all the movements

blend. Then ask your partner to turn over and lie on her back. When you feel that the time is right, lift her knees up towards her chest and, as you do so, gently and gradually slide your penis back into her again.

Rock your pelvis rhythmically but very slowly, so that your penis thrusts are tantalizingly sensuous, and at the same time use your hands to stroke, caress and massage every accessible inch of her body. Emphasize, if she starts to thrust in response, that she must take no active part, but should relax and let herself flow (mentally) into the bedclothes rather than move. The more she relaxes and leaves everything to you, the more profound will be her sensation. But don't forget that you are not aiming at orgasm.

BODY MASSAGE The first step in the Three-Handed Massage is a basic back massage. Spend about fifteen minutes on this, giving your partner slow, sensuous strokes and using plenty of warm massage oil or baby oil. Start with circling, swimming and glide strokes, and finish off with feathering to enhance the overall effect.

INTERCOURSE When you feel that the time is right for intercourse, gently penetrate her again. As you enter her, lift her knees towards her chest, and rock your pelvis slowly and rhythmically so as to thrust your penis in and out of her. At the same time, use your hands to stroke and caress and sensuously massage every accessible inch of her naked body.

PENETRATION Let your lower body massage her by gliding backwards and forwards over her thighs and buttocks. Then slip your penis into her vagina, and let it move in and out in time with the massaging movements of your body. Do the same when she turns over.

The slower your movements are, the more tantalizing the feeling will be for her

She should relax and resist the temptation to move

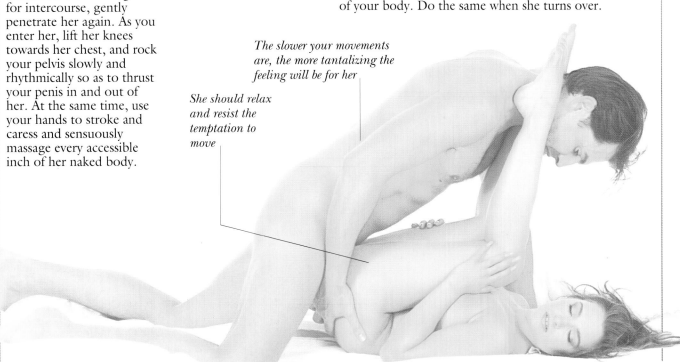

THREE-HANDED MASSAGE

The Three-Handed Massage, a concept developed by massage trainer Ray Stubbs, is a combination of sensitive hand massage accompanied by genital contact. For details of the Three-Handed Massage for a female partner see page 170: we focus here on the sex massage that a woman can give to the man in her life. Because it is his turn to receive, he is in no way to take any active part in what ensues.

SIT ACROSS HIM With your partner lying on his back, straddle him with your thighs across his abdomen. Begin by massaging his chest, arms and shoulders, and lean back to massage his thighs and as much of his legs as you can reach.

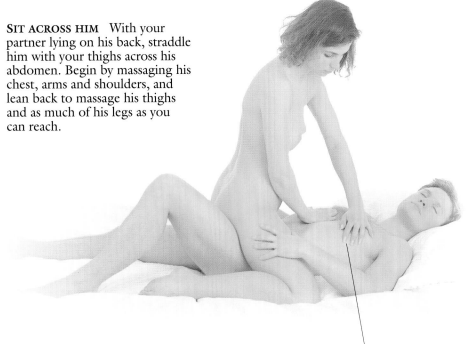

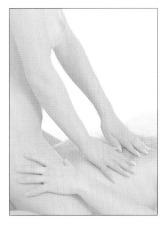

ALTERNATE TOUCHES When you first begin to massage an area, use the palms of your hands. Then, having massaged the whole area with your palms, knead gently with your fingers.

For a slippery sensuousness, oil your hands, genitals, thighs and abdomen before you begin, and re-oil them as necessary during the massage

USE SENSUAL BODY MOVEMENTS After massaging him with your hands for about 15 minutes, lightly and provocatively draw your breasts and nipples over his chest, moving them up and down and from side to side.

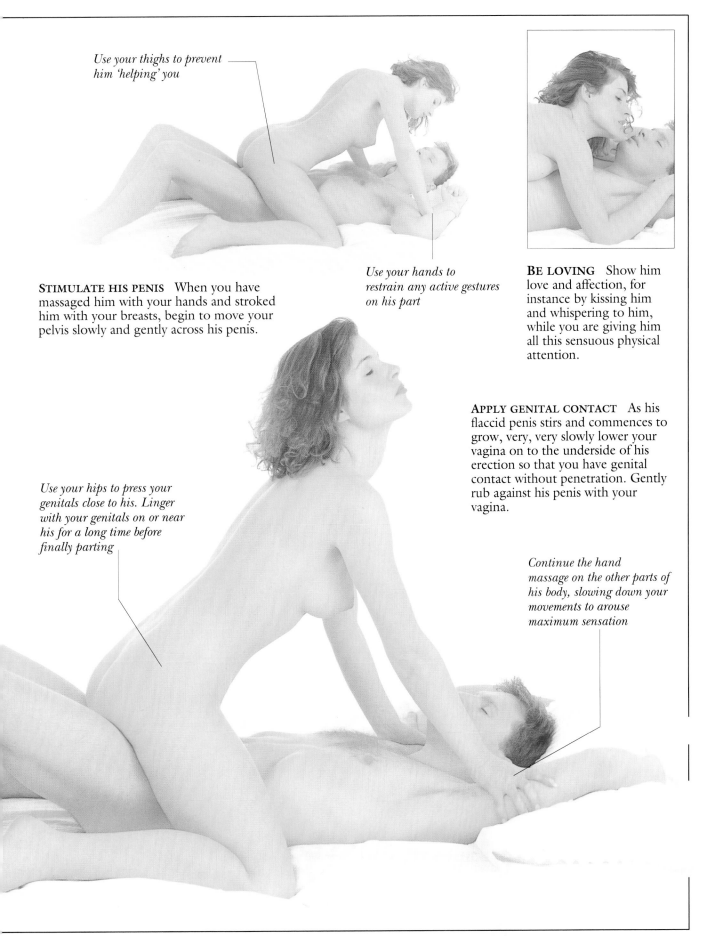

Use your thighs to prevent him 'helping' you

Use your hands to restrain any active gestures on his part

STIMULATE HIS PENIS When you have massaged him with your hands and stroked him with your breasts, begin to move your pelvis slowly and gently across his penis.

BE LOVING Show him love and affection, for instance by kissing him and whispering to him, while you are giving him all this sensuous physical attention.

APPLY GENITAL CONTACT As his flaccid penis stirs and commences to grow, very, very slowly lower your vagina on to the underside of his erection so that you have genital contact without penetration. Gently rub against his penis with your vagina.

Use your hips to press your genitals close to his. Linger with your genitals on or near his for a long time before finally parting

Continue the hand massage on the other parts of his body, slowing down your movements to arouse maximum sensation

LOVEMAKING ON A CHAIR

Even something as potentially exciting as sex can become boring. By making love on a chair instead of in bed you can try out a wide range of different lovemaking positions, and perhaps add some welcome variety to your sex life. As a bonus, many of these positions leave your hands free, allowing you to exchange caresses.

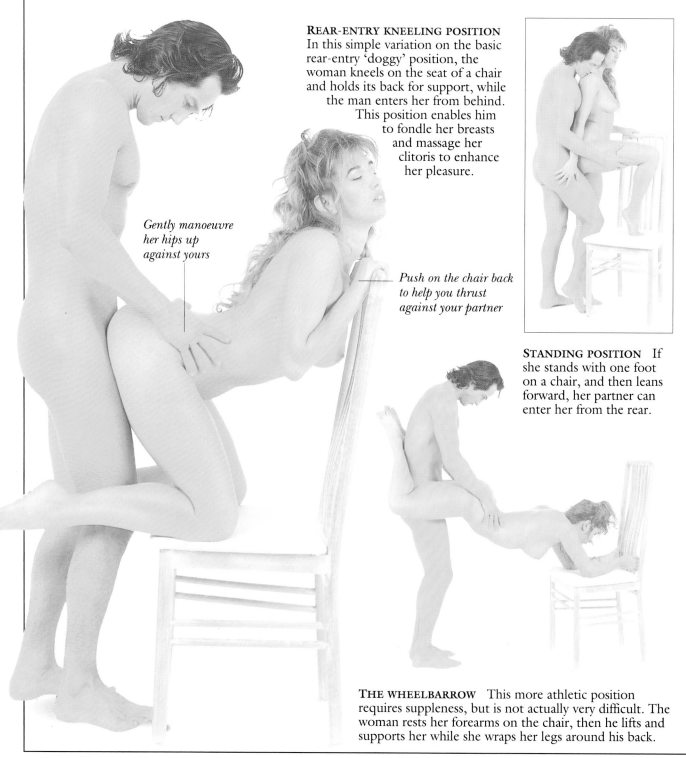

REAR-ENTRY KNEELING POSITION
In this simple variation on the basic rear-entry 'doggy' position, the woman kneels on the seat of a chair and holds its back for support, while the man enters her from behind. This position enables him to fondle her breasts and massage her clitoris to enhance her pleasure.

Gently manoeuvre her hips up against yours

Push on the chair back to help you thrust against your partner

STANDING POSITION If she stands with one foot on a chair, and then leans forward, her partner can enter her from the rear.

THE WHEELBARROW This more athletic position requires suppleness, but is not actually very difficult. The woman rests her forearms on the chair, then he lifts and supports her while she wraps her legs around his back.

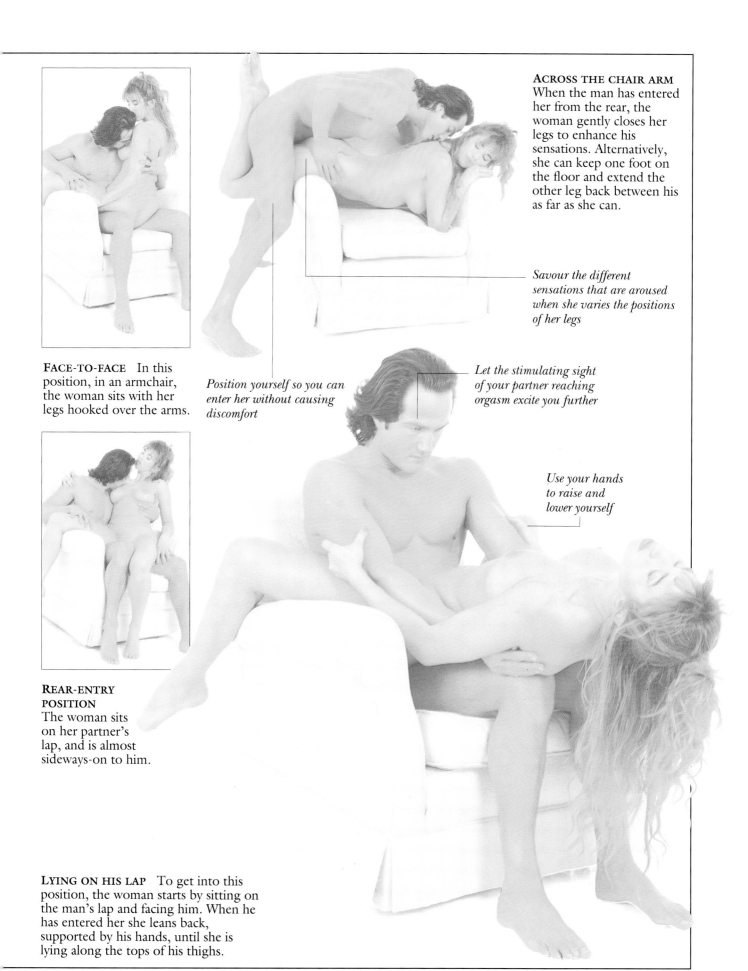

FACE-TO-FACE In this position, in an armchair, the woman sits with her legs hooked over the arms.

REAR-ENTRY POSITION The woman sits on her partner's lap, and is almost sideways-on to him.

LYING ON HIS LAP To get into this position, the woman starts by sitting on the man's lap and facing him. When he has entered her she leans back, supported by his hands, until she is lying along the tops of his thighs.

ACROSS THE CHAIR ARM When the man has entered her from the rear, the woman gently closes her legs to enhance his sensations. Alternatively, she can keep one foot on the floor and extend the other leg back between his as far as she can.

Savour the different sensations that are aroused when she varies the positions of her legs

Position yourself so you can enter her without causing discomfort

Let the stimulating sight of your partner reaching orgasm excite you further

Use your hands to raise and lower yourself

CHAPTER 16

HOW CAN WE FIND TIME TO BE LOVERS?

"If a relationship is important to you, you must ensure that you and your partner can both devote enough time to it to make it work."

IT DOESN'T MATTER how passionately you may love someone, and they you, if one of you never has time to spare for the relationship. It just won't work. Telling yourself that you can manage with few meetings and very little lovemaking is effectively lying to yourself. You may be able to survive such a restricted relationship, but it will be at a cost. And that cost will be a diminution of your sense of self-value and an erosion of your basic happiness.

In addition, if you and your partner cannot spend enough time together it is very likely that the development of your love affair will grind to a halt. For an affair to develop properly, the people involved need time to get to know each other better and love each other more. If insufficient time is available for this, the affair will probably stagnate and you and your partner will gradually drift apart.

You should also, of course, ensure that you spend sufficient time on your lovemaking so that the sexual side of your relationship works.

CASE STUDY *Liz*

After a long but increasingly unhappy relationship with a previous partner who was very dominating, Liz met Paul and this gave her a new lease on life. But it wasn't long before outside pressures began to intrude upon the relationship; Paul spent less and less time with Liz, and she started thinking seriously about having a new affair with an ex-lover of hers.

Name: LIZ

Age: 45

Marital status: SINGLE

Occupation: OFFICE MANAGER

Liz, who looked ten years younger than her age, had recently fallen passionately in love.

"After the bleakness of living with someone who for the past four years didn't really care if I lived or died," she said, "my new lover's appreciation of me was wonderful. I've blossomed thanks to Paul. I look prettier, feel glamorous. Feel a bit like a teenager, really. Loving him has brought back all my old sexuality and more. I know far more about sex at 45 than I did at 25. And I'm better at it. Ideally, I'd like to spend whole days in bed.

"And to begin with, that actually happened. We spent a whole morning just gently doing it. It was marvellous. I'd dreamed of that. We spent a few evenings where we went to bed as soon as we met, and took a very long time doing anything we felt like. It was wonderful.

"But then his business ran into problems and he became very worried about money. In order to keep his head above water financially he started to work very long hours; and he's been doing it ever since. He finishes now at half-nine or half-ten at night. He works just the same at the weekends, and if he isn't working he has to spend time with his kids. When we make love now, it's last thing at night, and although it's still lovely, he's tired. He passes out the minute he's had his orgasm simply because he's exhausted. Even though I've climaxed, I feel cheated. And I am being cheated — of time with him.

"This is a very tricky one to handle. I'm not sure there's anything to be gained by complaining. Paul's genuinely very pressurized to earn at the moment and I'm simply going to add to his sense of pressure if I start making demands which I don't think, quite honestly, he's in a position to do anything about.

"I feel so full of sexuality right now and I've arranged to meet up with a former lover who has remained a very good friend. The temptation to go to bed with him is extremely strong. But I genuinely feel that the love Paul and I have is so rare as to merit hanging on to him at all costs. However, I spent the previous four years denying myself love and affection through a misguided feeling of fidelity to someone else. Life is short. I'm not into denial any more."

THERAPIST'S ASSESSMENT

However pressurized someone is, it is always a mistake to take on too much of their pressure oneself. Unless Liz and Paul could arrange to spend more time together, and unless Liz could feel, despite everything, that Paul loved her enough to make some changes (even if they were only small ones), the love affair would come to a halt. Love affairs often survive all sorts of difficulties, but if they stagnate they usually fester and go wrong.

EXPLAINING
So I advised Liz that, before she got to the point where she felt sexually and verbally blocked off from Paul, she would find it helpful to explain her anxiety to him, choosing her words carefully to avoid misunderstanding or starting a row. She could do this by remembering that her needs were as important as his; by explaining how she felt (using a format such as "I feel unhappy about..." rather than accusing him of doing or not doing something); by asking him for constructive suggestions of how some changes might be built into the relationship; and by asking if he would consider suggestions she might offer.

ARRANGING TIME TOGETHER
Those suggestions might consist of a system of booking herself into his diary for a reasonable number of evenings a month. The evenings themselves would preferably be early rather than late and, just occasionally, the couple should plan themselves a full weekend away. Naturally, this would have to be negotiated to fit in with Paul's other requirements, but the sheer fact of negotiation would mean that Liz would be likely to end up with extra time that, so far, she hadn't been getting.

REWARDING TIME OFF
And just as she had worried about over-pressurizing him, Paul should be allowed to know he was in some danger of losing her so that his priorities might be sharpened up. If he remained anxious over sparing extra time for love-making, a Three-Handed Massage (see page 172) or a special lovemaking scenario (see page 142) could be made so rewarding that he wouldn't find further time off nearly so hard to contemplate!

My programme for
CLOSENESS AFTER THE
CLIMAX

Scant attention is paid to the end of lovemaking. Some people totally ignore each other, once they have achieved climax, while others commonly fall asleep almost immediately. Very few understand that a good experience has a beginning, a middle and an end, and that if lovemaking is deprived of its end, it feels staccato, incomplete and often unfulfilling. Learning to feel close to your lover after you have made love can enhance the sexual experience greatly. As one woman put it, "Among the best parts of lovemaking for me are those minutes of peace, after we have climaxed, when we are lying together in each other's arms, looking into each other's eyes, murmuring words of love and affection and just feeling completed by the love between us."

Stage | UNDERSTAND THE NEED FOR 'COMING DOWN'

Just as we need to carve out special times in which to be lovers, we need to devote some ten minutes or so to 'coming down' after the grand event. Orgasm doesn't always resolve sexuality as fully for women as it does for men: some women are able to continue to further orgasms, others may have experienced only minor orgasm as a result of the inefficient stimulation of intercourse. In other words, a woman may need a more cerebral ending to her lovemaking, since after intercourse her body may not always be as relaxed and free of sexual tension as her lover's.

Clients in psychotherapy learn that most events and relationships have a beginning, a middle and an end. That may seem obvious, but the reason that therapists like to bring it to the attention of their clients is because the way in which people deal with endings is often indicative of how they deal with relationships generally. Indeed, one of the tasks commonly required of a client undergoing

AFTER INTERCOURSE
Gazing lovingly at each other, and breathing together, will help to make you and your lover feel close and fulfilled.

therapy is to learn to end well. The same principle applies to any event in our lives, no matter how large or small that event may be, and lovemaking is no exception.

MEDITATION TECHNIQUES   Learning the experience of a loving and 'spiritual' resolution means acquiring another form of ending. US massage trainer Ray Stubbs teaches the value of enhancing lovemaking by using meditation techniques. He is practically unique among Western therapists in that he marries body touch and mind touch. "Quieting the mind and relaxing the body can be paths to fuller sexual expression," he writes. "Deepening our awareness, we can feel ripples of pleasure through our whole body. We touch not only with our lips, genitals and hands, we touch with our heart."

MEDITATION METHODS   Ray explores two simple meditation methods that attempt to bear this out. But he is the first to recommend that if, having tried them, they do nothing for you, it's sensible to drop them altogether rather than to burden yourself and your partner with something irrelevant.

Stage 2   BREATHING TOGETHER

For this stage of the programme, you and your lover should learn how to lie side by side, cuddled up in each other's arms, and breathe in and out together at the same time. As you breathe in, so does your partner. As your partner breathes out, so too do you.

This synchronized breathing may feel artificial when you first practise it, and some couples find it quite hard to do to begin with. This is perfectly understandable for two reasons. Firstly, the act of breathing in and out at the same time as someone lying next to us is not something we do naturally. And secondly, the normal rate of breathing of one person may differ quite a bit from that of another, and so a couple might have to learn to adjust their individual breathing rates.

BLENDING AND MERGING   But as you grow more used to the breathing pattern it will quite soon feel natural and effortless. A kind of blending and merging seems to take place, and it gets hard to distinguish your breathing from that of your partner. When that happens, it's easy to lose a sense of time. There's a feeling of oneness.

The only real prerequisites for this are that you lie in such a way that you are able to breathe without difficulty and that your body is comfortable enough to be relaxed (one lovely position for this is the spoons shape). If breathing together proves so relaxing that it is impossible to stay awake after having had intercourse, try the experiment before you make love. Breathing in unison calms the mind so that nuances of sensuality assume greater meaning.

Stage 3   GAZING TOGETHER

Gazing is a variation of a basic meditation technique, and in meditation it is often used as a method of mentally turning inwards. Do this simple gazing routine after intercourse, turning your gaze deliberately on to your loved one as he or she gazes back at you. Look softly towards each other's eyes. You don't have to try to focus on them, just let your vision be peripheral.

In this manner just allow yourselves to feel together. It may be difficult, at the beginning, not to laugh or fool around, but if that happens try to bring yourself back to that quiet, deliberate gaze. Focus your thoughts as much as possible on the intimacy and peacefulness of the experience

You may notice, after a while, that in your unfocused gaze your partner's face begins to look distorted. Don't let this become a distraction: ignore it, and try to bring yourself back to the quietness and stillness that you felt before it happened.

GAZING AND BREATHING   Combining this gazing with breathing together can be very rewarding, and as well as finding that it makes them feel closer after intercourse, many lovers find that gazing while lying next to each other on the bed, for about ten or fifteen minutes before lovemaking, both relaxes them and turns them on.

Since everyone's experience of meditation is different it is hard to predict how this will function for you and your lover. But for many people, calm and relaxation undoubtedly allow subtle thoughts and desires, which might not otherwise get the chance to come through, to take shape in their minds.

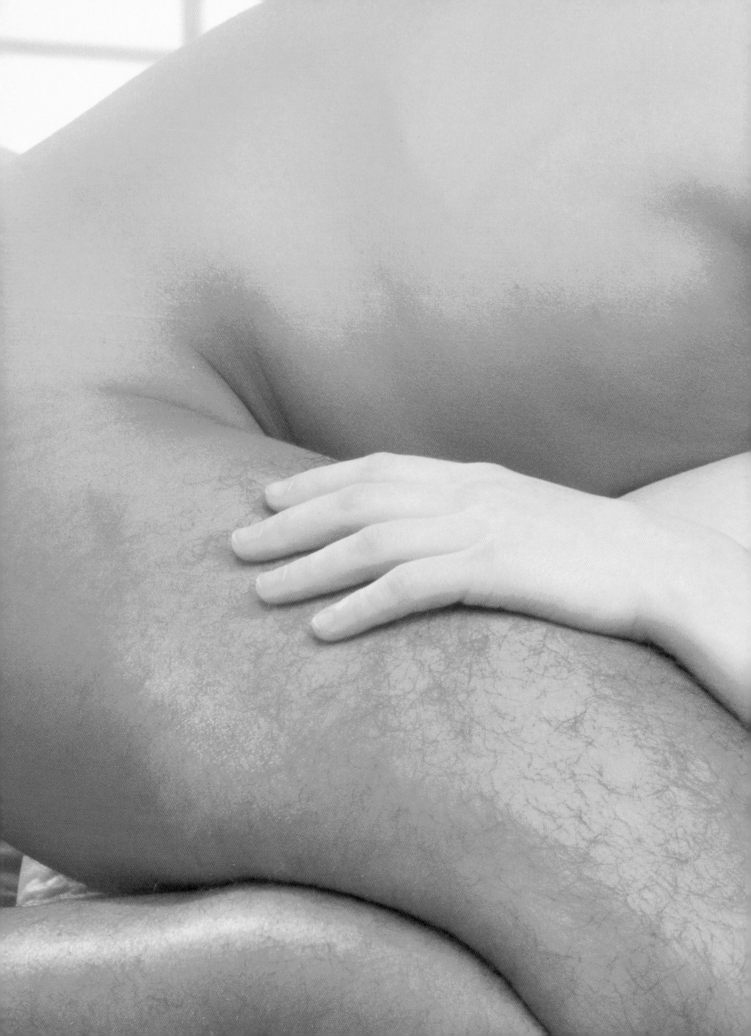

CHAPTER 17

RECHARG~ ING THE SEXUAL BATTERY

"Each of us has a limit to the amount of sustained sexual activity we can manage. Once that limit has been reached, our sexual functioning is restricted until we have given our bodies a chance to recover."

THERE IS A famous memoir by the American model, Viva, written in the early 1970s and based on her experiment of staying in bed and making love for three days without stopping. On Day Three she complains that she doesn't seem able to come any more.

What she was describing was an exaggerated version of what happens to any one of us should we try to make love constantly. The brain intervenes and enforces rest, to protect the body from death by orgasm.

Some young couples, however, expect their bodies to work like machines, and view the slowing down of their climaxes with dismay and, in some cases, anxiety. Their dismay is, of course, perfectly understandable, but this kind of slowing down is completely natural and nothing to worry about.

CASE STUDY *Steve & Linda*

Steve and Linda's sexual relationship started off spectacularly, but within a few months it was beginning to cause them problems. Steve found that he couldn't climax as easily and as often as he could before, and Linda had lost interest and was getting bored.

Name:	STEVE
Age:	19
Marital status:	SINGLE
Occupation:	STUDENT

Steve was in his first sexual relationship. He was anxious by nature and slightly greedy, and when he was keen on something or someone he bordered on the obsessive.

"In the early days of our relationship we made love all the time," he said. "It was wonderful. I came over and over again, it was almost like having multiple orgasms. The first weekend we spent together I had sixteen orgasms. I could hardly move on Monday. And Linda was just as keen as I was. But lately, and we've been going together for about seven months now, it hasn't felt so good. She doesn't want to make love so often and complains that it hurts.

"And I can't come as often as I used to before — it's got difficult to climax more than three times — but it feels awfully soon for my body to start running down like this. What's gone wrong with us?"

Name:	LINDA
Age:	18
Marital status:	SINGLE
Occupation:	STUDENT

Linda, also in her first sexual relationship, was a pale, thin girl. When I spoke to her away from Steve she showed that she was angry and upset, but in his presence she wrung her hands and was slow to speak.

"Steve just wants sex all the time," she complained. "We never do anything else together except go to bed. And to be quite truthful, I'm getting bored. He never asks me if I want to make love, just plunges on in there. I do like sex, very much, but now it really does hurt me when we have it. That's because I can't get properly interested and so I'm dry. When he spends hours on intercourse it's very painful for me, and also, he takes longer and longer to get to orgasm. The other night he was grinding away for nearly an hour before he managed to come. I was shattered. I don't know how to handle this."

THERAPIST'S ASSESSMENT

Most people, on first discovering sex, want a lot of it and manage more climaxes then than at most other times in their lives. It may be the sheer novelty, or the pent-up sex urge, or simply the fact that most people discover sex when they are young, and young people, particularly young men, have high sex drives.

So teenagers having sex sixteen times in a weekend, at the beginning of their first ever sexual relationship, may not be so rare. What would be unusual, though, would be if this average were to be maintained. The brain has its natural methods of slowing down the body for its own good. If, for example, sexual pleasure were completely addictive, we might be in danger of climaxing ourselves to death. The brain therefore provides a natural cut-out point, a sort of sexual thermostat, which puts an end to climaxes until the body regains its sexual energy.

RECHARGING
It helps, in this instance, to think of the body as a giant sexual battery which, if overloaded, runs out of energy. The simple answer to recharging is to wait a while and practise abstinence, or at least abstinence from orgasm. Many young people see their body as a machine and can't understand when it refuses to continue automatically with the desired response. But the body possesses a sensitive brain and sexuality isn't just about the pleasure of orgasm. It's about erotic buildup, too.

RECEPTIVENESS
The brain plays a strong part in how receptive you may be to a partner's overtures. If you begin to dislike that partner because of the bull-headed methods they use to go about securing their own pleasure, with no thought for your sensitivity, then not surprisingly you are going to get turned off. Linda, for example, felt she never had any choice in their sex life and that her feelings were stampeded over. If there was any hope for their future together, Steve needed to see Linda as an individual and not as a toy for his pleasure.

EXPLORING SENSUALITY
Together, the young couple decided to explore types of sensuality other than intercourse. They practised sensual massage (pages 128-131) and Taoist methods of love-making (page 186) in order to build up a sexual 'charge' again. Steve couldn't climax as often as he wanted to, but he could regain the intensity of orgasmic feeling.

My programme for
PSYCHIC SEXUAL HEALTH

The idea of 'recharging the body's sexual batteries' is not a new one. Thousands of years ago the ancient Taoists of China perceived the body as possessing an energy flow, and according to their observations this body energy can be both used up and restored. Just as the whole body possesses meridian points, which can be tapped or stimulated by acupuncture in order to restore a healthy balance of energy, so too, the Taoist philosophers argued, do the genitals. Like the feet and hands, the penis and the vagina are thus reflexology zones — areas that, if massaged in the correct way, will stimulate the flow of energy so as to benefit the energy levels elsewhere in the body.

Stage 1   RESTORE ENERGY

Science has so far been unable to verify that acupuncture meridian points exist or to explain why acupuncture works. But acupuncture does work — you need only watch film of a Chinese patient enduring an operation under the hands of a traditional acupuncturist rather than an anaesthetist to see for yourself. The patient feels no pain if the acupuncture is performed correctly.

ENERGY EMISSION In addition to acupuncture's demonstration of energy meridians, Kirlian photography may be used to demonstrate energy emission from the body. Kirlian photography is done with high-voltage equipment that is fast and powerful enough to show, in a photograph of a hand, for example, little shooting darts of energy, like tiny flames, coming from all over it. When a person with lesser energy touches your hand, the brilliance and height of your 'flame' diminishes, tapped by the other. It looks as if, simply by contact, energy becomes depleted.

Deer Exercise p188

ENERGY POINTS Sleep, of course, restores energy, but the Taoists say that, as with acupuncture and reflexology, so too do certain sexual practices that evenly stimulate the energy points on the penis and vagina. The Deer Exercise is one way of working towards this. As a result of this type of stimulation, certain glands in the body, which control sexual function, will be placed in an even balance and thus will act in a preventative way, safeguarding sexual health and vigour.

Stage 2   THE SETS OF NINE

Most people are familiar with the theory of Foot Reflexology. Practitioners of this believe that by applying stimulation to nerve endings in the foot, this will stimulate related organs. As previously mentioned, there are similar nerve endings or reflexology zones on the penis and vagina. The Sets of Nine is a Taoist exercise designed to massage these genital reflexology zones evenly and thus to benefit the related organs.

These organs — the Seven Glands — are the pineal, the pituitary, the thyroid, the thymus, the pancreas, the adrenal glands and the sexual glands (prostate and testes in the man and ovaries in the female).

GENITAL MASSAGE Regular and usual intercourse does not evenly massage the penis or the vagina since the folds of the vaginal canal and the uneven shape of the penis make this difficult. The Sets of Nine — one Set of Nine being a total of ninety strokes — aims to put this right. Many men may find it difficult to go the whole Set of Nine without ejaculating, and Taoist sex instructors encourage their pupils not to lose heart if this happens, saying that even part of the exercise is beneficial to the internal organs and that if they continue to practise comfortably, at their own pace, it will become easier to complete one Set of Nine. Serious students should aim at many further sets. The Taoist technique of 'injaculation' can be used in conjunction with the Sets of Nine, both for its beneficial effect on the man and for its usefulness in helping him to prolong intercourse.

Stage   INJACULATION

All men understand how to ejaculate, but in Taoist sex practice the man 'injaculates'. By pressing the Jen-Mo point — an acupressure point on the perineum, halfway between the anus and the scrotum — the ejaculation can, say the Taoists, be reversed and the semen recycled into the bloodstream and reabsorbed. The man still feels pleasurable sensations and these are, in fact, greatly accentuated since the pressure means that the orgasm happens in very slow spasms and so an orgasm may continue for as long as five minutes.

Although he still experiences orgasm, he retains his erection or can regain it quickly, allowing him to continue intercourse for far longer. Since he is not expelling his vital substances he will, according to Taoist principles, be preserving energy.

Pressing the Jen-Mo point is easy. Simply reach around behind you at the appropriate moment, and press so that the semen is not allowed to travel out of the prostate and through the urethra. You may like to practise this in private first. The pressure should be neither too firm nor too soft. If you apply pressure too close to the anus, the move won't work. If you press too close to the scrotum, the semen will go into the bladder, rather than the bloodstream, and make your urine cloudy when you urinate. Do not try injaculation if you have a prostate infection.

THE SETS OF NINE The Sets of Nine is a form of sexual intercourse that gives energy-restoring massage to the vagina and penis.

THE SETS OF NINE

To carry out the Sets of Nine, first decide on a comfortable position for intercourse. Then, for each Set of Nine, the man should begin a series of ninety deep and shallow strokes as follows:

1 He thrusts only the penis head into the vagina before withdrawing. He does this shallow stroke nine times, and then he thrusts the entire penis into the vagina once

2 He follows this up with eight of the shallow strokes (with the penis head only) and two deep strokes (with the entire penis)

3 Next, he makes seven shallow strokes and three deep ones

4 Six shallow strokes and four deep ones

5 Five shallow strokes and five deep ones

6 Four shallow strokes and six deep ones

7 Three shallow strokes and seven deep ones

8 Two shallow strokes and eight deep ones

9 Finally, he makes one shallow stroke followed by nine deep ones

Support yourself on your arms so you can control your strokes more effectively

Combinations of deep and shallow strokes are the key to the Sets of Nine

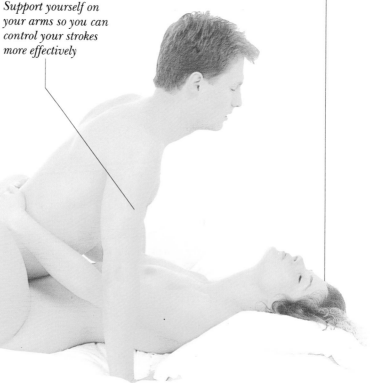

THE DEER EXERCISE

Over two thousand of years ago, in China, Taoist thinkers perceived that the deer, noted for its long life and its strong reproductive activities, exercised its anus when it wiggled its tail. Putting two and two together, they developed a 'tail-wiggling' concept for man — which they called the Deer Exercise — designed to rejuvenate him and to create conditions for increasing his sexual arousal. In a similar way, the version of the Deer Exercise for women is said by the Taoists to re-balance the female hormones, encourage sexual energy and keep a woman looking younger.

WARM HANDS The Deer Exercise involves self-massage, so before you begin, it is a good idea to make sure that your hands are warm, either by rubbing them vigorously together or by washing them in hot water.

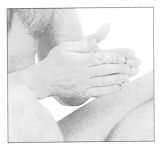

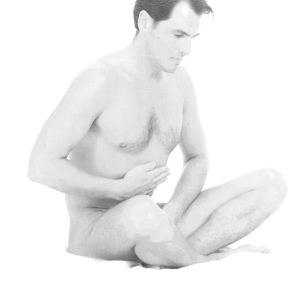

You will feel a brief tingling sensation ascend your spinal column, ending somewhere between your ears as you relax

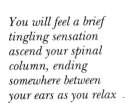

FACILITATING SEMEN PRODUCTION Cup your testicles gently in one hand and place the flat of the other on your abdomen, just below the navel. Using a circular motion, massage the left side of your abdomen 81 times, and then repeat on the right side.

Sit, stand or lie down to carry out this exercise; take off your clothes before you begin

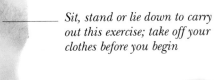

PROSTATE MASSAGE This part of the exercise strengthens the anal muscles which in turn massage the prostate. Squeeze the anal muscles tightly together and hold as long as you comfortably can. Relax for a minute, then repeat. Do this as many times as you can without discomfort. Taoist teachers say that anal contractions massage the prostate gland, producing hormone secretion and a natural high.

Sit cross-legged on the floor or bed; make sure you remove your clothes first

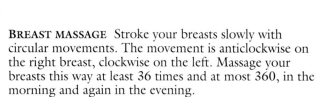

WARM HANDS Before you begin the self-massage part of the exercise, make sure that your hands are warm — either rub them vigorously together or wash them in hot water.

BREAST MASSAGE Stroke your breasts slowly with circular movements. The movement is anticlockwise on the right breast, clockwise on the left. Massage your breasts this way at least 36 times and at most 360, in the morning and again in the evening.

VAGINAL PRESSURE Sit cross-legged with the heel of one foot pressed up against your vaginal entrance. If this is difficult, place a small ball between your foot and vagina. The pressure from heel or ball stimulates sexual feelings and releases sexual energy.

DRAWING UP ENERGY Massage each breast in turn with one hand, using the other hand to press your vaginal opening. Contract the muscles in your vagina and anus as if you were trying to control a flow of urine, then focus hard on contracting the anus further. Hold this position for as long as possible then relax and repeat twenty times. Try to build up the number of times you are able to do this. To check that you are doing it properly, insert a finger into the vagina to see if you can grip it, or at least tighten on it.

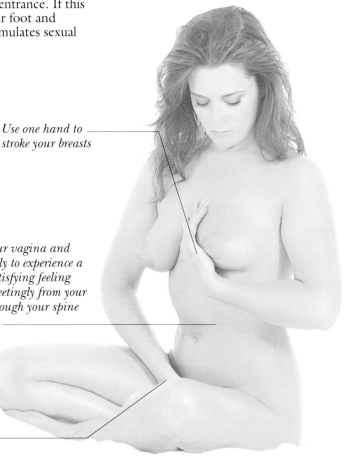

Use one hand to stroke your breasts

Contract your vagina and anus correctly to experience a deep and satisfying feeling travelling fleetingly from your anus up through your spine to your ears

Use one hand to press against your vaginal opening

CHAPTER 18

HOW CAN SEX MAKE US FEEL WHOLE?

"Learning the small aspects of sensuality as taught by ancient Oriental cultures is like being trained to be an outstanding performer in a team game."

AN INTERESTING fact of sexuality is that you don't have to be in love with a partner in order to experience ecstasy when lovemaking. Some lovers spontaneously achieve ecstasy when they hardly know each other, and old friends who occasionally have sex together have been known to feel intensely spiritual.

Yet even if you and your partner are fortunate enough both to love each other and to have sex together, this, alas, is not a guarantee of nirvana. An individual's sense of wholeness, of ultimate well-being, depends largely on that individual's state of mind rather than on a relationship with another person.

Eastern cultures, unlike Western ones, have always been very clear about the wholeness of the individual, and have traditionally associated sex with spirituality.

Oriental beliefs have it that flesh and mind are inextricably bound up in each other, a spiritual experience therefore being a very possible outcome of good sex. In Western terms, this might be experienced as a sense of wholeness and well-being.

2

CASE STUDY *Harry & Penny*

Harry was certain that there was more to sex than successfully achieving orgasm, but he was afraid to mention it to his partner, Penny. She, meanwhile, had sensed that he wanted something extra from their lovemaking. But although she was more than willing to go along with any suggestion he might make, she was afraid to ask him what it was he really wanted.

Name:	HARRY
Age:	34
Marital status:	SINGLE
Occupation:	STUDENT

Harry was a tall, serious, mature student who was working for a degree in Oriental Studies. Influenced by Japanese beliefs, his apartment and lifestyle were simple.

"I expected sex to have more meaning," he said. "I truly expected it to be a heavenly experience. I thought orgasm would be a glorious ascent, with sensations of clarity and light and immense well-being flooding through me. I've read many books about spirituality and sex and so I believe that this is possible, but with us, sex is somehow mechanical and too quick.

"I want to slow things down and be daft and soppy with her but I get the impression that if I tried it she'd think I was kinky somehow. For her, sex is about her orgasm, then my orgasm, and that's it. We have the orgasms all right, but afterwards I think, 'Is that all?' It's a curiously flat feeling, as though a huge dimension is missing."

Name:	PENNY
Age:	32
Marital status:	SINGLE
Occupation:	NURSE

Penny had a cheerful, matter-of-fact manner, but her over-loud voice concealed a personality considerably more sensitive than showed on the surface.

"I've been able to see all along that Harry is restless about something," she told me. "The trouble is, I haven't known what it's been about. I think he's been afraid of making me feel rejected. My problem is that Harry is my first lover, and although I've lots of ideas about sex, I've never actually done much of it.

"I believe that if you love someone deeply you'll do anything for them sexually, and I certainly feel that I do love Harry. But he never asks me for anything at all and yet I'm dying for him to do so. I'm open to new ideas, but how can I help Harry share his with me?"

THERAPIST'S ASSESSMENT

An interesting aspect of sexuality is that you don't have to be in love with a partner in order to experience ecstasy when making love. Some lovers spontaneously achieve ecstasy when they hardly know each other. Men and women, old friends who occasionally have sex together, have been known to feel intensely spiritual. Yet if you are fortunate enough both to love each other and to have sex together, this, alas, is not a guarantee of nirvana.

But when you do manage to combine love, sex and ecstasy, it's probably the best of all heavens. But the fact that virtual strangers can, through sex, experience what amounts to transcendental enlightenment means that the rather solemn, and almost unsexual-seeming, instructions of Oriental sex sages could actually work. These focus on the state of your own mind and body rather than on that of your partner.

SEXUAL STRENGTH
Put simply, the emphasis in Oriental sex practice on small aspects of sensuality, such as lying together quietly, breathing in unison, practising sexual exercises without a partner in sight, cultivates this independent sexual strength. Harry had derived his ideas of sexual wholeness from his knowledge of ancient Eastern cultures and was itching to try out the sexual instruction he'd read. When he understood that Penny's over-efficient exterior cloaked someone dying to be passionate and humble and powerful all at the same time, he lost his anxieties about alienating her. His more confident approach plus her immediate acceptance of some very different sex practices, where she felt wide open to him and he could see this and take advantage, totally altered and improved the quality of their bedtime experiences.

SIMPLE ROUTINES
I suggested that they try some simple routines to help them deepen the quality of their sexual activities. These were: to spend fifteen minutes simply lying next to each other in bed, stroking each other mutually; to spend five minutes each on kissing the ears, neck and shoulders; to breathe in unison and gaze into each other's eyes (see page 181); individually to practise the Deer Exercise (see page 188); together to practise some of the techniques that could help them achieve enhanced orgasms (see pages 194-197); and to abstain from orgasm one in four times they make love.

My programme for
ACHIEVING SEXUAL ECSTASY

In the Chinese Tao of sexology, a woman's orgasm is likened to a flower, uncurling from the centre, blooming in the sun as petal after petal unfolds. Inside herself she opens up entirely and surrenders to the man who can take her at any pace and bring her to the most intense ecstasy. The Tao view of sex is thus a sexist one, since this total giving of herself (amounting to a shedding of all hesitation, inhibition and tension, while offering the gift of humility) can only culminate through a man. Masturbation apparently isn't the same (although the body's orgasmic reactions can, of course, be identical to those experienced through intercourse).

Stage LEARN THE NINE LEVELS OF ORGASM

Western cultures have very little awareness of quality differences in a woman's orgasm although some years ago a debate raged about the merits of vaginal versus clitoral orgasm. In my book *The Body Electric* I identified a variety of climaxes: "A woman may have climaxes of different lengths and different strengths, experienced in different sites, both in the genitals and over the whole body, depending on her peace of mind and her physical state (e.g. whether or not she's tired, happy, etc)."

TAO SEXOLOGY Tao sexology goes further than this. It describes a woman's orgasm as a series of upward-rising steps followed by one declining step. These steps actually flow together in degrees of overlap, building on the experience of each former step. She thus experiences many levels of opening up to sensation until finally she is completely exposed to the man who is her server. These levels of orgasm — nine in all — have been listed in detail by Stephen Chang in his book *The Tao of Sexology*, and are summarized opposite.

INCOMPLETE ORGASM The typical Western man, apparently, not realizing there are so many further stages of orgasm to go, stops stimulating his woman at around Level Four and so her climax is frequently incomplete. By carrying on with the stimulation, she is likely to get a great deal more out of the orgasm.

Self stimulation p232

VARYING CIRCUMSTANCES It is fair to say, however, that since circumstances vary, so too may the emotional experience and this therefore would qualitatively affect a sense of completeness and wholeness. The Tao belief, however, is that upon reaching the Ninth Level of Orgasm the whole of the woman's body is energized.

FEMINIST ADAPTATION A modern and feminist adaptation of these ideas might list some of the body's reactions rather differently (for example, nowhere is the rigid stretching and pointing of the toes mentioned, although this is a very prominent feature of a woman's orgasm). It might also be mentioned that these are just as well experienced during masturbation or lesbian lovemaking. However, women who have experienced orgasms will recognize some or even all of the Nine Levels as a familiar sequence of reactions. The first four levels of female orgasm (those that, according to the Taoist view of Western sex, are all that most women are likely to have experienced) involve heavy breathing, passionate kissing, passionate embracing and finally a series of vaginal spasms accompanied by a flow of vaginal fluids.

During the remaining five levels, which can be achieved if a woman is given the correct kind of sustained stimulation after reaching Level Four, the body movements first become more vigorous and frantic. Then, at levels Eight and Nine, the woman's muscles relax totally and she finally collapses in a so-called 'little death'.

Stage REACHING THE NINE LEVELS

How, then, can a man bring his partner on from Level Four to these further stages of her climax? To begin with, of course, he must ensure that she reaches Level Four in the first place, and one very good way of doing this is through extensive, loving foreplay, including masturbation and, perhaps, tongue bathing and oral sex. This will help her to be well on her way to achieving an orgasm before intercourse even begins.

Better orgasm p196

CONTINUED STIMULATION Once she has reached her climax, he should not assume that it is quickly over and done with. He should continue with whatever stimulation has been effective so far, including intercourse, without varying the pace of it (neither speeding up nor slowing down) and without altering the strength of his movements.

RETURNING CONTRACTIONS As he continues to stimulate her, he will be able to see her orgasmic contractions return and he will be able to read in her face, and her body movements, the fact that the feeling is deepening for her. There may come a stage of climax where she is so helpless with sensation that he can alter the pattern of his stimulation, but he should ask her whether she likes this or not.

THE NINE LEVELS

Each level of orgasm energizes certain parts of the body and evokes a certain observable and predictable response in the woman.

• Level One (lungs): the woman sighs, breathes heavily and salivates

• Level Two (heart): while kissing the man, she extends her tongue out to him

• Level Three (spleen, pancreas and stomach): as her muscles become activated, she grasps him tightly

• Level Four (kidneys and bladder): she experiences a series of vaginal spasms at this time and secretions begin to flow

• Level Five (bones): her joints loosen and she begins to bite her partner

• Level Six (liver and nerves): she undulates like a snake, trying to wrap her arms and legs around him

• Level Seven (blood): her blood is 'boiling' and she is frantically trying to touch her man everywhere

• Level Eight (muscles): her muscles totally relax. She bites even more and grabs his nipples

• Level Nine (entire body): she collapses in a 'little death', surrenders to the man and is completely 'opened up'

REACHING THE NINE LEVELS
According to Taoist sexologists, few Western women get beyond about Level Four. This is because their partners stop stimulating them too soon.

Continue to stimulate her when she reaches her climax, so you can take her to higher levels

When you reach Level Nine of orgasm the whole of your body will respond

195

HELPING EACH OTHER TO AN ENHANCED ORGASM

A woman's orgasm differs from a man's in that it can go on and on in varying strengths. Most men experience orgasm as a sharp peak of orgasmic feeling, and don't know that their orgasms can be improved by slow, subtle beginnings. For both sexes, therefore, a sensual prelude to intercourse is an orgasm enhancer.

STROKING AND TOUCHING
At the beginning of lovemaking, sensuous, provocative stroking and touching will heighten your arousal and strengthen your desire and longing for each other.

Kiss lovingly, look into each other's eyes, and tell each other your thoughts and feelings

Enjoy the sensual pleasure of the close contact between your bodies

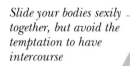

Slide your bodies sexily together, but avoid the temptation to have intercourse

TEASING AND TANTALIZING
While cuddling and rolling around on the bed, extend your loveplay to include mutual masturbation but resist the temptation to have intercourse too soon: there is yet more enjoyable stimulation to be had before penetration.

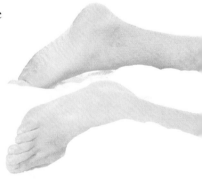

ROLLING AND CUDDLING After arousing yourselves with stroking and touching, closer physical contact in the form of playful rolling around and cuddling will take your mutual physical arousal to an even higher level.

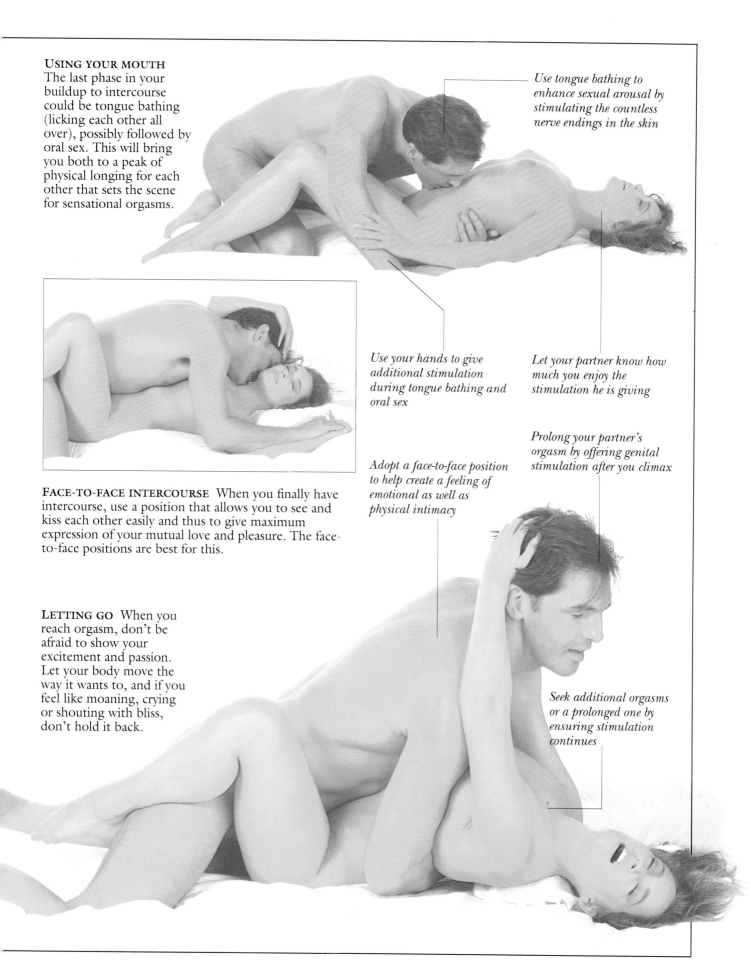

USING YOUR MOUTH
The last phase in your
buildup to intercourse
could be tongue bathing
(licking each other all
over), possibly followed by
oral sex. This will bring
you both to a peak of
physical longing for each
other that sets the scene
for sensational orgasms.

*Use tongue bathing to
enhance sexual arousal by
stimulating the countless
nerve endings in the skin*

*Use your hands to give
additional stimulation
during tongue bathing and
oral sex*

*Let your partner know how
much you enjoy the
stimulation he is giving*

*Prolong your partner's
orgasm by offering genital
stimulation after you climax*

FACE-TO-FACE INTERCOURSE When you finally have
intercourse, use a position that allows you to see and
kiss each other easily and thus to give maximum
expression of your mutual love and pleasure. The face-
to-face positions are best for this.

*Adopt a face-to-face position
to help create a feeling of
emotional as well as
physical intimacy*

LETTING GO When you
reach orgasm, don't be
afraid to show your
excitement and passion.
Let your body move the
way it wants to, and if you
feel like moaning, crying
or shouting with bliss,
don't hold it back.

*Seek additional orgasms
or a prolonged one by
ensuring stimulation
continues*

CHAPTER 10

HOW CAN WE BRING BACK DESIRE?

"Even when desire has dwindled away almost to nothing, if both partners really want to rekindle it then there are ways in which that can be done."

THE ONE single ingredient that has proved to be the most difficult to quantify in human sexual response is that of the desire of one individual for another.

What exactly is sexual desire? How do we get it? Is it something caused by our hormones or is it a psychological phenomenon, or is it perhaps a combination of both of these factors? Why doesn't it last? And when it fades away, as it so often does, how can we get it back?

These are all questions that sex researchers have been asking for years, but they have yet to come up with any completely satisfactory answers to them.

More importantly, they are also questions that are asked by ordinary men and women who love each other but, without really knowing why, are finding it hard to raise the enthusiasm for making love to each other.

CASE STUDY *Jan & Elaine*

Jan and Elaine's long and loving marriage was coming under strain because Jan, despite his love for his wife, had lost interest in making love to her and no longer got the thrill from sex that he once did. This left Elaine feeling undervalued and, as the children were now grown up and had left home, made her think of leaving him and finding a new lover.

Name:	JAN
Age:	45
Marital status:	MARRIED
Occupation:	SERVICE MANAGER

Jan was a tall, thin, greying individual with pebble glasses, a sharp stare and a charming smile. He had come to this country as a child refugee, married young, and had two grown-up children.

"I had very precarious beginnings in this country," he said. "I arrived at the age of ten, with parents who had nothing. But in spite of doing well — first in school, then with my career — I still felt insecure until I met Elaine, who gave me an almost physical sense of relief. With her, my fears vaporized. Now, it feels as though she's part of me. I love her and there's no way I want the marriage to end.

"But in the past few years our sex life has declined. It has got harder and harder to make the effort. Admittedly, when I have done so, usually because Elaine has got frantic, it's been as lovely as ever. But I just don't get that sense of need for her body any more, and I don't get the buzz out of sex I used to."

Name:	ELAINE
Age:	47
Marital status:	MARRIED
Occupation:	SYSTEMS ANALYST

Elaine, youthful-looking with soft red hair, a slim, willowy figure and an obvious zest for life, was stylishly dressed and managed to look designer sexy.

"He's not the only one to be concerned," she told me. "I'm sure I ought to rid myself of the belief that sex represents love, and therefore Jan doesn't love me any more — I can see that logically this doesn't follow. But underneath I'm feeling more and more undervalued. As I see it, the problem isn't on my side. I still fancy Jan. I still try and initiate sex. And once every few months I finally goad him into doing something about it. But that isn't enough and I'm thinking of just giving up. I'm reaching a dangerous age. My kids have left home. My career is blossoming again, and although I haven't been tempted yet, I can see, so easily, how women fall in love with other men in these circumstances."

THERAPIST'S ASSESSMENT

Nobody knows what makes lovers lose desire for each other. The cause could be familiarity, or resentment over past hurts, or the changing appearance of a lover as the years pass. Or it could be because of parenthood, or seeing a spouse as a companion or sibling rather than a lover. The list goes on and on.

The options for people in Jan and Elaine's situation are straightforward. They can separate amidst great pain and form new partnerships, which may indeed restore their 'joie de vivre'. They can remain together but tacitly agree to condone each other's affairs elsewhere. They can continue as they have been doing but with the danger that the marriage will become so stagnant it will die of inertia. Or they can take a shot at reviving the sensual side of life together. This doesn't guarantee orgasms, but it does mean that the partners learn to build up the amount of time they spend on sensual enjoyment. This goes a long way towards reviving warmth and tenderness.

MEDICAL PROBLEMS
There are occasionally medical or hormonal reasons why men and women lose desire, and naturally medical advice should be sought if this is the case. But both Jan and Elaine were in good health, so they decided to try and learn new tactile skills together, giving themselves an attractive common platform of sensuality.

WEEKLY EXERCISES
They agreed to embark on a weekly series of exercises, starting with mental self-examination to reveal their inner fears and desires. The second week's exercise was mutual physical self-examination (see pages 80-83) and that was followed by regular weekly touch sessions, at first with intercourse forbidden but, as time passed, eventually including it.

SELF-HELP THERAPIES
There are two other therapy models that couples can choose from to assist themselves with solving the problem of waning sexual desire. The first is the sexual enhancement programme (page 60) and the second the three-day Tantric programme (see page 202). The emphasis in both of these is in building up tactile pleasure without, at first, a sexual imperative, so that sensuality becomes a strong bond once more between the lovers, and a sound basis upon which desire can be rebuilt.

My programme for
REKINDLING DESIRE

The dampening or death of desire may be countered by experience of a different order. Tantric philosophy, which believes that through sex we can experience expanded and enhanced being, can offer new sexual vistas. Tantra, like yoga, originated in India; nicknamed the 'science of ecstasy', it heightens and prolongs the special rapport that exists between a man and a woman when making love. The point of the exercises practised over this three-day programme is to aim consciously at merging yourself ecstatically with your partner and, through him or her, with the rest of the world. If that sounds a tall order, it's worth remembering that in your mind, anything is possible.

If you were the complete student of Tantric philosophy, you would have to go through an extensive programme of training your senses to detect subtle nuance and change. You would practise physical exercises to strengthen the muscles needed to make extended intercourse a pleasure rather than a pain, and explore mental exercises to extend your imagination. In this way you would train yourself to be aware of not only your own feelings but also those of the man or woman with whom you wish to become one. The three-day programme described here is not as rigorous as a full Tantric programme, but it will help to bring you and your partner closer together and to reawaken your desire for each other.

SEXUAL CONTINENCE The three-day programme comes with a strict rule about sexual continence: there will be no intercourse or orgasm until the latter part of the third day. It is best carried out away from your everyday circumstances, preferably somewhere quiet, private, comfortable and in the countryside so that the beauty of the surrounding scenery enhances the experience.

Read the instructions for each day while lying close together, and do your best not to give way to longings that lead to coupling — some of the practices can be deeply arousing. But since the Tantric ideal is to prolong the entire sex act so that it becomes greatly enhanced, there is method in this abstinence.

THE FIRST DAY The object of the first day of the programme is to get you and your partner to relax and talk freely and candidly about yourselves and your relationship. You should be completely open with each other, but avoid saying anything hurtful.

On the first day you both remain clothed and close physical contact is restricted

You may hold hands, but you should not kiss or caress each other

Stage I THE FIRST DAY

The first day of the three-day programme is a day for getting to know each other. No matter that you may have lived together for ten years: today you will begin to tear aside the veil of privacy that, over the years, you have instinctively but unconsciously placed between yourself and your lover, and you will dare to expose yourself without reservation.

After a light breakfast, go for a walk in the beautiful countryside in which you are staying. Enjoy the scenery and the peace and quiet, and try to relax and forget about the problems of your everyday life. Spend the time talking, and reminisce about what it was like when you first met. Remember the beauty of your love in the beginning, the way you felt about each other in those early days of your relationship, and the things you did together.

OPEN UP When you talk with your partner about yourself and your relationship, let down your defences and be completely open about your feelings. Don't be afraid to show emotion: hold hands, laugh, cry, and talk freely of your fears, fantasies, hopes and hates. Speak of anything and everything — but do not say anything that might hurt your partner.

For example, if you discuss a former lover or partner, stress that the affair is over and done with, and don't talk about it too regretfully because that might give your partner the impression that he or she is some kind of second best. And if you decide to mention that you find fault with something about your partner, hasten to add that the fault is really a minor one and that his or her good points far outweigh the bad.

NO INTERCOURSE On the first night, sleep in each other's arms if you can do so comfortably, but do not fondle or caress each other and avoid intercourse — abstinence will intensify your feelings.

USE RESTRAINT During the first day, you should refrain from kissing until you go to bed, and should avoid caressing or fondling each other and making love.

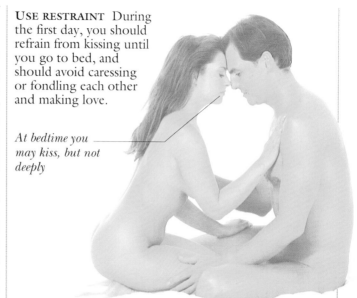

At bedtime you may kiss, but not deeply

Give each other plenty of time to speak and to express opinions, thoughts, hopes and fears, and pay attention to what is said. Make each other feel good, and do caring things like making each other little gifts.

USE RESTRAINT Although you may hold hands, or walk arm in arm, that should be the extent of today's touching. Hold back from kissing, fondling and making love. In the evening, talk a little more. Share your feelings about this exercise and its progress, and talk about what it is like to be together without making love.

When you go to bed on the first night, kiss if you must, but not deeply, and do not caress. Sleep in each other's arms, but hold back from caressing and lovemaking. There is plenty of time ahead in which to make love.

The spoons position is a comfortable one in which to sleep closely together

Put your arms around your partner, but do not caress or fondle

Stage 2 THE SECOND DAY

All being well, you will have resisted any temptation to make love on the first night of the programme. But sexual pressure will be tingling in the air around you, and your desire for each other will have been thoroughly awakened by the combination of intimacy and abstinence you are experiencing.

On the morning of the second day, after you have bathed and eaten a light breakfast, ensure that you will not be disturbed and close the door and windows to your room. Sit opposite each other naked, and close enough to touch easily. Very gently and lightly, reach forward and begin to stroke each other lightly and lovingly. You may stroke anywhere except on the breasts or the genitals.

STAY SILENT Do not speak as you stroke but simply carry on, stroking your partner as lightly as you would if you were caressing a delicate flower. You may become exceedingly aroused by this, to the extent that you may even tremble, cry out or break into a fine sweat. But despite your arousal, continue the stroking for half an hour if you can. When you have finished, lie down on your backs, side by side, and relax together so as to allow the intense sexual feeling that has built up to decline and gradually disperse.

After a while, when you are both feeling completely relaxed, and the sexual feeling has dispersed, bathe separately in warm water. Then once more sit opposite each other, naked, and do the stroking exercise again for a further quarter of an hour.

Later, eat a light lunch and go for another walk. Hold hands as you walk, and be quiet if you want to or else share your feelings. If one of you feels that the exercise is useless, just try and hang on to enjoying the feelings for the moment alone.

REPEAT THE STROKING In the evening, after a light meal, begin the stroking exercise again. Only this time, as you do it, imagine that the touch you are bestowing on your partner can be felt by you.

Stroke each other all over, but not on the breasts or genitals

THE SECOND DAY The second day of the programme focuses on mutual stroking and touching exercises. These are designed to enhance the empathy between you and your partner.

If, for instance, you stroke your partner on the arm, imagine it is your own arm that is being stroked and try to think what it would feel like to be touched in that manner. And while you are doing this, deaden yourself to the actual touch that you are experiencing in return from your partner's hands.

The point of this exercise is to encourage you, by using your imagination, to experience your partner's feelings rather than your own. Try to spend at least half an hour on the exercise, even though it may not feel as intensely erotic as that of the previous night. It may even make you feel a little unreal, because in your imagination you and your partner are exchanging personalities, but the most important thing about it is that you are also increasing the telepathic bond between you.

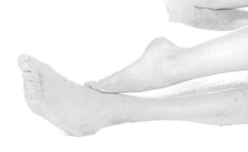

Stage 3 — THE THIRD DAY

Begin the third and final day of the programme with a bath or shower and a light breakfast. Then as on the second morning, ensure that you have total privacy and carry on with the empathic stroking.

GENITAL TOUCH Sit naked and close together and, without speaking but allowing yourselves to moan, gasp or cry out if your arousal becomes intense, stroke each other very lightly and lovingly. This time, you may stroke each other all over — and you should include the breasts, labia, vagina, penis and testicles in your caresses — but the strokes should continue to be as light as you can make them.

EMPATHY Empathize with your partner, as on the previous evening, by trying to imagine that you can feel the touches you are giving in the same way that he or she can feel them. Pay particular attention to the touches on the breasts and, more importantly, to those on the genitals, because these touches were not part of the empathic stroking exercise that you did before.

Keep on with these caresses for about an hour, and then take a five-minute rest before moving on to the next part of the exercise, which involves penetration.

Tantric strokes p206

Tantric intercourse p208

PENETRATION After that five-minute rest, the man should lie down flat on his back. Then, his partner should sit astride him and gently lower her vagina on to his erect penis. (If he does not already have an erection, either he or his partner should masturbate him by hand so that he achieves one.)

Once she has inserted his erect penis into her vagina, there should be no more movement from him and no thrusting or other sexual movement from her. She simply sits, then stretches out and lies face-down on him, with his penis contained within her. Then you both simply lie there peacefully, without moving, until his erection has subsided. Do not let yourselves be tempted to move or to come to orgasm.

After this, wash and dress and go for a walk together before taking a light lunch. While you are walking, talk over your thoughts and feelings about the programme so far and discuss the effects it has had on your feelings for each other.

During the final afternoon or evening, do the stroking and penetration exercise again for an hour at least, concentrating on the empathic quality of your touch until you feel that you have virtually merged identities with your partner. Then you may have uninhibited intercourse to complete the three-day session in a joyous, satisfying way.

THE THIRD DAY The third day of the programme builds on the empathic stroking exercises of the previous day, repeating and extending them to include penetration, and further strengthening the empathy between you.

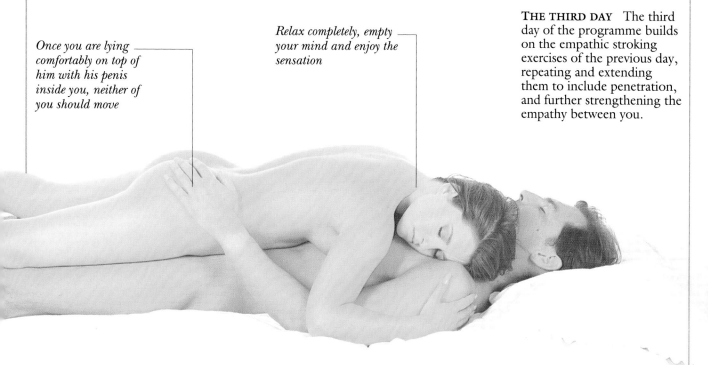

Once you are lying comfortably on top of him with his penis inside you, neither of you should move

Relax completely, empty your mind and enjoy the sensation

TANTRIC STROKING

Tantric stroking is an Eastern version of Masters and Johnson's 'sensate focus' therapy. But it is a version with a major difference. The first half of the exercise echoes the 'touch for pleasure's sake' principle, but the second moves on to something more profound that touches the spirit as well as the body. There are two sensations to be appreciated. The first is your own — what you feel when you touch your partner. The second is what your partner feels when touched by you, and the Tantric lovestroke exercise will teach you how to tune in to that sensation as if it were your own.

After stroking the arms and legs, sit closer and stroke each other's back

Begin by stroking each other's shoulders, arms and legs

1 BASIC STROKES
Without speaking, lightly stroke each other first with a circling action and then up and down. Avoid the breasts and genitals. Stroke slowly for about 15 minutes, take a break, then repeat the stroking for another 15 minutes. Later in the evening repeat the stroking for 30 minutes, and imagine that you feel the touch you are giving your partner as if it were you receiving it.

2 AFTER COMPLETING THE FIRST STAGE
Lie quietly together closely but chastely in the spoons position (if that is too tempting, simply lie facing each other with foreheads together but bodies not quite touching).

Enjoy the closeness of your bodies, but do not have intercourse

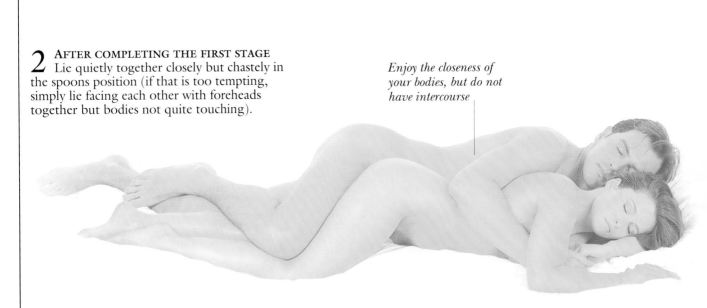

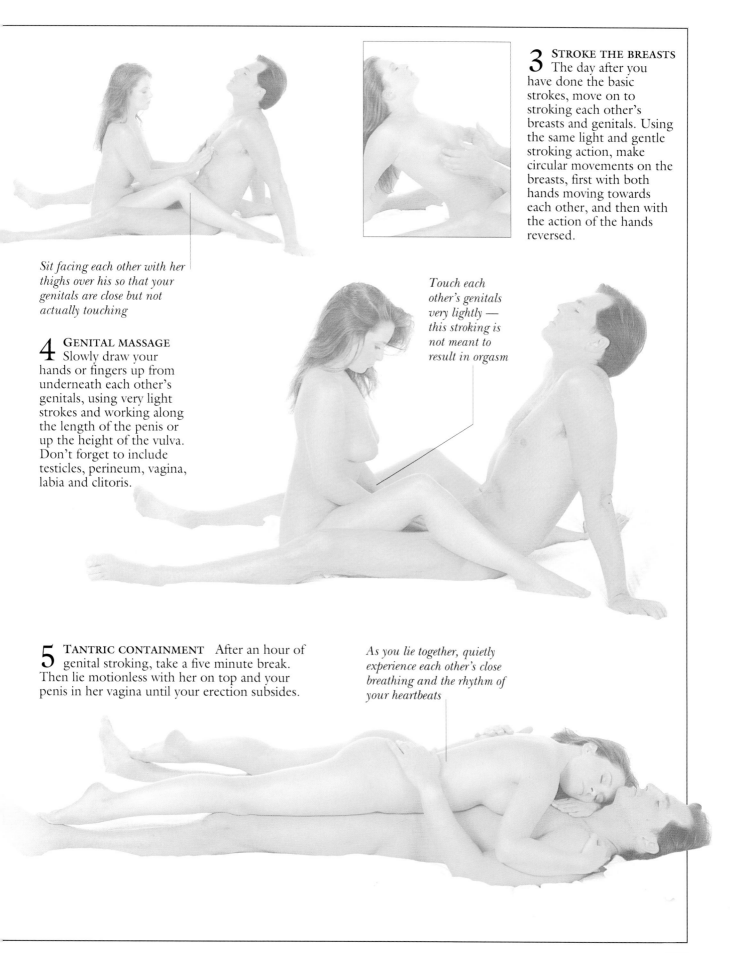

Sit facing each other with her thighs over his so that your genitals are close but not actually touching

3 STROKE THE BREASTS The day after you have done the basic strokes, move on to stroking each other's breasts and genitals. Using the same light and gentle stroking action, make circular movements on the breasts, first with both hands moving towards each other, and then with the action of the hands reversed.

Touch each other's genitals very lightly — this stroking is not meant to result in orgasm

4 GENITAL MASSAGE Slowly draw your hands or fingers up from underneath each other's genitals, using very light strokes and working along the length of the penis or up the height of the vulva. Don't forget to include testicles, perineum, vagina, labia and clitoris.

5 TANTRIC CONTAINMENT After an hour of genital stroking, take a five minute break. Then lie motionless with her on top and your penis in her vagina until your erection subsides.

As you lie together, quietly experience each other's close breathing and the rhythm of your heartbeats

TANTRIC INTERCOURSE

Tantric sex aims to prolong sexual arousal. The stroking described on the previous pages is followed by very slow intercourse. The penis penetrates the vagina by only a couple of centimetres, stays there for a full minute, withdraws and rests in the clitoral hood for a further minute and then slides back in. During subsequent rest minutes the penis first waits on the outside of the vulva for the next strokes, and then eventually waits just inside it.

THE LATERAL POSITION
Prolonged intercourse is facilitated if the couple lie on their sides facing each other. She lies with one leg between his and the other over him.

Lie partly on your back, with your partner lying partly on her front

Pass your lower arm underneath her, pulling her towards you

THE MISSIONARY POSITION This use of this versatile position is intended to facilitate prolonged intercourse. The advantage of the missionary position is that he can raise himself slightly to one side so that one of his hands can reach back to grasp his testicles and pull them downwards should he need to control an impending orgasm.

ORGASM CONTROL
Many men find it easier to reach between their legs to grasp their testicles than to reach around behind to get at them.

Lift your hips slightly while tightening your buttocks

To free one hand to grasp your testicles, use the other to raise yourself and support your weight

As you near orgasm, prevent it happening by firmly but gently pulling down on your testicles

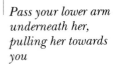

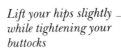

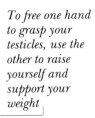

Draw your feet back and bend your knees so that you can easily lift your buttocks clear of the bed

Support your weight on your arm, pressing your body close to hers

FEMALE HIP ROTATION This, like the two techniques shown below, is intended to trigger orgasm when both partners are ready for it. Lying on her back, she tenses her buttocks, lifts and swivels her hips as she thrusts upwards, tightening her vaginal muscles on the downward movements.

MALE HIP ROTATION This is the same as the female hip rotation technique, only this time it is the man who lies on his back and tightens the muscles of his buttocks while lifting his hips and giving them a slight 'hula-hoop' movement as he thrusts upwards. The woman experiences a highly arousing, corkscrew-like sensation.

The slow and flowing movements of Tantric intercourse allow her to savour the sensations fully and without distraction

Tighten your anal muscles to make him exquisitely aware of your orgasmic contractions

REAR ENTRY The advantage of the man entering the woman from the rear is that he can easily reach her clitoris to stimulate her to orgasm with his fingers. His proximity to her anal muscles means that when she climaxes his penis will be particularly affected by the strength of her orgasmic contractions.

CHAPTER 20

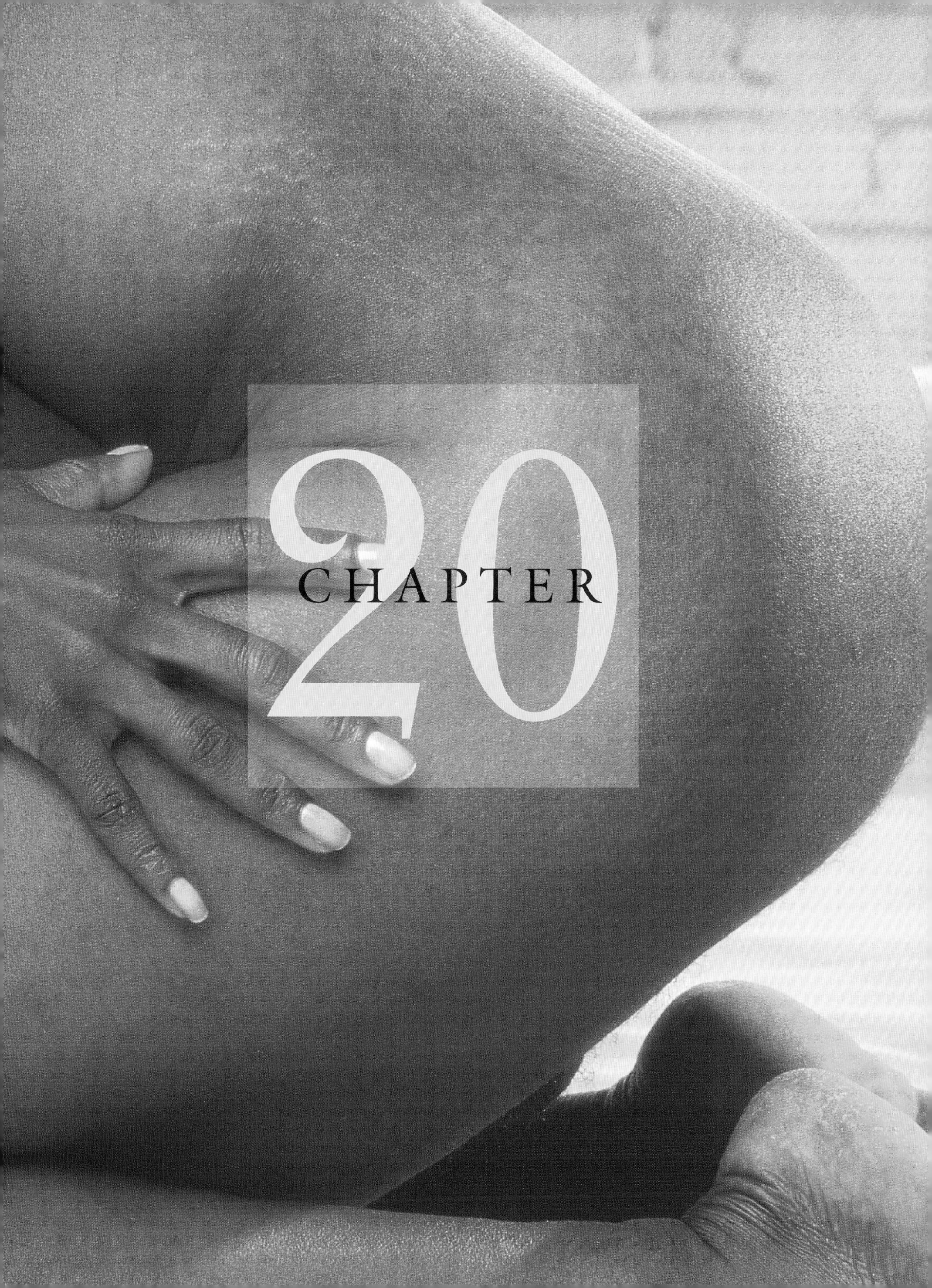

HOW CAN I HAVE MORE FUN IN BED?

"Enjoying sex isn't only about trying out new love positions. It is also about developing a sense of humour so that what goes on between the sheets stimulates your mind as well as your body."

AFFICIONADOS OF FENG SHUI may be fascinated to discover that the ancient Chinese didn't just re-arrange the furniture or the shape of the garden in order to get the 'chi' going. They focussed very particularly on the 'chi' generated between man and woman during the ultimate togetherness of sex.

Just in case there is anyone left out there who doesn't understand the concept of 'chi', it is, quite simply, a Far Eastern concept of energy. This energy or 'chi' lies everywhere. How we tap into it, or how we learn to live with it and around it, is presumed to affect our personal sense of well-being.

If the 'chi' of certain surroundings or certain actions is not taken into account, we won't feel so good. On the other hand, if we take it seriously and re-arrange our lives accordingly, life will feel great. Here then is a brief Feng Shui of sex.

CASE STUDY   *Tom & Yasuko*

Tom and Yasuko's bedtime experience was loving, varied and sensual. Yet each partner admitted to wanting more from love-making. Tom was a straight-forward lover, doing what came spontaneously. Yasuko, on the other hand, missed a thoughtfulness she had experienced with a previous lover.

Name:	TOM
Age:	24
Marital status:	LIVING TOGETHER
Occupation:	WEB DESIGNER

Tom was a broad, healthy and sportive individual, with an open manner, to whom women instantly felt they could relate. He took sex in a very relaxed way, enjoying what came spontaneously while not worrying too much about minor setbacks.

"I've been living with Yasuko for two years now," he said. "I adore her but I can see that she feels somehow sex should be more substantial. I'm willing to try anything new but feel at a loss to know exactly what. My Mom always says of me that I take my time to learn anything new, but that when I have managed it, I usually embrace it whole-heartedly.

"I value Yasuko, I truly want to keep her happy. She is very intelligent and I worry that if I can't sustain her interest she will move on to someone new."

Name:	YASUKO
Age:	26
Marital status:	LIVING TOGETHER
Occupation:	WEBSITE MANAGER

Yasuko had emigrated to the US from Japan at the age of 17 and had adapted to life in California very rapidly. At the age of 23 she emerged from a traditional Japanese marriage and since then had had two relationships with very modern young men. Now that she had lived with Tom for two years she was thinking in terms of long-term commitment. But she admitted to a small anxiety about the quality of their sex.

"Tom is a lovely person," Yasuko reveals. "He's what my mother used to call wonderful husband material. I've grown to love him. I never expected to do so because our life experience is very different. I've already been married once and there are times when Tom feels like an innocent baby compared with myself.

"My previous marriage ended because I got bored – my ex-husband was quite a dull man. Tom has much more going for him – what I particularly like is his willingness to learn and adapt. I think that is rare. But why can't he ever come up with any new ideas about sex? This bothers me."

THERAPIST'S ASSESSMENT

No-one can force a partner to grow a new imagination. But… it is possible to feed the imagination in such a way that new behaviour is stimulated. An example of this is when non-orgasmic women are taught to fantasize in order to assist climax. What Yasuko seemed to be asking for was that Tom should be taught how to develop new sexual ideas.

MENTAL RESTLESSNESS
But Yasuko also needed to look inside herself and question her need for novelty. Therapy revealed that this search for all things new was a major theme in her life and underlay most of her behaviour. So far Yasuko had concentrated on external possessions and had equipped a home with the most modern belongings. Was she in danger of seeing Tom as one of these possessions?

Nature had provided Yasuko with a good brain. She had graduated easily from college in spite of having to study in what was originally a foreign language to her. She was quick, intelligent and already so skilled at her management job that she had been offered a share option in the website that employed her.

DIFFERING TYPES OF INTELLIGENCE
Tom also possessed a good brain but worked more slowly. It wasn't that he couldn't understand new concepts but rather that he took longer to get round to them. One of Yasuko's needs therefore was to cultivate 1) an awareness of his different mental system and 2) a better tolerance of the difference in pace between the two of them.

FASTER IS NOT SUPERIOR
This difference in type of intelligence was especially relevant to sex. Yasuko learned that faster does not mean superior. It simply meant she worked to a different mental system. Yasuko remembered this principle at times when she felt impatient. Tom, needing some new ideas about sex to build on, took a closer look at the system of Yin and Yang. The thoughtful concepts this focuses on provided rich material for exploration, thought and fun.

SLOW EXCITEMENT
This couple were pleasantly surprised by how varied their sex life became. By building up sensuality under every inch of the skin, Yasuko in particular grew more turned on. Part of her excitement lay in delaying her climax through the slow application of touch.

My programme for
FENG SHUING YOUR SEX LIFE

A serious belief on the part of the ancient Chinese was that as well as providing pleasure, sex also acts as a healer. Healing power, it is thought, comes from Yin and Yang energy. These energies co-exist as equals inside the human body but should they be thrown out of kilter, the individual doesn't feel so good. It helps to understand just how 'chi' functions sensually.

Male PENILE 'CHI'

'Chi' systems differ considerably between men and women, according to the ancient Chinese. With men, 'chi' is considered to be focused on the penis, building up in four successive stages. These are known as the Four Signs of a Man.

SIGN ONE FIRM As the penis erects and becomes firm, a man's 'chi' moves from the kidney to the heart. When a man is stressed, tired or older this takes longer and thus the penis takes longer to grow strong.

SIGN TWO LARGE Next the 'chi' moves from the heart and begins circulating through the body's muscles. This means that, amongst other things, the man's penis expands in size. If this fails to happen or if it takes a great deal of time before it happens, it means that the man may be subject to strong emotions that are distracting him or a poor immune system.

SIGN THREE HARD Although a man may get an erection, it may only be a partial one because it does not get hard enough for intercourse. This means that the 'chi' has not yet reached the body's bones. Blocking the 'chi' may be a weak immune system, an illness or depression.

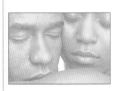

SIGN FOUR HOT When the penis is ready for intercourse it will be firm, large, hard and hot – literally hot to touch. Penile heat is reached when the 'chi' affects the man's inner spirit. If the penis is not hot it may be because the spirit is opposing the body. Incidentally, the ancient Chinese believed that this fourth stage means that the man is ready for sex – not that he should instantly climax.

Sexual Tao p218

Female WHOLE BODY 'CHI'

'Chi' and sexual excitement are irrevocably intermingled. As sexual 'chi' starts flowing through the body, men and women become increasingly turned on. The ancient Chinese thought women experience sexual 'chi' not just in their sex organs but in nine separate sites of the body. These are the Nine Sites of the Woman.

SITE ONE SKIN When a woman strokes and caresses and invites the male to do the same to her, her 'chi' is thought to be flowing through her skin and the flesh underneath.

SITE TWO BREATHING When the flow of 'chi' reaches the lungs the woman begins breathing harder and generating more saliva.

SITE THREE LIVER As the 'chi' expands throughout her body and reaches her liver, she presses her whole body against her partner's, thus generating a flow of 'chi' between the two of them.

SITE FOUR SPLEEN Next, as the 'chi' flows to her spleen she pulls him tightly to her and kisses him.

SITE FIVE BONE As the 'chi' bathes her bones with energy she strains her man harder to her and kisses him with great passion.

SITE SIX TENDONS Since the tendons are thought be one of the most powerful sources of energy, once the 'chi' reaches them her actions become aggressive to the point of even using her feet to hold her man hard against her.

SITE SEVEN HEART The ancient Chinese considered the heart to be responsible for emotion. Naturally once the 'chi' reaches the heart the woman becomes extremely moved; she may sigh, she may say words of love, she may kiss her man all over.

SITE EIGHT BLOOD Next the woman's blood is suffused with 'chi' and heats up. As a result she may pay special attention to her partner's penis. At the same time her skin takes on a rosy glow.

SITE NINE KIDNEY The kidney is believed to control the front Yin, which according to the ancients is situated at the front of the vagina, making it especially moist.

Couples CONTEMPORARY CHI

Modern sexology tells us that sexual response is far more alike between men and women than we ever previously suspected. Taking this into account, 'chi' probably does not affect males and females as differently as previously believed. Many males, given half a chance, revel in their woman's touch, feeling the sensuality that this evokes just as sensitively as their partner. Equally, many females seem to experience very similar 'chi' arousal on their labia and clitoris as do males on their penis and testicles.

Differences aside, what the old-fashioned concepts of male and female 'chi' tell us is that if sex does not seem to be instantly right, we should stop and think why this might be. The idea of 'chi' blockage is a useful one because it introduces the concept that emotional state can influence what happens physically in the body. In Yasuko's case, for example, it is possible that her mind was actually putting emotional blocks between her and her spontaneous sex partner Tom. Becoming really intimate with someone means opening up emotionally and for some wounded lovers, this can be just too frightening.

TOUCH TIPS

• If something doesn't feel right, stop, go back a step and relax. When you feel better, take a look at your emotions. Don't feel ashamed or embarrassed by your withdrawal. Use those feelings boldly. Bring them out and talk about them. If you don't share anxieties, you don't give your partner a chance to repair things.

• Use touch to facilitate any difficult conversation. Touch, provided it doesn't go too far too fast, is reassuring and according to the ancient Chinese is responsible for provoking an easy and rapid flow of 'chi'. So use as much touch as possible.

• The Chinese believe that for sexual touching to stimulate 'chi' successfully, it needs to be done in a particular order. It should, they say, begin on a woman's arms and neck, continue to her legs and breasts and end with her genitals.

• Before beginning touch, always ensure that your hands are clean and warm. This is because even a speck of dirt can feel like a sharp grain when drawn across the skin. And cold hands make the body tense so that touch is experienced as pain not pleasure. So wash your hands in hot water first.

SENSUAL TOUCH
We touch, with soft strokes, to show both tenderness and sensuality, while sitting with legs and genitals intertwined.

FENG SHUI SEX POSITIONS

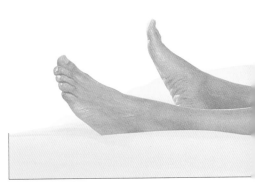

Sex, according to the ancient Chinese, is both a pleasurable and a healing activity that nourishes the spirit of both partners by promoting the flow of 'chi'. Sexologists in ancient China felt so strongly about this that they carefully designed a number of just-for-fun love positions that would ensure maximum well-being. The following poses, which were created 5000 years ago, will help individuals to best supply their partner's needs. Common to all these positions is that they will help a couple foster a sense of tenderness and care.

BAMBOO
The woman and the man stand face to face. The man inserts his penis and thrusts gently, embracing his partner. The Bamboo enables the man's penis to stimulate the front of his partner's vagina. Because the couple is standing, this position resembles two bamboo stalks.

PHOENIX AND CHICK
The woman sits on the end of the bed with her legs opened wide. The man stands or kneels in between his partner's legs, facing her. He inserts his penis and gently thrusts, while she rests her feet on his shoulders. In ancient China, the position was recommended for a large woman (phoenix) and a small man (chick).

GOAT AND A TREE
With her back to her partner, who is kneeling down, the woman lowers herself onto the man's lap and onto his penis. The woman then starts to move up and down. To help the movements, the man holds the woman's hips and lower legs close. The position is named after a goat scratching itself on a fallen tree.

APE HOLDS THE TREE
The man sits with his legs stretched out in front of him, slightly more than shoulder-width apart. The woman stands facing her partner, legs either side of his hips, and lowers herself onto his penis, holding his neck. The man can grasp her hips to help. This position was named after the resemblance to an ape holding a tree.

BUTTERFLY
The man lies on his back with his legs straight and apart. The woman faces the man and lowers herself into a sitting position on top of his hips. After inserting her partner's penis, she reaches behind her and grasps her partner's knees, which she uses to anchor herself. In this position the woman slowly rises and descends, using her legs to propel herself. With the woman moving on top of the man, the couple resembles a butterfly in flight.

The woman lowers herself onto her partner's hips

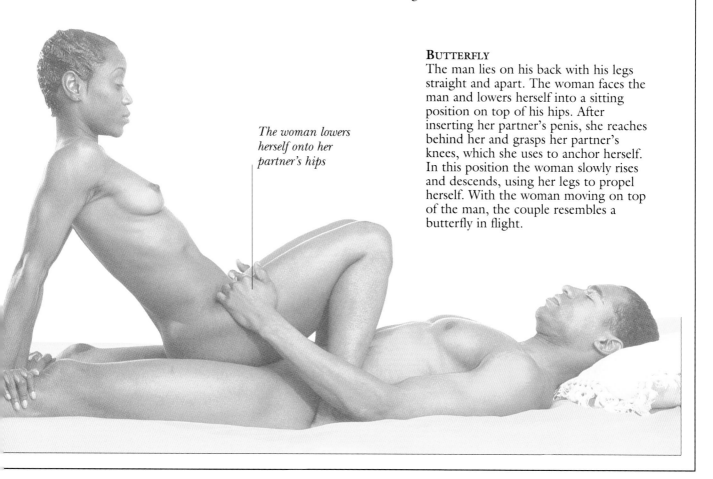

THE PATH OF SEXUAL TAO

The Ancient Chinese revelled in the vigour and ardour of young lovers. Instead of dismissing the sex activities of birds and beasts as diminishing the human spirit, they actually encouraged young lovers to look and learn from the natural behaviour of animals. The pure raw sensuality of the wild tiger or even the domestic donkey were to be sought after and embraced. The same 'chi' that flows through man and woman also flows through all of life and so, far from seeing creatures as objects to be disliked and dismissed, humans were taught to seek and channel the same vigorous energy.

SPRING DONKEY

With the woman kneeling down on her hands and knees, the man positions himself at the woman's hips; he grasps them and inserts his penis. The man should experiment with shallow and deep thrusts, trying faster and slower speeds. This position frees partners from having to support each other's body weight, while allowing the man to caress the woman's thighs, back and breasts. In China, donkeys often mate in spring, which is how this position got its name.

WHITE TIGER

The woman crouches forward, resting on her forearms, with her legs bent at the knees and held shoulder-width apart. The man then lies on top of her, using one hand to hold her neck while inserting his penis. His thrusts should be a combination of fast and slow. White Tiger was so named because in this position the man moves like a male white tiger.

The man can massage the sensual nerves at the base of his woman's neck as he thrusts

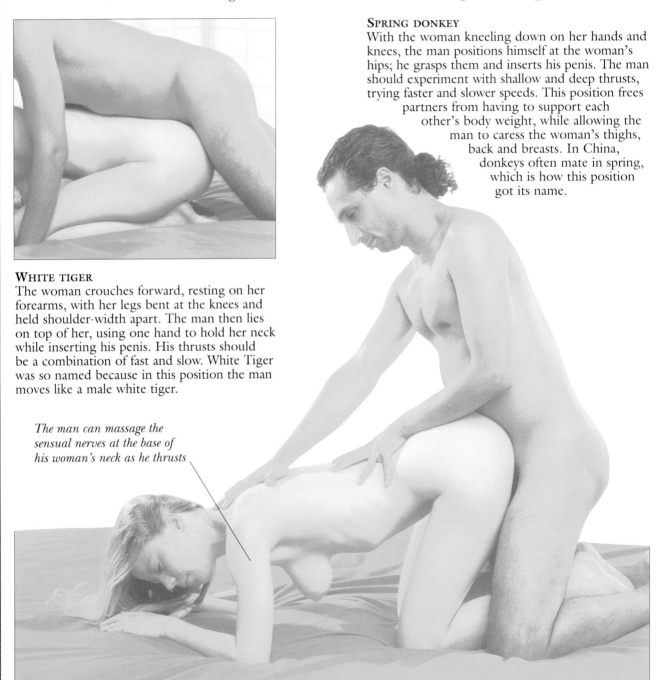

JADE JOINT

The woman lies on her back, bending her legs at the knee and pulling them up to hip level. The man kneels below the woman's hips and inserts his penis. This position enables the man's penis to touch the back of the woman's vagina, and is so named because the couple resemble a jade joint.

DRAGON TURN

The woman lies on her back with her legs bent at the knees and held against her chest. She holds her feet away from her body. Facing the woman, the man kneels below her hips. Holding her tight, the man inserts his penis, alternating between deep and shallow thrusts. The Dragon Turn is so named because the Chinese believe it resembles the mythical creature, which has long limbs and a flexible body.

HORSE CROSS FEET

The woman lies on her back and bends her left leg at the knee. The man faces the woman and kneels below her hips. Once he is in place, he grasps her neck with his left hand, clasps her left leg with his right hand and inserts his penis. The man will thrust fast. Because the woman has one leg bent, some think that the couple performing this position resembles a running horse.

The man clasps the woman's left leg and grasps her neck

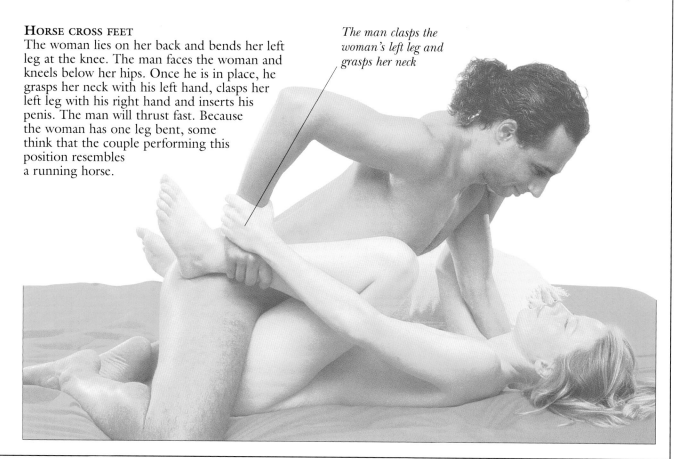

SEX AS HIGH ART

The fact that sex was seen as healing and pleasurable did not prevent it from also being used as a version of art. The Chinese thought that sex at its best might become a form of beautiful display. In the dance between male body and female form, intricate shapes are formed, by the intertwining of sinuous limbs and the stretch and shudder of rhythmic movement. Out of this creative undulation might flow the shapes and poses of birds and beasts in movement. Capturing movement is never easy on any canvas but here is one that provides a live display of art in action.

MANDARIN DUCK
The woman lies on her back with her left leg bent and her right leg straight. The man then kneels forward on his right leg with his left leg out behind. He tucks her left leg over his right thigh and inserts his penis. Because they mate for life, mandarin ducks are considered the Chinese lovebirds.

TWO FLYING BIRDS
The woman lies on her back. Facing her, the man lowers himself over his partner, supporting himself with his hands and knees. The man inserts his penis, then the woman wraps her legs over and around the man's buttocks, crossing her feet. The position is called Two Flying Birds because some believe that this is what it resembles.

CICADA
The woman lies face down, raising her hips slightly above the bed. The man, also face down, lowers himself above her, supporting his weight with his elbows and feet. He penetrates her and gently thrusts, being careful to keep the movements shallow. Though the woman's movements are restricted, she still can move her hips to coordinate with the man's movements. The movement of both partners' legs resembles the beating wings of two mating cicadas.

The man must take care not to crush his partner during this gentle stroke

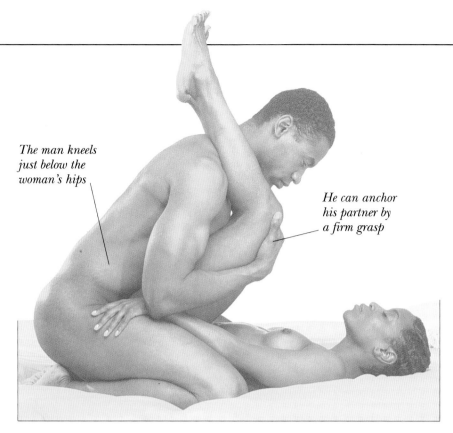

The man kneels just below the woman's hips

He can anchor his partner by a firm grasp

WILD HORSE JUMP

The woman lies on her back. The man faces the woman and kneels below her hips. Once the man is in place, the woman raises her legs and rests her ankles on his shoulders. The woman can hold her hand over the bed post or brace her palm against the wall or headboard to help hold her body steady. The man then holds the woman's thighs, inserts his penis and thrusts hard and fast. With the Wild Horse Jump, the penis is in contact with the back of the vagina. When the woman moves in this position, it almost appears as if she is bucking like a wild horse.

TWO FISH

The couple lies side by side, facing each other. The woman wraps one leg around the man's hip. He inserts his penis, then holds onto her raised leg. Since the length of the man's penis and the depth of the woman's vagina affect each partner's sexual sensations, the man should experiment with both shallow and deep thrusts until finding a type of thrust that suits both individuals. This position is thought to resemble two flounder fish swimming side by side.

After sex, the couple can rest and relax

CHAPTER 21

HOW CAN I GET OVER SEXUAL REJECTION?

"One of the most important steps in getting over sexual rejection is to regain confidence in your own sexuality."

REJECTION, whether it happens during the course of a relationship or when one is breaking up, is never easy to cope with. It can lead, on the part of the one who is rejected, to feelings of inadequacy and worthlessness, and can make them so afraid of further rejection that they find it hard to form new relationships.

When sexual rejection happens during a relationship, it may be because of straightforward sexual incompatibility or it may be that one partner rejects the other for reasons not directly connected with sex. For instance, some people reject their partners as a method of punishing them for some real or imagined offence, while others grow to dislike their partners so much that the idea of having regular sex with them becomes unthinkable.

Whatever the reason for it, sexual rejection can be hard to handle, but if it happens to you there are positive steps that you can take to help you get over it and to restore your sexual self-confidence.

CASE STUDY *Diana*

Diana's husband, Monty, to whom she had been married for ten years, had left her for another woman. During their marriage he had often criticized her sexual performance, and when she came to see me she was so lacking in sexual self-confidence that it was holding her back from forming new relationships.

Name: DIANA

Age: 37

Marital status: SEPARATED

Occupation: CHEMIST

Diana was a perfectionist, who ran her home and her job immaculately; she had no children, felt very wounded by Monty's rejection of her and, although longing for a new relationship, was scared of risking her emotions again.

"Every time I think about dating a new man, I feel terrified," she confessed. "Even though I keep telling myself this can't be the case, I know I must be a complete failure in bed. Monty spent a lot of time telling me how awful I was. How does one ever risk finding out what it's like with someone else when the upshot might be to face that again?

"I gave myself heart and soul to Monty, did everything for him and it was just never good enough. And apart from everything else, I still care about him. I actually still fancy him — God knows how or why. I can't imagine being able to go to bed with anyone else.

"Monty used to accuse me, among other things, of being very passive in bed, and it's true that I was passive with him. But I've often fantasized about doing all kinds of things to a man I've really fancied. I honestly think Monty was so critical he frightened me from taking any initiative. I may not be very versatile in bed but I've always enjoyed sex. Also, I've always had the sneaking suspicion that I might be better at sex with someone who genuinely made me feel good. No-one's ever done that. How do I ever let go with someone new after all this? And what do I do with my sex drive?"

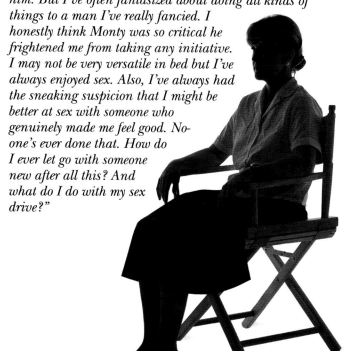

THERAPIST'S ASSESSMENT

There were two components to Diana's problem: her feelings of rejection and sexual inadequacy, and her perfectionism. Perfectionists who set themselves impossible targets make failure unavoidable, and it is always worth looking into a perfectionist's background and working out where that need for perfection comes from. Inevitably, it turns out to be the result of trying, in childhood, to please a demanding parent for whom the best was never enough.

CONTINUING PATTERN
Even when we leave home the pattern of trying to please continues, transferred from parent to teacher, lover or boss. Sometimes we may be lucky and feel rewarded by someone who appreciates what we are doing. In this way, we grow to relax and to understand that perfectionism is not vital. More often than not, though, we will have unconsciously picked a partner who feeds into these insecurities and plays on them, probably because they feel familiar, rather like that impossible parent we tried so hard to please.

COUNSELLING AND ASSERTIVENESS
Counselling would help Diana to make connections with her belief system in the present and understand how it linked with her childhood. And simple assertiveness (see page 72) would enable her to do what she really felt like doing, without feeling guilty about it, rather than blindly following early patterns.

SEXUAL SELF-KNOWLEDGE
Sexually, Diana needed to find out about herself. She had never masturbated, even as a child, and had only ever experienced orgasm through intercourse. Possessing a solid background of knowledge about her own sexual responses and sexual interests would give her increased confidence so that when she came next time to a new relationship, she would have more, sexually, to feed into a new love affair.

SEXUAL SELF-PLEASURING
More importantly, through a self-pleasuring routine (see page 226), she could find out how it is possible to be a highly sexual individual without relying on a partner. Of course, masturbation has different emotional dimensions to it than intercourse, but it can be a powerfully arousing and satisfactory experience in its own right.

My programme for FEMALE SELF-PLEASURING

Women are brought up and educated to look after others. They are taught to be support systems: mothers, secretaries and nurses. With all that caring to do, it can often be difficult for a woman to remember that she deserves to give herself time, too. This self-pleasuring programme for women is therefore aimed at helping you to put a little self-indulgent luxury back into your life. Details of a similar self-pleasuring programme for men are given on pages 228-229.

Stage THE RAG DOLL EXERCISE

Prepare your surroundings so that they are warm, private and comfortable. Give yourself at least an hour. Enjoy a warm bath, with luxury soaps and sweet smelling bath oils. (If you are going to use massage oil for the final stage of this programme, float the bottle in the bathwater so that it warms up.) Then dry yourself in warm, fluffy towels and do the rag doll exercise to help you relax.

DEEP BREATHING You do the rag doll exercise sitting upright in a comfortable armchair. Breathe deeply, and once you are comfortable with a breathing rhythm, relax your body so that slowly but surely you let it slump over until, finally, you look as limp as a rag doll.

RELEASE TENSION As you slump there limply in the armchair, explore your body for tense spots. If you find any, deliberately tense and relax them until you have eliminated all

the muscular tension from your body and you truly feel as though you are made of floppy material. When you have stayed relaxed in that position for at least five minutes, slowly raise first your torso and then your head again, starting from the waist and leaving the head to roll back up into place last.

Stage THE PELVIC LIFT

The pelvic lift is a bioenergetic exercise that enables you to feel energy flow in your thighs and pelvis. It is also a soothing exercise for the relief of tired backs.

Lying on your back, draw your knees up so that your feet are squarely on the floor. Then put your arms along your sides, palms flat down on the floor. Push your abdomen upwards and arch your back so that your buttocks are high off the ground. Your body's weight should be supported almost entirely by your shoulders and feet so that you are actually

THE PELVIC LIFT This exercise enables you to feel energy flow in your thighs and pelvis. It is also soothing for tired backs.

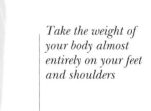

Take the weight of your body almost entirely on your feet and shoulders

resting on your shoulders. Hold this position for a couple of minutes, and then let your body gently down on to the floor again. Lie there on your back for a couple of minutes or so, peacefully relaxing, and then do the squatting exercise.

Stage — THE SQUATTING EXERCISE

Squat down Australian bush fashion, but with your arms inside your legs and your feet flat on the floor. It isn't easy to maintain your balance doing this, but after a little practice it becomes much easier.

GENITAL RELAXATION The object of the squatting exercise is to open up your genitals and relax them. Breathe deeply, and as you do so imagine that the breathing is coming from your genitals. Continue for three minutes, then lie on your bed and relax for a minute or two before giving your body and genitals a sensual massage.

SQUATTING EXERCISE
The object of the squatting exercise, which becomes much easier to do after a little practice, is to open up your genitals and relax them.

If you find it difficult to balance, put a book under your heels to give support

Stage — SELF-MASSAGE

Begin your sensual self-massage, using warm massage oil if you want your hands to feel especially slippery and sensuous, by lying on your back and caressing your arms, shoulders and thighs. Then run your fingers and hands over your more erogenous zones, such as your breasts, before turning your attention to your genitals, sliding your fingers into and around your vagina and stimulating your clitoris.

Self-stimu-lation p232

FURTHER SESSIONS Try to treat yourself to further self-pleasuring sessions at regular intervals. Use these hours of privacy to escape from the pressures of everyday life and to do absolutely anything you want to, provided that it pleases only you — one woman I know of chose to spend her sessions lying naked on a sheepskin rug in front of a roaring fire, listening to lyrical music through headphones while reading an exciting novel.

FEMALE MASTURBATION

Many women use masturbation as a regular and enjoyable part of their sexual activities, but others feel guilty about doing it — usually because they have been told, wrongly, that masturbation is unhealthy or sinful.

• Masturbation, and the urge to masturbate, are now known to be completely natural urges in both men and women. And there is no truth in the old but persistent myth that female masturbation leads to concupiscence (unbridled lust) or to nymphomania

• That story may have arisen because a woman with a high sex urge is more likely than others to masturbate and to be sexually active, and in less enlightened times such behaviour would have made her the target of much sexual innuendo and slander

• Most women who masturbate regularly use their understanding of masturbation to boost their love lives. If you know you are capable of orgasm, you don't let yourself get put down easily by a partner who is a poor lover, and if you love someone who is inexperienced, you can help him by letting him know what turns you on

• And you can guess intuitively, from your own knowledge of turn-on, what might appeal to others, although there can be some discrepancy between the sexes here

My programme for
MALE SELF-PLEASURING

The basis of the self-pleasuring concept is to learn how to spend time on yourself that is purely for the purpose of pleasure. For those men brought up to believe you should always look out for others first, this can be surprisingly difficult to practise, but self-pleasuring is worth the effort not only for the enjoyment it gives you, but also because it enables you to know your own sexual response and allows you to be a fully-functioning sexual being regardless of whether or not you have a partner. Details of a self-pleasuring programme for women are given on pages 226-227.

Stage RELAXATION

Prepare your surroundings so that they are warm, private and comfortable. Give yourself at least an hour. Enjoy a warm, relaxing bath, taking your time over sensitively soaping and rubbing yourself. If you are going to use massage oil to make your hands feel slippery and sensuous in the final stage of this programme, float the bottle in the bathwater now so that it warms up.

TENSE-AND-RELAX After the bath, make yourself comfortable on a towel on the floor of a warm private room and carry out the tense-and-relax relaxation exercise (page 45).

Stage GROUNDING

Grounding is a bioenergetic exercise that lets you feel in touch with the earth and helps you to sense the energy that flows through both the ground and you. It enables you to feel the power in your body, in particular in your upper legs and pelvis.

BREATH CONTROL Stand with your legs 20 centimetres (8 inches) apart and your knees slightly bent, fists pressing into your back just above your waist. On an in-breath let your head fall back, and at the same time press your heels firmly down into the ground (the floor).

Hold this position for as long as you can bear, breathing regularly but lightly as you do so. When the time comes when you can no longer maintain the position and you have to stand upright, do so on an out-breath.

Once you are standing upright again, pause for a very brief rest and then let the upper half of your body flop over forwards so that the tips of your hands are reaching down and nearly touching the ground, but still keep those heels grounded. After a couple of minutes, stand upright again and relax.

You should, after a couple of grounding sessions, start to feel a vibration in the tops of your legs. Once you get this feeling of vibration, you know that the exercise has worked — the energy flow has been released.

MALE MASTURBATION

Contrary to Victorian propaganda, masturbation does not make you blind, deaf, give you the flu, send you mad or kill you. The notion that each teaspoonful of lost semen weakens you to the equivalent of a pint of blood lost is totally without foundation. Masturbation is a natural and harmless expression of sexuality.

• The fear about masturbation most often voiced to sex therapists is: "If I masturbate, will I get stuck in a pattern of sexual response that won't work when it comes to intercourse?" The truthful answer is that a few people do get stuck because they are inhibited about disclosing their masturbatory activities to a partner, and therefore can never break emotional barriers, which would allow them to relax and climax

• What about addiction, the other masturbation fear? The only people who are truly addicted to masturbation — they can't leave themselves alone, day or night — are seriously disturbed men and women who are suffering from a form of mental illness and who demonstrate this with unacceptably overt self-stimulation. Masturbation is not the cause here, but the effect

Stage   PELVIC CIRCLING

This bioenergetic exercise helps you to feel energy in your genitals. While standing, move your hips in a circular fashion as if you were hula-hooping. Move your hips first to the right and then to the left, and then eventually weave them in a figure-of-eight shape. Breathe evenly throughout the exercise.

    When you have finished the exercise, lie down on your bed and allow yourself to relax for a minute or two before giving your body and genitals a sensual massage.

Stage   SELF-MASSAGE

Male stimulation p230

Begin your sensual self-massage, using warm massage oil to make your hands feel especially sensuous, by lying on your back and running your hands and fingers over your arms, shoulders and thighs, including erogenous zones such as your nipples. Then turn your attention to the stimulation of your genitals. At further sessions do anything you want, provided it pleases only you — self-stimulation, reading, watching TV, anything.

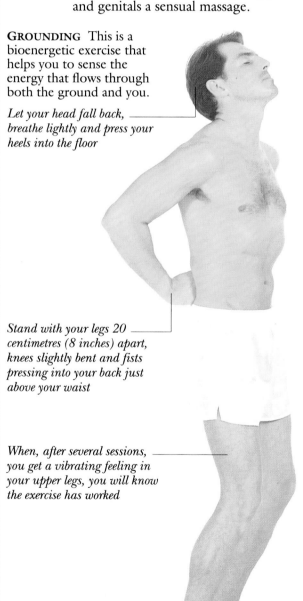

GROUNDING This is a bioenergetic exercise that helps you to sense the energy that flows through both the ground and you.

Let your head fall back, breathe lightly and press your heels into the floor

Stand with your legs 20 centimetres (8 inches) apart, knees slightly bent and fists pressing into your back just above your waist

When, after several sessions, you get a vibrating feeling in your upper legs, you will know the exercise has worked

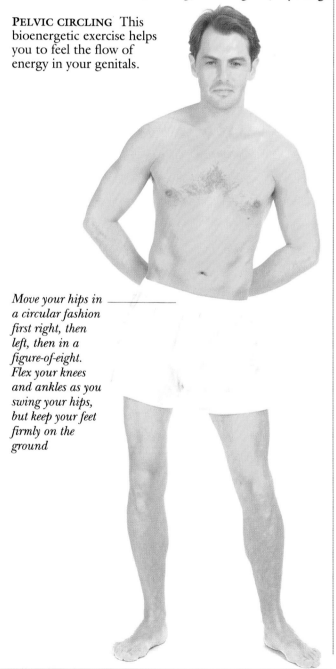

PELVIC CIRCLING This bioenergetic exercise helps you to feel the flow of energy in your genitals.

Move your hips in a circular fashion first right, then left, then in a figure-of-eight. Flex your knees and ankles as you swing your hips, but keep your feet firmly on the ground

MALE SELF-STIMULATION

The knowledge of your own body and its sexual responses that self-stimulation teaches you can form the basis of a good sexual relationship with your partner. More importantly, self-stimulation can provide you with a solid sexual foundation upon which you can build up your overall feeling of self-confidence. It can thus help to establish you, in your own eyes, as someone of value.

COMFORT AND PRIVACY
Ensure that you have total privacy in a warm bedroom. Lie on the bed and make yourself comfortable.

Relax before you begin, to clear your mind of other thoughts

Undress completely and adopt any position that feels comfortable

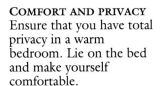

LIGHT TOUCHING Begin by running your hands and fingers lightly over your body, arms and thighs, but not your genitals.

Use massage oil to make your hands feel slippery and sensuous

EROGENOUS ZONES
Stimulate your most sensitive spots, including the area around your genitals. Indulge in sexual fantasy to help arouse yourself.

Experiment with different types of touching and stroking

Let your mind wander to scenarios that excite you

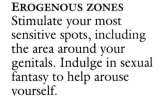

GENITAL STIMULATION Begin to masturbate, either by using your hands or by rhythmically thrusting your penis against the bed.

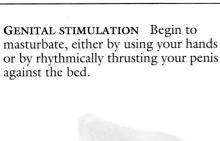

If you are masturbating face-down, use a pillow to support your head

PELVIC MOVEMENT As you masturbate by hand or by rubbing yourself against the bed, stroke your testicles and perineum and make pelvic thrusts.

For extra sensation, hold your penis as you thrust against the bed

Squeeze your legs together rhythmically to increase the sensation

LET YOURSELF GO Thrust your pelvis up and down and from side to side, making your movements rhythmical. As your feelings grow in intensity, let your breathing become heavier and don't hesitate to moan or shout if you feel like doing so.

Let your hand linger against your limp member. Don't be in a hurry to clean yourself up

If you don't normally express yourself vocally, shout as loud as you can when you reach orgasm

FEMALE SELF-STIMULATION

Self-stimulation enables you to explore your body and gain detailed knowledge of your own sexual responses, knowledge that you can use as the basis of a good sexual relationship with your partner. In addition, by providing you with a solid, reliable sexual foundation upon which you can build up your self-confidence, self-stimulation can help to make you feel good about yourself.

COMFORT AND PRIVACY
Ensure that you have an hour of total privacy in a warm bedroom, and lock the door if necessary. Lie on the bed and make yourself comfortable.

Relax for a while before you begin, to clear your mind of other thoughts

Make sure you are comfortable with room to move about

LIGHT CARESSES Begin by running your hands and brushing your fingers lightly over your shoulders, arms, body and thighs, but do not touch your genitals.

Use massage oil to make your hands feel more slippery and sensuous

EROGENOUS ZONES
Stimulate your most sensitive spots, including your breasts and nipples but not your genitals. Indulge in sexual fantasy to help arouse yourself.

Experiment with different types of touching, stroking and fondling

Use fantasies if they help to stimulate you

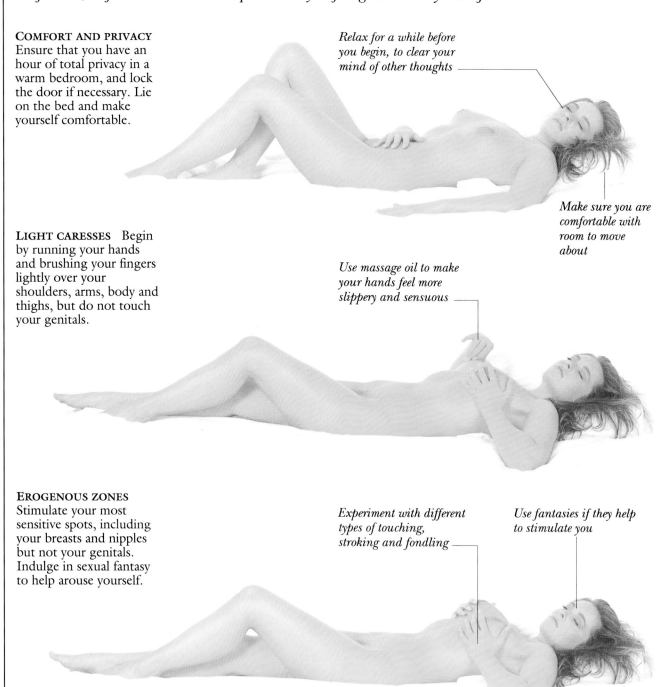

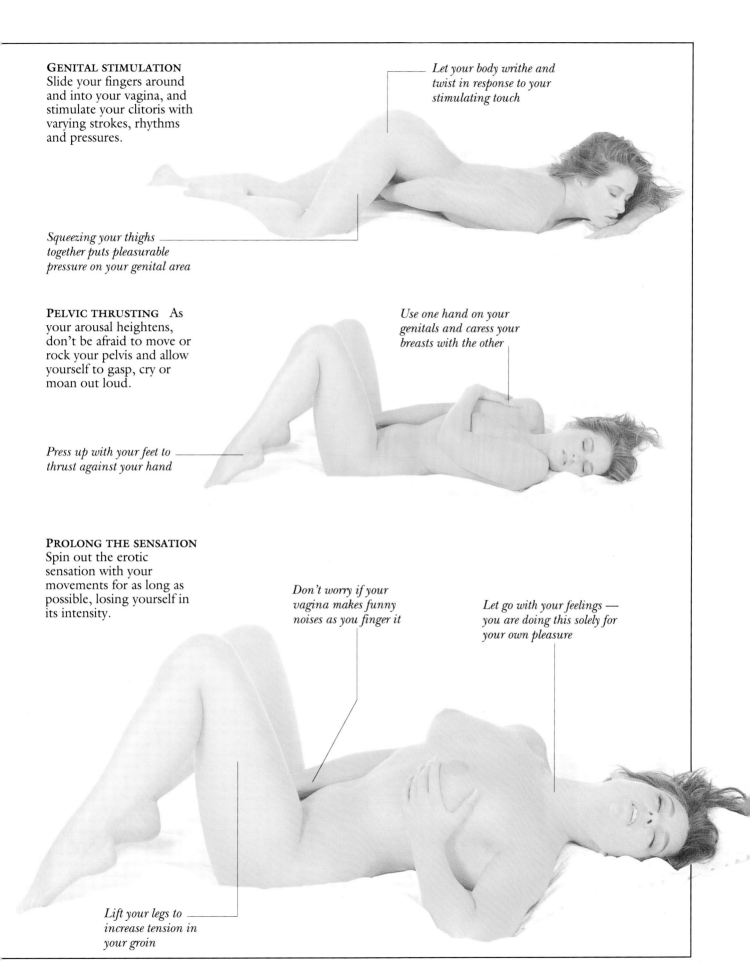

GENITAL STIMULATION
Slide your fingers around and into your vagina, and stimulate your clitoris with varying strokes, rhythms and pressures.

Let your body writhe and twist in response to your stimulating touch

Squeezing your thighs together puts pleasurable pressure on your genital area

PELVIC THRUSTING As your arousal heightens, don't be afraid to move or rock your pelvis and allow yourself to gasp, cry or moan out loud.

Use one hand on your genitals and caress your breasts with the other

Press up with your feet to thrust against your hand

PROLONG THE SENSATION
Spin out the erotic sensation with your movements for as long as possible, losing yourself in its intensity.

Don't worry if your vagina makes funny noises as you finger it

Let go with your feelings — you are doing this solely for your own pleasure

Lift your legs to increase tension in your groin

CHAPTER 22

USING

SEX

AIDS

"One man was so intrigued by his partner's use of a vibrator to give herself a climax that he learned to use it on her during intercourse so that she came with him inside her."

WE ARE NOT brought up to think of vibrators as natural additions to the act of sex, mainly because these objects are patently artificial. Yet vibrators, used sensitively, provide women with more stimulation than either penis or fingers and act as a catalyst to the elusive orgasm.

Vibrators are especially useful to women who suffer from what is called 'automatic switch-off': because of unconscious anxiety during intercourse, their minds are distracted from sex into thinking negative thoughts that prevent climax. They may be able to become very sexually excited and reach a level — which Masters and Johnson aptly called the 'plateau phase' — from where, if they could relax mentally, they could take off into the heights of climax. But sometimes, that unconscious anxiety holds them back.

In many such cases, all that the woman needs to overcome this anxiety and have an uninhibited climax is more stimulation, and the use of a vibrator will often provide her with that.

CASE STUDY *Pauline*

Pauline and her husband had an excellent relationship and they both enjoyed sex. But Pauline rarely climaxed and she had resorted to faking orgasms so as not to disappoint her partner, Laurie, and make him feel inadequate as a lover. This strategy of faking orgasms was effective in that it encouraged Laurie's self-confidence and his belief that he was a good lover, but as time went by Pauline began to feel increasingly dissatisfied at her own lack of real orgasms.

Name: PAULINE
Age: 28
Marital status: MARRIED
Occupation: PHYSIOTHERAPIST

Pauline, married to Laurie, a welfare officer, was sexily dressed in a low-cut blouse and very vivacious. She and her husband had been married for three years, had no children and were very open with each other about sexual matters.

"Laurie and I make love often," she told me. "He makes me feel very sexy. But I think I've only ever come with him twice, and each time the orgasm has been very faint. Laurie buys sex manuals and we read them together. I've taught myself to masturbate from them and I get very turned on by some of the 'naughty' stories in them. But although masturbation feels nice, I don't climax from it.

"Laurie has been keen for me to get help with this. He's very supportive. He hasn't had other lovers since we've been together, but he did once help me go to bed with a woman I fancied. He took her partner out drinking so that I could go to bed with her. It was very exciting. In fact, we made love on more than one occasion. I still didn't come, though.

"Laurie and I are very loving and cuddly with each other. When we're in bed together, sometimes I know I'm near to orgasm. But then part of me seems to turn off at that realization. I find it hard to relax because I'm being watched by Laurie. That turns me off. I'm frightened Laurie is going to be so upset by my not climaxing that in the end we'll split up. I love him a great deal. I don't want that to happen.

"I have to confess that I do fake orgasm with Laurie sometimes. I don't do this very often. Maybe one in four or five lovemaking sessions. I don't want him to feel he's not a success in bed. It's important for him to think of himself as a good lover. And quite a lot of the time I feel satisfied by him coming. He's had such obvious pleasure from his climax and he's been so loving to me as a result of it, that I've felt a pleasure and satisfaction through him even though I myself don't technically come. But recently that hasn't been enough for me."

THERAPIST'S ASSESSMENT

What Pauline described were several common problems that get in the way of sexual enjoyment for many people. Always feeling that Laurie was watching her meant that she had performance fears. When you are focusing on your performance there isn't space left in your brain to focus on heightened sensations. She needed to learn how to cut out her over-awareness of Laurie and focus instead on herself.

FAKING ORGASM
Faking orgasm may sometimes be expedient for the reasons Pauline outlined. But if you do it too often, it produces not only the negative effect of never allowing you to find out how to climax through intercourse but it actually teaches your partner the wrong methods of getting you to orgasm.

Naturally, if he thinks a particular method of lovemaking works well for you he's likely to carry on using it, thereby compounding the problem. Having the courage to confess sometimes that things aren't working quite right and to ask for his patience and for different stimulation is the road to opening up trust and of course to orgasm. This is where vibrators can help. Sometimes, what is needed in order to get to orgasm is quite simply more stimulation. And a vibrator can provide that when a penis and fingers are flagging. But raising the subject with your partner, and persuading him to let using a vibrator become a regular part of your lovemaking, can often be a difficult move to make.

USING A VIBRATOR
I recommended that Pauline carry out the self-pleasuring programme (see page 226) over a period of about four weeks, incorporating vibrator use towards the end of that time. I also suggested that she practice assertion exercises (see page 72) so that she could pluck up enough courage to ask Laurie if they might include use of the vibrator in their lovemaking (see page 238) Use of the vibrator, plus learning to focus on some especially sexual thoughts (see page 136 on sexual fantasies), helped Pauline to overcome her performance fears and reach orgasm.

My programme for
INTRODUCING SEX AIDS

The answer to the question "Why use sex aids?" is "Why not?" They are fun to use, and sex should, as often as possible, be fun. It doesn't have to always be heavy, or deeply romantic or full of spiritual meaning. Sometimes it can be wonderful when it's just 'messing about'. And the great advantage of sex aids is that you can use them privately on your own to assist your light-hearted experience of self-pleasuring, as well as use them on an inventive and playful partner.

Sex aids are not a recent invention: they have been around for at least the last 2500 years. The ancient Egyptians used dildos, and a Greek vase of the 5th century BC shows a woman putting one enormous dildo into her mouth while a second one penetrates her vagina. The Romans made candles designed to look like huge penises, and ancient Chinese scripts tell of the custom of binding the base of the penis with silk, a method of retaining erection (an early cock ring).

The Chinese 'hedgehog' was a circle of fine feathers, bound on to a silver ring that fitted over the penis. This enabled the lucky woman in question to be tickled to orgasm. Even the idea of a vibrator probably had its origin in the 19th century when mill girls, leaning against the vibrating handles of the mill machinery, discovered an unexpected work bonus.

Sex aid prediction for the future is the sex robot. It will be programmed to overcome any sex problem — you will simply plug yourself in to it and the machine will do the rest. (Remember Woody Allen and the 'Orgasmatron' in *Sleeper*?)

Stage 1 FIND OUT WHAT'S AVAILABLE

Perusal of any sex aid catalogue (available from sex aid shops or by mail order through advertisements in sex magazines) will show a plethora of dildos, vibrators, cock rings, play balls, fruit-flavoured massage oils, inflatable plastic dolls and other masturbation aids, and usually a selection of harmless bondage items such as silken cords, blindfolds and handcuffs. These items are relatively inexpensive and, in terms of the endless hours of enjoyment they can provide, they are generally good value for money.

DILDOS AND VIBRATORS There are any number of dildos designed in varied shapes and sizes, including the double-headed dildos used by lesbian couples. The vibrator is a modern variation of the dildo and is undoubtedly the most successful sex aid ever invented.

There are vibrators that simply vibrate, and there are multi-speed ones that vary in their speed of vibration from slow to very fast. There are soft rubber ones that twist and undulate, and double ones intended for vagina and anus, with a special attachment for the clitoris, that both twist and vibrate.

There are small, slim anal vibrators with a safeguard across the top to prevent them disappearing at an inappropriate moment. There are small cigarette-shaped vibrators designed solely for intense clitoral stimulation, and there are pink vibrating eggs which can be inserted into the vagina and switched on as you type your masterpiece.

COCK RINGS AND PLAY BALLS Cock rings are rings designed to fit closely around the base of the penis, so that the blood flow of erection is trapped inside the penis for as long as possible, should it show signs of wanting to leak away. Play balls are small weighted balls for women to slip inside their vaginas, where they roll around and produce erotic sensations. The ancient Japanese were the first to use these, and Japanese women would swing in their hammocks enjoying the turn-on.

OILS, DOLLS AND BONDAGE Fruit-flavoured massage oils are specially manufactured to make oral sex tasty, and plastic inflatable dolls are designed for men who want to pretend they are making love to a partner when one is not available. There are versions of these which can be filled with hot water while, at the small end of the scale, there are rubber labia and vaginas which meet the boast of being 'the easiest lay in the world' since they can be carried around in a pocket and produced anywhere. The items of bondage equipment speak for themselves.

Despite the variety of aids now on the market, though, a vibrator is probably the best choice for a couple.

Stage 2 CHOOSING A VIBRATOR

There are two principal sorts of vibrator: those that are battery operated and those that are mains operated. The cigar-shaped battery vibrators with varying speeds of vibration are the most convenient. You don't need a great variety of heads to make their stimulation work successfully, but you do need a suitable speed of vibration.

VIBRATOR POWER English research has shown that the optimum vibration speed for facilitating a climax is 80 cycles per second. Some women need such intense stimulation, which is almost impossible to obtain by hand, and this greater frequency of vibration is best obtained on the expensive mains-operated Japanese vibrators.

If you are using a battery-powered vibrator, invest in the long-life alkaline batteries, since although these are more expensive than the standard carbon type they are more powerful and last longer. Vibrator batteries lose power surprisingly quickly, and often, when a woman thinks she has lost the facility of climaxing when using her vibrator, it turns out that the batteries have run down and so the vibrator is running at well below its proper speed.

Stage 3 USING A VIBRATOR

Vibrators are a useful means of ensuring that some women climax who might otherwise never manage it. But they are also a means of enjoying wonderful clitoral sensation without having to rely on a partner. If there is a partner in your life, it is easy to include a use of a vibrator in masturbation and loveplay and to slip it between your bodies, focused on that strategic point, during intercourse.

Mutual masturbation p106

What many people forget, or perhaps never knew, is that men also enjoy the sensation of vibration. There are circular vibrators designed to slip over the penis and rest at the base, capable of bringing the man to climax too.

VIBRATORS AND LOVEMAKING At a warm and loving moment during lovemaking, try using a warmed-up vibrator on each other's body. Take turns at running it over each other's shoulders, neck, chest and breasts, down the sides of the body, and around the abdomen and buttocks. Dart it in and out of the inner thighs, which for most people are sensitive erogenous zones. Explore and probe the vagina with it, and press it very gently in among the folds of the testicles and then around the base of the penis.

INTENSE SENSATIONS The areas that produce the most intense sensations when stimulated by a vibrator are for a woman, the clitoris, and for a man, the frenulum of the penis. The rim of the anus, for both men and women, is another good spot to stimulate, and many men get great pleasure from stimulation of the prostate, inside the anus.

VIBRATORS Vibrators are one of the most popular of all sex aids, and can be used by both men and women, alone or together.

CHAPTER 23

HIS SEX ORGANS

In terms of loveplay and sexual intercourse, the most important single part of a man's genitals is undoubtedly his penis. However, the common belief that a man's virility and his effectiveness as a sexual partner depend on the size of his erect penis is totally misguided — what really counts is the skill and consideration with which he makes love to his partner.

MALE GENITALS The male genitals or sex organs are partly external and partly internal. The external organs are the penis and the scrotum (which contains the testicles, epididymis and vas deferens) and the internal organs include the prostate gland and the seminal vesicles. During erection, an intricate network of vessels within the penis fills with blood, causing it to swell and stiffen. The urethra, a tube running right through the length of the penis, discharges urine from the bladder and also carries the seminal fluid during ejaculation.

VAS DEFERENS Each vas deferens (there are two) carries sperm from the epididymis to the seminal vesicle ducts, where it is mixed with seminal fluid for ejaculation.

SEMINAL VESICLE The two seminal vesicles (one each side of the bladder) produce most of the seminal fluid discharged during ejaculation.

Anus

PROSTATE GLAND Within the prostate gland, which is situated below the neck of the bladder, ducts from the seminal vesicles join the urethra. Manual stimulation of the gland creates intense arousal.

GLANS The glans, the head of the penis, is rich in nerve endings which make it very sensitive to touch.

FRENULUM The highly sensitive frenulum is a small fold of skin between the glans and the shaft.

SHAFT The ridge along the underside of the penis shaft is often very sensitive to touch and stroking.

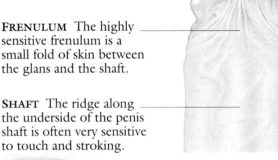

Bladder

Pubic bone

Penis

Urethra

Epididymis

Glans

Foreskin

TESTICLES The testicles (or testes) produce sperm and the male sex hormone testosterone. Sperm, after production, is stored in the epididymis, a long, extensively-coiled duct.

SCROTUM The scrotum has two parts. Each contains one of the testicles, suspended by a spermatic cord containing the vas deferens, blood vessels and nerves.

HER SEX ORGANS

The external parts of a woman's genitals, and the area immediately surrounding them, are highly sensitive to physical stimulation. This sensitive region extends from the mons pubis (or mound of Venus), the padding of fatty tissue beneath the pubic hair that acts as a sort of cushion during intercourse, back to the perineum, the area between the vulva and the anus.

FEMALE GENITALS Although the female genitals are partly external, most of the organs are hidden away inside the body. The external organs (the vulva or pudendum) comprise the clitoris, two pairs of skin folds called the labia, and the openings of the vagina and urethra. The complex internal organs include the ovaries, fallopian tubes, uterus, cervix and vagina. The fallopian tubes connect the ovaries to the uterus or womb, and the cervix connects the uterus to the vagina, into which the man's penis is placed during sexual intercourse.

CLITORIS The abundant nerve endings of the clitoris make it extremely sensitive to stimulation, and when stimulated it swells and becomes even more sensitive.

LABIA MAJORA The outer, larger pair of lips or skin folds that protect the openings of the vagina and urethra are the labia majora.

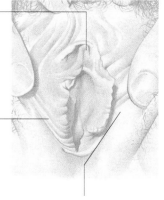

LABIA MINORA The inner labia, the labia minora, secrete a substance called sebum that helps to lubricate the vagina, and meet at the top to form the hood of the clitoris.

OVARIES The two ovaries each produce eggs, the female hormones oestrogen and progesterone and small amounts of testosterone.

UTERUS After an egg has been fertilized, it moves down into the uterus or womb where it eventually develops into a foetus.

FALLOPIAN TUBES The fallopian tubes transport the eggs from the ovaries, and the fertilization of eggs by sperm takes place within them.

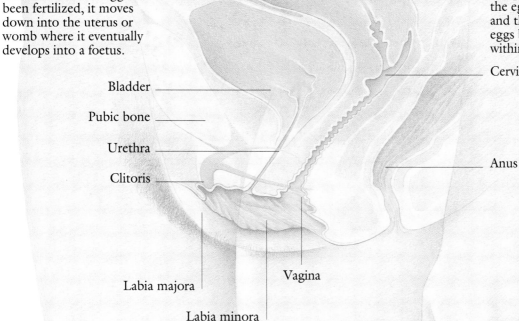

Cervix

Bladder

Pubic bone

Urethra

Clitoris

Anus

Labia majora

Labia minora

Vagina

INDEX

*ANNE HOOPER'S
ULTIMATE SEX GUIDE*

Typesetting: Debbie Rhodes
Film outputting: DTP
Production direction: Lorraine Baird

CARROLL & BROWN LIMITED
would like to thank Bruce Garrett and
Madeline Weston for their editorial
assistance; Tim Kent and Tula Whitlow for
their photography assistance; and all the
models for the enthusiasm, co-operation
and professionalism they displayed in
helping us to produce this book.